MAGNIFICENT AN[

CW01432535

CRIME MAGAZINE CHARACTER INDEX

Magnificent and Beggar Land

Angola Since the Civil War

RICARDO SOARES DE OLIVEIRA

HURST & COMPANY, LONDON

First published in the United Kingdom in 2015 by
C. Hurst & Co. (Publishers) Ltd.,
41 Great Russell Street, London, WC1B 3PL
© Ricardo Soares de Oliveira, 2015
All rights reserved.
Printed in England

The right of Ricardo Soares de Oliveira to be identified as the
author of this publication is asserted by him in accordance
with the Copyright, Designs and Patents Act, 1988.

A Cataloguing-in-Publication data record for this book
is available from the British Library.

ISBN: 9781849042840

This book is printed using paper from registered sustainable
and managed sources.

www.hurstpublishers.com

To Devika

CONTENTS

CONTENTS

ACKNOWLEDGMENTS

I have been fascinated by Angola for more than fifteen years and incurred extraordinary debts in the process of trying to understand its paradoxical history of tragedy and immense promise. On the basis of my own experience and expertise, the book seeks to make sense of this "magnificent and beggar land", to borrow Joseph Brodsky's words, as it left a long war behind. My greatest thanks goes to the many Angolans who spoke to me with candour, especially between 2009 and 2013. Most of these interviews and conversations were confidential. It goes without saying that neither they, nor anyone thanked below, share any responsibility in regard to the interpretation put forward in this book or any mistakes that may have crept in.

A project on this scale would not have been possible without the generous support of the Leverhulme Trust, which granted me a Research Fellowship during the academic year of 2011–12. As a result, I was able to conduct the necessary fieldwork and gather material for this book. The Leverhulme Trust did not hesitate to support the high costs of fieldwork in Angola and kept bureaucratic matters to a minimum. I thank the Master and fellows of St Peter's College and the Department of Politics and International Relations at the University of Oxford for the granting of research leave on this occasion. I am also pleased to acknowledge a 2009 Small Research Grant from the British Academy that financed three trips to Angola and the productive time spent at Sciences Po as OXPO Visiting Professor during March and April 2012. An associated senior researcher position at the Christian Michelsen Institute in Bergen since September 2013 has provided me with access to an outstanding group of researchers, many of whom with more than a decade of experi-

ACKNOWLEDGMENTS

ence in Angola. Lastly, I want to express my continued appreciation of the work of the Global Public Policy Institute, to which I have been attached since 2005, and in particular to Wolfgang Reinecke and Thorsten Benner.

While in Luanda, I benefited from the wonderful hospitality of my friend Alexandre Manuel Santos and his late mother, Dona Maria Alice Santos. Dona Alice, the former director of the celebrated Santa Teresinha School in Sumbe, was a formidable character and an Angolan patriot. Manuel's house was like home to me, and I do not have enough words to thank him and his friends for welcoming me in such a way. Also in Luanda, I was privileged to be able to discuss energy-related matters with José Oliveira. Manuel Alves da Rocha, the director of the Centro de Estudos e Investigação Científica (CEIC) at the Catholic University of Angola, an island of excellence and the country's major research center, was generous with his time and knowledge, as were Nelson Pestana and Regina Santos. The following people have offered valuable observations over many conversations: Fernando Pacheco, Jerónimo Belo, Rafael Marques, Sérgio Calundungo, Miguel Gomes, Carlos Leite, Carlos Rosado de Carvalho, Cesaltina Abreu, Arlindo Barbeitos, Maria Alexandre Dáskalos, Belisário dos Santos and the late João Van Dunem.

I also owe a debt of gratitude to Angola scholars Didier Péclard, Michel Cahen, Justin Pearce, Assis Malaquias, António Tomás, Paulo Inglês, Chloé Buire, Ana Duarte, Cheryl Schmitz, Claudia Gastrow, Paula Roque and Sylvia Croese, who provided me with valuable insights, as well as Jon Schubert and Marissa Moorman for sending me two important, then-unpublished papers. Mathias de Alencastro was a source of knowledge about the Lundas as well as a great travel companion in the east of Angola. In particular, I'd like to acknowledge the generosity of the late Christine Messiant, whose outstanding work on Angola continues to influence me. I met Christine in 2003 during a five-month stay in Paris, and she gave me precious advice in the following two years about research on Angola.

Perhaps the most exciting aspect of researching and writing this book was the opportunity to see a new generation of researchers emerge whose work is changing our knowledge about Angola and placing this crucial African state at the forefront of academic and policy debates about the continent as a whole. Research in Angola remains a difficult and very expensive enterprise but the excitement more than compensates for the

ACKNOWLEDGMENTS

drawbacks. In collaboration with Manuel Ennes Ferreira, I organized a conference on Angolan research in Oxford in July 2011. In March 2014 we co-organized a follow-up event with Aslak Orre and Mathias de Alencastro. These events were collaborations with Lisbon's ISEG, CMI, and three Luandan universities, the Catholic University of Angola, Lusíada University and the Economics Faculty of Agostinho Neto University. I am grateful to the participants in the two conferences for their excellent contributions and hope that such gatherings of scholars become more frequent and increasingly take place in Angola itself.

Kathryn Allawalia of *Foreign Affairs*, Tom Burgis of the *Financial Times*, and Rosemary Bechler at *Open Democracy* kindly commissioned or accepted to publish short pieces on Angola that were helpful in clarifying my thinking on this subject. In addition, the first section of Chapter 1, parts of Chapter 2, and the last section of Chapter 3 are based on papers I published in the *Journal of Modern African Studies* (2007 and 2011) and in *Politique Africaine* (2013). Michael Dwyer at Hurst Publishers, as well as Jon de Peyer, Rob Pinney and Fatima Jamadar, were once again a wonderful team to work with, and I thank them for the dedication they have shown towards this book.

Manuel Ennes Ferreira has for more than ten years been a privileged interlocutor on matters Angolan and I have greatly enjoyed our long conversations in Lisbon, Luanda and Oxford. Manuel patiently read this manuscript and gave detailed advice. Aslak Orre did likewise, despite the fact that he had his own deadlines to keep. Gavin Williams, Michel Cahen and Zaheer Kazmi also read parts of the book and gave precious feedback. I have had enriching conversations about diverse aspects of this book with Peter Lewis, Anne Pitcher, Manuela Franco, Chris Alden, Marta Magalhães, Kjetil Hansen-Shino, José Cutileiro, David Sogge, Pedro Rosa Mendes, Michael Watts, Roland Marchal, Pedro Aires Oliveira, Richard Banégas, Raufu Mustapha, Naomi Chazan, Jocelyn Alexander, Kate Meagher, Philipp Rotmann, General Carlos Branco, Yossi Melman, Richard Caplan, Richard Dowden, Nic Cheeseman, Mats Berdal and J.R. Mailey. My discussions with Harry Verhoeven and Will Jones on Africa's illiberal statebuilders added an exciting comparative dimension to think out the Angolan experience. At Oxford, several colleagues provided me with indispensible advice, especially David Anderson, Neil MacFarlane and Nancy Bermeo. James Mayall, Yezid Sayigh, and Christopher Clapham were behind this project from the very

ACKNOWLEDGMENTS

start and I thank them for their unwavering belief in my work. Thorsten Benner and Daniel Large were, as always, unfailing in their support.

The research and writing of this book owes considerably to my family's support as the task dragged on. In Portugal I especially thank Adelina, Miguel and Tomás. In Paris I am grateful to Anne, who has been endlessly patient and kind. My biggest debt, however, is towards Devika, to whom this book is dedicated.

Oxford, February 2014

LIST OF ACRONYMS

AATA	Associação Angolana de Autoridades Tradicionais
AJAPRAZ	Associação dos Jovens Angolanos Provenientes da República da Zâmbia
ANIP	Agência Nacional de Investimento Privado
BAI	Banco Angolano de Investimentos
BFA	Banco de Fomento Angola
BNA	Banco Nacional de Angola
BPI	Banco Português de Investimento
BPN	Banco Português de Negócios
BRINDE	Brigada de Informação e Defesa do Estado
CABGOC	Cabinda Gulf Oil Company
CACS	Conselhos de Auscultação e Concertação Social
CASA-CE	Convergência Ampla de Salvação de Angola-Coligação Eleitoral
CIF	China International Fund
CITIC	China International Trust and Investment Corporation
CPLP	Comunidade dos Países de Língua Portuguesa
CNPC	China National Petroleum Corporation
CSR	Corporate Social Responsibility
ENSA	Empresa Nacional de Seguros de Angola
FAA	Forças Armadas de Angola
FALA	Forças Armadas de Libertação de Angola
FAPLA	Forças Armadas Populares de Libertação de Angola
FESA	Fundação Eduardo dos Santos
FLEC	Frente de Libertação do Enclave de Cabinda

LIST OF ACRONYMS

FLEC-FAC	Frente de Libertação do Enclave de Cabinda—Forças Armadas de Cabinda
FNLA	Frente Nacional de Libertação de Angola
FOCAC	Forum on China-Africa Cooperation
FRELIMO	Frente de Libertação de Moçambique
FSDEA	Fundo Soberano de Angola
GOSPLAN	State Committee for Planning (USSR)
GRN	Gabinete de Reconstrução Nacional
IDP	Internally Displaced Person
IMF	International Monetary Fund
INAR	Instituto Nacional de Assuntos Religiosos
IO	International Organization
JES	José Eduardo dos Santos
JMPLA	Juventude do MPLA
JURA	Juventude Unida Revolucionária de Angola
LIMA	Liga da Mulher Angolana
MAT	Ministério de Administração do Território
MINARS	Ministério da Assistência e Reinserção Social
MPLA	Movimento Popular de Libertação de Angola
OAU	Organization of African Unity
OECD	Organization for Economic Cooperation and Development
OMA	Organização da Mulher Angolana
OPEC	Organization of Petroleum Exporting Countries
OSI	Open Society Institute
PAIGC	Partido Africano da Independência da Guiné e Cabo Verde
PEP	Politically Exposed Person
PIR	Polícia de Intervenção Rápida
PRESILD	Programa de Reestruturação do Sistema de Logística e de Distribuição de Produtos Essenciais à População
PRC	People's Republic of China
PRI	Partido Revolucionario Institucional
PRS	Partido da Renovação Social
PSA	Production Sharing Agreement
SADC	Southern African Development Community
SIE	Serviço de Inteligência Externa
SIIND	Sonangol Investimentos Industriais

LIST OF ACRONYMS

SINFO	Serviço de Inteligência e Segurança do Estado
SME	Small and Medium Enterprises
SONANGOL	Sociedade Nacional de Combustíveis de Angola
SONATRACH	Société Nationale pour la Recherche, la Production, le Transport, la Transformation, et la Commercialisation des Hydrocarbures
SONIP	Sonangol Imobiliária e Propriedades
SWAPO	South West Africa People's Organization
SWF	Sovereign Wealth Fund
TAAG	Linhas Aéreas de Angola
UEA	União de Escritores Angolanos
UNAC	União Nacional dos Artistas e Compositores
UNAP	União Nacional de Artistas Plásticos
UNAVEM	United Nations Angola Verification Mission
UNDP	United Nations Development Programme
UPA	União dos Povos de Angola
UNITA	União Nacional para a Independência Total de Angola
ZEE	Zona Económica Especial

Map 1: Luanda

Map 2: Angola

INTRODUCTION

"ANGOLA STARTS NOW"

As night falls, stand at the tip of the Island of Luanda, the pleasure peninsula that separates the bay and the city from the open sea, and you will be awed by the prospect that lies ahead. The shantytowns and their inhabitants are almost invisible in the darkness. Instead, you will be dazzled by the brightly lit skyline of the modern city, with soaring skyscrapers added monthly, and by the new Copacabana-style bayside avenue. On the Island itself, Africa's priciest restaurants and bars entertain a cosmopolitan crowd, and far into the Atlantic Ocean, dozens of idle ships await the privilege of discharging their cargo in Luanda's harbour. From this perspective, Angola's oil-fuelled decade of peace is nothing short of an economic miracle.

Yet, not so long ago, Angola was a ravaged country where few outsiders dared to venture. A former Portuguese colony, Angola was isolated from the wider world by a vicious war that lasted more than four decades and only ended with the death in 2002 of the rebel leader Jonas Savimbi. The conflict, which killed up to a million people, was tightly linked with international dynamics such as the struggle against colonialism and apartheid, the Cold War, and commercial appetite for petroleum and diamonds. Many external actors—Western oilmen, Cuban soldiers, Israeli gem dealers, mercenaries from the world over—played important parts in this protracted drama. But the war's complexity and remoteness meant that it never inserted itself in the global consciousness. In Paul Theroux's words, Angola remained "a foreign land without a face",[1] virtually unknown to all but a handful of experts.

This makes Angola's postwar experience all the more remarkable. In a short space of time, this so-called failed state became one of the world's fastest-growing economies and sub-Saharan Africa's third largest, with a GDP of US$121 billion in 2013. It is now China's principal trading partner on the sub-continent and the USA's second. Luanda, a magnetic metropolis pulling in 6 million Angolans and hundreds of thousands of expatriates, is routinely awarded the dubious title of the world's most expensive city amidst a Dubai-inspired urban reinvention and a veritable onslaught of luxury consumer goods. Angola's all-powerful regime, under President José Eduardo dos Santos's (JES) firm control since 1979, defines the peace at home and plays its part on the international stage in a manner that is rare for African political elites. This book explores this extraordinary yet under-studied story.

Compelling in its own right, Angola's decade of reconstruction also holds important lessons for the comparative study of state trajectories in the developing world. The outsized dimensions of Angola—of its resource endowment in particular, and all that flows from it—bring into stark relief dynamics that play out more discreetly elsewhere. Angola shows that there are robust visions of postwar political order that deviate from donor expectations of liberal state-building and choose not to converge with Western models.[2] It also shows that elites, far from being weak or in need of capacity-building, have a strong degree of agency in defining the shape of institutions and the direction of their societies. Moreover, the study of postwar Angola sheds light over the political economy of resource-rich states in an era of high commodity prices. It provides a prism from which to assess the impact of resource wealth on the consolidation of regimes, the expansion of African capitalism, the prospects for economic diversification and the likelihood of the rise of states able to foster broad-based development. Lastly, as one of the star performers of the "Africa Rising" decade, and amidst a geopolitical transition that has seen China and other states emerge as major players on the continent, Angola is a pivotal case for inquiring about the changing position of African states in the international system.

THE PROMISE OF PEACE

The manner in which Angola's civil war ended is key to understanding the power of the MPLA[3] regime in the postwar era. Many African conflicts are halted by foreign-brokered truces that entail some sort of power-sharing between belligerents. These arrangements frequently do not last, as was the case with Angola's failed peace processes in the 1990s. The Angolan war's eventual resolution, however, came about with the government's ferocious vanquishing of the UNITA rebellion.[4] Through the old-fashioned medium of destroying the enemy, the ruling party achieved an uncompromising mastery over Angola.

This military victory soon benefited from an economic bonanza without parallel in Angolan history. Angola had for years been sub-Saharan Africa's second largest oil producer after Nigeria, and petrocarbon revenue played a critical role in financing the government's war effort. But the windfall provided by the postwar increase in oil prices and doubling of oil production to almost 2 million barrels per day by 2008 decisively strengthened the MPLA's domestic and international positions. For its part, the Angolan population, yearning for order and exhausted by a conflict that consumed two generations, was acquiescent towards the victors and placed no restraints on the MPLA leadership. The regime now had both the political space and financial means to pursue its own reconstruction agenda. It could ignore the peacebuilding policies favoured by the West and engage with the foreign private sector rather than the usual NGOs and international organizations.

The result of Angola's uncommon degree of leeway in defining the postwar agenda is one of the world's most capital-intensive and spectacular reconstruction processes of recent decades. Tens of billions of dollars have been spent on infrastructure development, including the road and railway networks, vanity projects such as sports stadia and shopping malls, and the recasting of cityscapes. In the process, Western and East Asian workers marched in, with pride of place given to significant numbers of Portuguese and Chinese. Formerly inaccessible Angola now hosts a global hotchpotch of service providers. The blueprint for recasting Angola, however, is the Angolan elite's own: a grandiose, boom-era vision of state-led modernization and, at least rhetorically, inclusive development, which is barely recognizable to those who had termed Angola a "non-governmental state" only a few years earlier.[5] This goes much beyond mere reconstruction: this well-entrenched regime seeks to build the state and shape Angola in its own, finally hegemonic, image.

As with other oil-rich states undergoing a boom, this self-confidence spills into the international setting. Few trajectories in present-day

Africa are more illustrative of the apparent shift in the continent's fortunes than Angola's successful recasting of its external status. Yesterday's basket case now behaves with the optimism and aplomb of an emerging power and cultivates relationships with rising states in the developing world. Angola has become a major foreign investor with interests spanning the globe, buying off choice morsels of its former imperial power's economy to boot. Beset by criticism of its governance record in the late war years, the MPLA successfully renegotiated relations with Western states. For all the pieties about global reform of the extractive industries, these actors did not hesitate to recalibrate their Angolan presence around business interests and away from normative concerns. This was made easy by Angola's allure for foreign investors in oil and gas, the financial sector and the many profitable reconstruction opportunities it offered.

The postwar conjuncture provides this magnificent country with an unequalled opportunity. Encompassing vast forests, deserts, and lush highlands and as large as Italy, Germany and France combined, Angola has staggering economic prospects, even bearing in mind the extensive and costly destruction wrought by the war. Angola's population, at an estimated 20 million, is sizeable yet manageable. Its present-day wealth, impressive though it is, relies almost exclusively on oil and diamonds production. The entire resource endowment extends across world-class mineral reserves and tremendous agricultural, hydroelectric and fisheries potential. War-weary Angolans have embraced the hopes of development and sense of possibility of the postwar era. Even if only a fraction of this promise is realized, Angola will be in a class of its own amongst emerging economies. And in a decade of renewed optimism about Africa's development potential, the ultimate course of one of the continent's major players and commodity exporters—whether it is able to successfully transition from war to peace, from poverty to prosperity, and from oil dependence to a diversified economy—matters far beyond its borders.

Yet Angola's endowment and the promise it holds are inseparable from the country's tragic legacy of exploitation, foreign meddling and unremitting suffering. Angola was first disfigured by 250 years of transatlantic slave trade that left a deep imprint on the culture of the state and society. Later on, white settler colonialism worked against the emergence of a strong African bourgeoisie, any dabbling in pluralist politics or, until very late in the day, much development—however defined. The postcolonial experience of Afro-Stalinism in the cities was matched by the tyrannical order of rebel areas, both laced with extensive outside involvement in the civil war. Like many other resource-rich states in the developing world, Angola has conspicuously failed to place its mineral wealth at the service of economic diversification or inclusive prosperity, even if a minority of insiders always benefited from it. Its population remains one of the world's poorest. A thread running through Angolan history is the disregard, even cruelty, with which the powerful have treated the powerless: whether reigning locals or venal outsiders, the enduring design has been the extraction of the riches of the land, with most Angolans counting for nothing.

At this exceptional juncture, the challenge for Angola is whether this harrowing historical pattern can be overturned. Taking the first ten years of Angolan reconstruction as its subject, and focusing on the Angolan elite and the actions of the party-state, *Magnificent and Beggar Land* asks the following questions: what is the nature of this victor's peace and the regime's reconstruction and state-building agenda? What is the MPLA's project of modernity and who is it for? Is Angola's newfound international status sustainable? Can the country harness its resource endowment and unusual autonomy from external pressures to create broadbased growth and a diversified economy? Will Angolans, for the first time in history, be treated as citizens and allowed self-realization in a decent society?

This sense of possibility was perfectly encapsulated in the motto often proclaimed by Angolans from all walks of life in the early postwar years: *Angola começa agora*—"Angola starts now."[6]

LEGACIES

Of course, 2002 was not Angola's zero hour, for the country carried into the postwar era burdensome legacies that did not dissipate with the defeat of UNITA. But the historical nuances of the civil war never quite registered with most outsiders who knew very little about Angola and projected onto it just about any theory of conflict that seemed to make it legible. During the Cold War, the country was seen as a proxy arena for the superpowers by way of their client states, Cuba and South Africa. In the 1990s it epitomized the greed-driven "new war", its protagonists gorging on oil and diamonds; and every so often the spectre of "tribal conflict" was bandied about. Wrong when pursued as single explanations, these factors are not entirely wide of the mark. The Cold War contributed to Angola's plight, natural resources played a role in sustaining the belligerents, and there was an ethnic dimension to the conflict.[7] These factors exacerbated the civil war, but did not cause it. The roots of the conflict are instead primarily to be found in Angola's long and disjointed insertion in the world economy and the domestic political patterns of power and exclusion that accrued over centuries. This resulted in a late colonial and early postcolonial contest for control of the state by competing elites articulating different nationalist projects. Angolan history, Christopher Cramer writes, "reverberates with continuity".[8] This history did not dictate that the war must occur, but one cannot make sense of the conflict without putting it into historical perspective.

First and foremost, this means acknowledging the significance of Angola's violent inclusion into the world economy from the late fifteenth century onwards. One of the ironies of Angolan history is the extent to which this corner of the African continent has been tightly linked to the outside world from the very beginnings of European imperial expansion. Because colonial propagandists concocted the myth of five centuries of Portuguese rule, scholars have instead emphasized the weakness and lateness of effective occupation of what would become Angola. There is no doubt that, as late as 1904, the Portuguese controlled barely 10 per cent of the territory, with some societies in the east and the south not subdued until the 1920s.[9] However, the coastal enclaves of Luanda (founded in 1575) and Benguela (1617), as well as a thin corridor along the Kwanza River, had been under Portuguese rule for centuries.[10] Amongst Africa's most important enclaves of the Atlantic trade, their economic pull eventually extended across great areas of Central Africa and may have sucked into captivity, in alliance with inland kingdoms, a larger percentage of the African population than in any other catchment area on the continent.[11] Puny they may seem in retrospect, but these continuously occupied beachheads of Portuguese power were the embryo of the later domination of the hinterland, and remain the political and economic epicentre of Angola until the present. Their importance for the history of Angola cannot be overstated.

Most significant was the slave ports' spawning of an Afro-Portuguese community that would long play a leading role in articulating relations between the Angolan interior, especially the Mbundu areas abutting Luanda and the Kwanza river, and the outside world. While Europeans were scarce and their population constantly depleted by tropical diseases, the slave trade and the running of the colony were effectively in the hands of local dynasties who spoke Portuguese, lived in lavish palaces, enjoyed prestigious administrative positions and saw themselves as loyal subjects of the Portuguese Crown well into the nineteenth century. In recent years scholars have come to label these coastal communities as "Creole". The term has never been deployed as self-definition, and some Angolan intellectuals recoil from it.[12] But it is helpful in two ways. First, it conveys the fact that these communities are the product of colonialism and that a new, hybrid culture resulted from it. Though often associated with the mixed-race offspring of the Portuguese, Creole-ness is in fact a multiracial category defined by culture. Most important, Creoles are defined by what they are not, that is "indigenous/natives".[13] Second, the term "Creole" places the Angolan pre-colonial experience in the wider context of the European trading enclaves that dotted the Western African coast from Senegal and Sierra Leone to Benin and Lagos and beyond from the early modern period until the scramble for Africa. However, only in Angola have these people emerged as the postcolonial elite and only in Angola did their highly particular culture come to define the nation.

This was not meant to be so. The social standing of the Creoles nose-dived in the aftermath of the scramble for Africa that started in the 1880s. At the onset, the Creoles still thought of themselves as civilized, denigrated the peoples of the hinterland as savages, and even participated in the Portuguese occupation of the interior. But the arrival of white settlers soon relegated non-whites to subordinate roles in the civil service and resulted in wider social downgrading. The anguished, articulate reactions of the *filhos da terra*[14] in the small Luanda press of the 1890s contains some of the earliest iterations of "*Angolanidade*",[15] and would in time be turned into a nationalist narrative by anti-colonial ideologues in search of a genealogy. But the character of their complaints was always problematic. Creoles mixed affirmations of Angolan pride with rights claims as Portuguese subjects; they railed against metropolitan mercantilist policies that underdeveloped the colony but defended the slave trade and the subsequent long-lasting commerce in indentured labourers. As the historian Malyn Newitt has pointed out, "their main orientation was always the interests of their own group [...] the real nature of these movements was an expression of the interests of an urban class, once influential and even dominant, which was now in decline".[16]

However, and this is key to understanding later Angolan politics, this decline was relative to the Creoles' hitherto dominant status. Their social distance vis-à-vis the African majority remained vast. In the absence of a formal colour bar, the Creoles' presence in the lower ranks of the civil service still placed them above illiterate poor whites and those deported to Angola for criminal offences (Angola was a penal colony until 1934). More important, Creoles were given *assimilado* status, according to which they were deemed to have risen to the cultural standard of Europeans. While they faced daily challenges to their social status, in legal terms they were Portuguese citizens exempted from the extremely harsh demands made upon the estimated 98 per cent of Angolans labelled as "indigenous", with emphasis on the compulsory labour requirements that would last until the outbreak of the anti-colonial war in 1961. From this liminal yet somewhat privileged location in Angolan colonial society, two generations of Creoles would nurse memories of past greatness and deplore their predicament.

The social position of Creoles is a vantage point from which to make sense of the pecking order of colonial (and postcolonial) Angola. In much the same way that access to the "material and ideological resources" emanating from the world economy[17] had long given Creoles a paramount status, the standing of individuals and communities in Angola depended on their proximity to the externally connected "central society" and the extent to which they had become "Portugalized". The Portuguese authorities measured this quite strictly when it came to allowing access to the coveted *assimilado* status.[18] Conditions included the holding of property, perfect mastery of Portuguese without a hint of African intonation, European table manners (to this day, even Luandans in shantytowns eat with forks and knives—an essential feature of "having left the bush behind"), personal hygiene, general "civilized" deportment and in most cases, the dropping of an African surname and its replacement by a Portuguese one.

Unsurprisingly, the long colonized areas, including the Mbundu hinterland of Luanda, fared better in this regard. The Creole/Mbundu *assimilados* provided the "standard of civilization" for non-whites, having been schooled together with the Portuguese in the major cities, lived in uneasy intimacy with them, and monopolized the little Angolan upward mobility that was to be had. In turn, this deepened the abiding divide in Angolan society between the city and the bush. This was not simply a physical divide between the rural areas and the core colonial areas where social opportunity beckoned; it was a cosmological one corresponding to a barbarian/civilized dichotomy, with Creoles and urbanites sharing with the whites a contempt "for the ignorant African".[19]

In view of this, those unable to access the scarce fruits of colonial modernity to the same extent, or at all, necessarily held a lower status in Angolan society, even if they were prestigious in their own communities. In areas outside the colonial core, access to education was mostly through missionary stations, often Protestant North American or northern European. This meant that Bakongo elites in northern Angola and Ovimbundu elites in the central highlands, while receiving modern education, did not much socialize with the Portuguese and had only oblique contact with the settler culture until relatively late. Populations in even remoter regions that were colonized later and saw little Portuguese investment had no access to schooling or any form of colonial modernity. This divide was made greater by the character of colonial Angola until the 1950s: it was less an integrated territory than a multiethnic and multilingual patchwork of different societies with contrasting and sometimes loose rapports with Luanda.[20]

This disjointed character meant that no integrated pan-Angolan elite arose. Although not strictly ethno-regional, the patterns of elite sociability were so narrow that, with rare exceptions, these people rarely even met.[21] Except for FLEC,[22] the small separatist movement in the oil-rich Cabinda province, secessionism has always been a marginal force in Angolan politics. The three major movements that eventually challenged the Portuguese—FNLA, MPLA and UNITA—accepted the colonial territory and saw Luanda as the focal point of linkage with the world system.[23] But as they emanated from such strikingly dissimilar corners of society, they inevitably came up with very different ideas of Angola as well as of their own roles and those of others in it.

The subsequent story of Angola's competing nationalisms is well known.[24] The MPLA was created by young *assimilado* and *mestiço* Angolans, primarily in exile and in Luanda. Nurtured in the politics of Portugal's leftist opposition and the anti-colonial trends of the era, the MPLA phrased itself as a modern, inclusive liberation movement that transcended narrow (ethnic, racial) affiliations within Angolan society. Lurking behind this discourse, however, was the will to power of "a social elite [wanting] to be a political elite as well".[25] For their part, Bakongo notables from northern Angola, who had flocked to the Belgian Congo from the late 1940s to escape the aggressive takeover by settler coffee planters, created the UPA[26] (later called FNLA).[27] Led by Holden Roberto, a relative by marriage of Zaire's President Mobutu, UPA was a predominantly Bakongo movement with secondary roles for non-Bakongo and a message focused on its core constituency.

* * *

The anti-colonial war was launched in February 1961 with a locally organized attack on Luanda's main prison, the first shots of which were to herald more than four decades of conflict. The assault was immediately claimed by the MPLA but its involvement is questionable for, at that stage, it amounted to little more than a few exiled cadres without the sustained contact with Luanda needed to engineer this uprising.[28] But UPA was clearly the mastermind of the next step of the insurgency in mid-March 1961: guerrillas moving in from the Congo attacked coffee plantations across the northwest of Angola, killing hundreds of settlers. Ominously, UPA also slaughtered several thousand Ovimbundu workers and other African employees of the Portuguese, giving this anti-colonial revolt a schismatic character from the very start. Initially stunned, the Portuguese responded by sending in a large expeditionary force to preserve the empire. By the end of 1961, the northwest had been reconquered. Low-level insurgencies by UPA/FNLA and the MPLA ensued, with new fronts in Cabinda, Moxico and other peripheral regions. On Christmas day 1966, Teixeira de Sousa (now Luau), a town near the Congolese border, was assailed by hundreds of men wielding machetes and homemade shotguns. Though easily repulsed, this was the first sign of UNITA's existence. Its subsequent anti-colonial war exploits were unremarkable, partly on account of a secret agreement with the Portuguese that allowed UNITA breathing space in exchange for collaboration in attacking MPLA forces, but a third movement had joined the struggle for Angola.

None of the three movements, which were prone to internal dissensions and spent much time fighting each other, met with success against the Portuguese.[29] At some cost in lives and cash, the Portuguese contained them, a very different situation from those in the parallel anti-colonial conflicts in Guinea and Mozambique. Far from damaging the economy, the war was a major stimulus for sustained growth and late colonial reform. In the end, it was a coup in Lisbon on 25 April 1974 that broke the stalemate. Portuguese military officers committed to end the African wars and grant independence to the colonies. In the subsequent months, as the MPLA, UNITA and FNLA streamed from exile and the maquis into the cities, the clash of their mutually exclusionary ambitions became unavoidable. After a fleeting attempt at brokering a unity government in early 1975 failed, the country slid into chaos and, by the middle of the year, civil war. The settler exodus was in full swing.

Henceforth the struggle for control of Angola would become an international conflict. The USA and the USSR supported their respective clients through proxies: South African and Zairian troops invaded on the side of UNITA and FNLA while Cuba airlifted a major expeditionary force to help the MPLA, which had already benefited extensively from assistance by the departing Portuguese military. This Cuban presence proved instrumental in securing Luanda and scattering the competing movements and their foreign allies.[30] By early 1976 the MPLA was in control of the Angolan state. The FNLA soon collapsed as a major political-military movement, its remnants dispersed; UNITA, though battered, managed a "long march" towards the border areas protected by South Africa. From 1978 onwards, their alliance would return in full to relentlessly pummel the MPLA state, which became ever more dependent on Eastern Bloc support. The subsequent decade of South African- and US-sponsored insurgency culminated in the spectacular battle of Cuito Cuanavale in January 1988, where Cuban and South African troops faced off. Although Cuba gained the upper hand on this occasion, both sides were soon convinced of the futility of the war. But while the role of international forces and sources of funding was key during this period, the domestic sources of the conflict—the visceral enmity between the Angolan belligerents—were always present.

A major consequence of the first postcolonial war (1975–91) was the takeover of the country by "two single parties",[31] both of which presided in an authoritarian manner over what Christine Messiant saw as distinct "societies".[32] The MPLA society was the tightly circumscribed, mostly urban society inhabited by millions of Angolans, dominated by the single party and presided over by José Eduardo dos Santos after the death of President Agostinho Neto in 1979. Its survival ensured by the military presence of the MPLA's Eastern Bloc patrons, the MPLA society was at the same time implausibly financed by Western oil corporations such as

Chevron, which continued a profitable and pragmatic engagement with socialist Angola in oblivion of Cold War politics. The political space of the MPLA society was not contiguous. The MPLA's power hinged on the control of urban and coastal enclaves and areas of resource extraction but it had next to no foothold in much of the countryside and did not govern the vast majority of the country's nominal territory.

For its part, the extremely insular UNITA society was constituted by pockets of the rural world where hundreds of thousands of people lived under the direct control of the rebel movement. UNITA's ambitions to govern led it to engage in statist rituals and "behave like a state". It provided public goods in its core areas of administration, including health and schooling, separated its large and increasingly mechanized armed forces, the FALA, from its civilian structures, and sought to establish a complex bureaucratized organization with a youth wing (JURA), a women's organization (LIMA) and other structures. This UNITA society was, until the late 1990s, a world unto itself, with its own values and political imagination, intensely patrolled by a secret police, BRINDE,[33] and jealously protected from unregulated contact with the outside. Although it was meant partly for external consumption, UNITA's bush capital of Jamba, with its compulsive emphasis on order personified by the iconic traffic policeman standing on a traffic-less roundabout, hinted at this craving for total control.[34]

It is widely acknowledged that the personality and choices of Jonas Savimbi, the movement's founder and leader until his death in February 2002, are more important for understanding UNITA than its loosely defined ideology or formal decision-making structure. At every juncture, this charismatic, intelligent and brutal man dictated UNITA's course, and with it Angola's fate. Born in 1934, the son of a Bié rail station chief, Savimbi availed himself of the meagre, mission-based educational opportunities obtainable at the time. But his path was quite different from those of university-bound Creoles whom he always loathed.[35] Initially a senior member of the FNLA, Savimbi broke away on account of its "tribalism" to create UNITA. For four decades, his ideology was entirely situational, as were his alliances with, *inter alia*, the Portuguese, Mao's China, apartheid South Africa, the Reagan administration, and assorted European Christian Democrats. Savimbi's professions of faith in democracy were always dubious but he was a useful man at a certain point, and many chose to take him at face value. He could certainly dazzle interlocutors with his multilingual erudition, and seemed a cut above the rest of the anti-Soviet "freedom fighters" of the 1980s: how many of them could boast a "spacious and serene" bunker containing a presidential library of more than 2,000 well-thumbed volumes?[36]

For all of Savimbi's opportunism, there were constant themes to his long pursuit of absolute power. He built upon deep-seated town-country divisions and a sense of victimhood and social resentment against Luanda and its Europeanized elites, whether phrased as a Maoist peasants' war, as payback for the forced labour system of the colonial era, or in chauvinistic terms for Ovimbundu and other "African" audiences. UNITA's message had traction in part because it opened up an alternative path towards Angolan modernity, which the Protestant missions had already put forward, that did not entail the "detribalization" (and implicit convergence with elite culture) preached by the MPLA.[37] Dismissed in the cities as "primitives from the bush",[38] UNITA supporters in turn demonized the "minority regime"[39] of the Creole bourgeoisie as "non-Angolan".[40]

This language resonated in quarters of Angolan society. Yet many Angolans were tactical in their engagement with either movement, and coercion played a big role in eliciting support. On the side of the MPLA, the forced conscription, bordering on kidnapping, of teenagers into the armed forces was widespread. This coercive aspect is certainly crucial for understanding UNITA, which came close to the ideal-type of a totalitarian organization, its policies a direct, unmediated result of the will of the leader. The abject humiliation of senior cadres was routine, as was their show of public repentance. Contrary to the MPLA's portrait of its enemy as rural and backward, UNITA had modernist aspirations and educated elites; but even self-confident, worldly men trembled in Savimbi's presence. Accounts of his court are reminiscent of Stalin or some despot who would dispose of henchmen on a whim. The execution of Tito Chingunji, hitherto a favourite and architect of UNITA's high standing in 1980s Washington, and more than twenty members of his family, is well known, and the MPLA made much of Savimbi's penchant for witch burnings. But a focus on these moments of terror must not obscure the routine *modus operandi* of what was in effect a totalitarian society.[41] While it was exceedingly brutal and presided over the bloodiest campaign of repression in independent Angola, the 1977 internal purge that followed the failed Nito Alves coup, the sloppier MPLA never achieved the same degree of social control.

As the Cold War drew to an end, the external sponsors of the Angolan conflict sought an orderly extrication and some sort of closure. By December 1988, a US-brokered agreement simultaneously attained South Africa's retreat from Namibia, which became independent in 1990, and Cuba's from Angola.[42] UNITA and the MPLA were unhappy at this turn of events, and far from pushing for a resolution, spent much of 1990 in high-intensity fighting in the hope of upsetting the balance on the ground, to no avail. With US and USSR support, a Portuguese-negotiated peace agreement was finally signed at Bicesse, Portugal, in May 1991, Savimbi and dos Santos limply shaking hands. The advent of peace was met with elation. But soon, even the most optimistic observers noticed that the UN mission overseeing the peace process was under-resourced and had a vague and weak mandate.[43] Elections, scheduled for September 1992, were clearly premature in view of the fact that there was no time to disarm and demobilize the two movements.

Most important, the warring parties were not interested in peace. The MPLA had been bullied by the changing geopolitical climate into signing the peace accords, but the leadership was initially convinced that it could not manage the transition (amongst other things, this was said to have resulted in a minor real estate boom in Lisbon, where MPLA barons quickly took their money). Savimbi, at the height of his international standing and benefiting from American support, was convinced that he would win the elections, a mere formality before his takeover of the state. But the situation shifted imperceptibly over months. The MPLA's adoption of capitalism and image makeover led many Westerners to realize that these Europeanized urbanites could be engaged with. For its part, UNITA did not demobilize its army; the leadership was notoriously aggressive and seemingly unaccustomed to the media. In early 1992, the defection of Tony da Costa Fernandes and Miguel N'zau Puna, two Cabindans who were then numbers two and three of UNITA, brought out revelations about the killing of UNITA cadres like Tito Chingunji.[44] The MPLA made expert use of these tales of repression, rebuilding its support amongst constituencies that felt threatened by Savimbi's anti-urban, anti-*mestiço* diatribes.

Elections in late September 1992 went off peacefully, but the results were devastating for UNITA. The presidential elections gave more votes to dos Santos but Savimbi's high score meant that there would have to be a second round (this never took place). The legislative elections, however, gave a clear majority to the MPLA. Refusing to accept the results, UNITA moved to occupy much of Angola, including vital diamond areas in the east that would now become the movement's lifeline. After weeks of tension, Luanda exploded just before All Saints' Day. The MPLA, making use of its heavily armed *poder popular* militias and the Spanish-trained Rapid Intervention Police, unleashed a horrific pogrom against UNITA militants and cadres remaining in the city. Thousands of people, including top UNITA politicians such as Vice-President Jeremias Chitunda, were slaughtered in only three days. Images of their battered, decomposing bodies were broadcast by Angola's public television, with voiceover justifications of the government's actions.

The Luanda massacre sped up Savimbi's countrywide offensive, and by early 1993 UNITA had taken control of 80 per cent of the country. Towns that would not submit, like Huambo, Malanje and Cuito, were subjected to large-scale bombardments that cost thousands of lives.[45] Despite this, the government's fiscal lifeline—the offshore oil sector run by the likes of Chevron, Elf Aquitaine and other Western companies—continued to thrive. As the oil money kicked in and the government revamped its armed forces, including through the hiring of mercenary outfits staffed by former apartheid soldiers such as Executive Outcomes, UNITA's gains were slowly reversed.[46] However traumatic the previous thirty years of war had been, the last decade would be of an entirely different order of magnitude, with hundreds of thousands killed and most of Angola levelled to the ground. In 1993, the UN famously deemed Angola's "the worst war in the world" in reproach for the international community's disregard of it.[47]

The post-election war was suspended by a new peace accord signed in Lusaka in late 1994, but this again proved to be no more than a lengthy lull in the fighting. A beefed up UN mission revealed itself entirely inept at preventing UNITA from rearming. Violent incidents in which thousands of people were killed multiplied across the country.[48] The MPLA leveraged its position as *de jure* government and the erosion of UNITA's foreign support—at this stage, even the Savimbi enthusiasts of Republican Washington had peeled away—to win the international struggle for recognition, which resulted in crippling UN sanctions against the rebels. Far-reaching military interventions in the DRC and Congo-Brazzaville in 1997, besides helping to replace the pro-UNITA Mobutu and Lissouba regimes by pliable allies, also gave the FAA serious logistical muscle. Threats against Zambia to discourage any further assistance to UNITA, and a friendly SWAPO government in Namibia, guaranteed that the region was now safely in the MPLA camp.

But the endgame proved horribly protracted. President dos Santos' presumptuous "war for peace" announcement of a return to fighting in December 1998 was immediately countered by the mangling of several FAA battalions[49] amid rumours that UNITA had created a capable mechanized unit (in some accounts, even an air force) under the supervision of Ukrainian mercenaries. The odds were entirely against the rebels but instead of swiftly bringing to bear its crushing superiority in resources and international legitimacy, Luanda took three more years to destroy UNITA. This included the resort by the FAA, by this stage one of Africa's largest armed forces replete with foreign "security consultants", to the countrywide, large-scale removal of populations, and extensive bombing. The former FAA commander-in-chief, General João de Matos, did not hesitate to label the 1998–2002 conflict, "in human and material terms, the most destructive of all [the wars] Angola has known in the last half century".[50] By the time of Savimbi's death in an ambush in Moxico province on 22 February 2002, which finally brought the war to an end, the country was in tatters.

It was a vastly transformed Angola that emerged from four decades of conflict. Nothing was left of the relatively diversified economy of the early 1970s; Angola was a major exporter of oil and diamonds but otherwise needed to import everything, including its food supply. But in addition to the destruction it had wrought, the war worked as a vast agent of social change and uniformity. The war did not do away with racial, ethnic or regional identities but a third of the population had become internally displaced, with millions flocking to the precarious outskirts of the provincial capitals and Luanda. By 2002, Angola, historically an overwhelmingly agricultural society, had a rural landscape scarred by millions of landmines and a primarily urban population, in a permanent upset of the dynamics of the rural world. Portuguese, spoken by only a minority of Angolans in 1975, had become the *lingua franca* of this unsettled multiethnic land; in the cauldron of Luanda, Kimbundu was fast receding and the colonial language was now the mother tongue for most young people. By the end of the war, more Angolans were in contact with each other than ever before.

The political consequences of the war were also formidable for the MPLA-run state.[51] Much of the public administration remained incapable of performing basic tasks and had next to no territorial coverage outside the cities. The state provided few public goods and welfare tasks were carried out instead by the UN system and a plethora of churches and humanitarian NGOs. But the war strongly affected the institutional design of the state. It incentivized the development of state capacity in areas of structural importance such as fiscal consolidation (the creation of the competent national oil company, Sonangol, a major player throughout this book), war fighting (the well-resourced armed forces, amongst Africa's largest, which the government would not demobilize after 2002) and the maintenance of public order in the cities (the police and intelligence apparatus). This institutional capacity was firmly controlled by President José Eduardo dos Santos, who lost no opportunity to tighten his grip over the country.

* * *

In the history of the conflict now being actively manufactured by the MPLA, the first decades of independence are presented as the story of a "national" state confronted by a parochial insurgency that brought *confusão* and destruction to the country. This does not accord with the wartime reality: the MPLA's legitimacy was tenuous in much of the country, and the party was assumed by many to be in the hands of a small, unrepresentative clique. Especially after the late 1980s, the government was missing from the lives of many Angolans, save for the vicious role of marauding army units. For its part, UNITA's claims to "stateness", its denying the MPLA a consistent foothold in the rural world, real control of a segment of the population, and popularity amongst others created something approaching parity between the two forces, with the MPLA state less than a real state, and the UNITA insurgency more than an insurgency.

This situation—the divided nature of Angola and the existence of an alternative UNITA society—disappeared in 2002. For the first time since independence, Angola was, in the words of MPLA historic figure Lopo do Nascimento, "truly reunified", with an end to "not only two armies, but literally two states and two administrations [...] Angolans are now effectively within the same territory, unified and indivisible, under the same symbols and the same state authority".[52] In this sense, 2002 was a foundational moment for the MPLA itself: the moment in which it vanquished the last major challenge (UNITA having been preceded by the FNLA and the Portuguese colonialists) to its bid for control of Angola. A minor secessionist insurgency tumbled along in the oil-rich Cabinda province, but this posed no major threat to the regime, and a mix of cooptation and army crackdowns was quickly brought to bear on the FLEC and its splinter groups.

The MPLA's peace was not vindictive. Savimbi's family was taken care of in a dignified and generous manner. There were no reprisals and UNITA cadres were quickly integrated into Angolan public life and allowed a subordinate stake in the postwar order, some even serving in the "national reconciliation" government until 2008. For good measure, an amnesty was declared that encompassed everyone's putative war crimes. But Angola's pluralist façade and holding of elections in 2008 and 2012 could not mask the unequivocal domination of the MPLA: in Juan Linz's terms, the regime is better conceived as a diminished form of authoritarianism than as the young, partial democracy it claims to be.[53] For almost half a century, rival social groups had competing ideas of Angola, of what the country was, should aspire to become, and who should lead it. Now, the vast legitimacy afforded by the war victory, the establishment of political order for the first time, and the unprecedented oil boom jointly meant that only one of these competing ideas of Angola would hold sway. The MPLA would get to dictate what the nation is.

Why is this important for our understanding of the reconstruction era? Simply put, because the way in which the MPLA conceives of the nation—whom it includes and excludes, its social and geographical biases—directly affects its state-building and development agenda for the country as a whole. The MPLA's idea of Angola is therefore crucial for making sense of its postwar project. It conceives of the country first and foremost as the historical product of Portuguese imperialism.[54] The focus is very much on "Angola" to the detriment of the "Africa" of most twentieth-century African and diaspora intellectuals. The MPLA may use figures of the African past as nationalist tropes but it doesn't exalt the pre-colonial world as the direct antecedent of contemporary Angola. It acknowledges that the territory has no pre-colonial unity, and sees the experience of Portuguese rule and the Portuguese language as the common threads of an otherwise immensely diverse patchwork of cultures. Moreover, the MPLA sees the cultural and political convergence of "Angola" as a work in progress. Some parts of the country and society represent "Angola" more than others. Luanda and the long-colonized

areas that enjoy privileged access to the outside world constitute the pinnacle of both what is "modern" and "national" and the historical
"Angolan" culture favoured by the MPLA. This is undergirded by an
unstated standard of civilization whereby some Angolans, by their
Portuguese language proficiency and "cosmopolitan" deportment, hold a
higher status, while others whose behaviour and culture are, in one word,
more "African" are deemed to be backward and of lesser social import.
This dichotomy is a defining, if implicit, tenet of Angola-ness as perceived by the MPLA leadership.[55] Viewing itself as the only movement
whose nation-building aspirations transcend exclusionary (that is, ethno-
regional and racial) boundaries, the MPLA has a "visceral belief"[56] in its
own legitimacy to guide Angola into the modern world.

Those hostile to the MPLA see this as a smokescreen for the ambitions of a handful of Creole families who are both historically preemi-
nent and overrepresented at the summit of the postcolonial party-state.
This caricature of the MPLA avoids the fact that the party is now a
catchall organization with a national footprint. Yet it is not entirely
wrong, for the Creole/*assimilado* elite model remains "a shaping force over
anyone aspiring to power and control of the state".[57] In this sense it is
less a discernible clique of "great families", although they do exist and are
at the core of the MPLA, than a compelling social logic whereby Angolan
upward mobility is historically equated with hoisting oneself to the level
of these elites, behaving in accordance with their standards—and seeing
the country through their eyes and from their perch in Angolan society.

In sum, the MPLA's agenda for postwar Angola much transcends the
ambitious task of national reconstruction to encompass an ideological
project of transforming the country in its own image. This project has a
tool—the oil-rich state—and a vanguard: the urban, civilized, Portuguese-
speaking Angolan. At its centre resides Luanda, the MPLA's city-state
during the long years of the war. Luanda is more than the power centre
and controller of the nation's wealth: it is the setter of its parameters.
Fashion, youth culture, patterns of consumption, aspirations for personal
success, the right Portuguese accent, the comportment one aspires to
master: all emanate from Luanda, the swallower of men where a fourth
of the population already resides and most others aspire to join. Luanda's
monopoly on Angolan modernity means that anything that is not
Luanda's is by definition narrow-minded. Every innovation radiates out-
ward from Luanda, and the expansion of state power, the reconstruction

of the country and the systematic incorporation of its diverse regions and peoples are conceived in terms of assimilation of the city's culture, outlook and directives. In the era of MPLA hegemony, Angola was finally to become "the Republic of Luanda".[58]

OUTLINE OF THE BOOK

Magnificent and Beggar Land is neither a history of modern Angola nor an encyclopedic study of the peace era. Put simply, it seeks to provide an account and interpretation of postwar Angola centred on the victors and the political and economic order they have sought to build. I have thus made choices about the focus of the analysis that reflect the strong degree of state power and autonomy from society prevalent during the first decade of peace. There is no attempt at symmetry between the MPLA and UNITA. The book is overwhelmingly focused on the MPLA party-state, its elites and the political economy they control; the episodic presence of UNITA and its people is testimony to their marginality and subordinate integration in the MPLA order between 2002 and 2012.[59] As to the Angolan masses, they were quietist actors in the Angolan drama throughout this period: they were happy not to be shot at and did not challenge the status quo. Also, despite the fact that I have travelled and conducted research across twelve of Angola's eighteen provinces, this book is unequivocally written from the vantage point of Luanda. Needless to say, a book written from Huambo or Cuando Cubango would be entirely different and certainly cover in much greater detail matters that I deal with only peripherally here. In this regard, the book contributes towards a conversation about postwar Angola that will doubtless elicit divergent interpretations in the years to come. Lastly, the book seeks to introduce Angola to a broad readership interested in contemporary Africa and the politics of resource-rich states in the developing world. It therefore includes some material and analysis that the specialists will be familiar with but are essential for understanding the Angolan trajectory.

A brief word on sources: this book is primarily the product of fieldwork, encompassing both interviews and participant observation in Angola and elsewhere (primarily in Portugal, the United Kingdom, France, and the United States) between 2009 and 2013. I also benefited greatly from a much longer scholarly engagement with Angola dating back to the late 1990s. The vast majority of the close to 200 interviews I conducted (and a large number of informal conversations over several years) were confidential. Almost everyone not speaking in their official capacity, whether Angolan or expatriate, feared the negative consequences of being identified as in any way critical of the status quo. Their invaluable insights are quoted throughout this book. In addition, I have made use of the existing secondary literature and of sources such as Angolan government reports, MPLA documents, NGO reports, the Luanda newspapers and the occasional foreign media coverage, a handful of memoirs by Angolan public figures and the grey literature produced by international organizations active in the country.

One cannot overemphasize the centrality of dedicated, long-term fieldwork and local knowledge for the goals this book aims to achieve. The Angolan government's legendary distrust, indeed aversion, towards foreign researchers seems to have mellowed somewhat in recent times. Angola's increased accessibility, particularly in the last five years, has both allowed the carrying out of research for this book and brought in a new generation of scholars who are unearthing new knowledge about the country. This said, research for this book suffered from the lack of authoritative data and credible statistical information on a country whose last census, at the time of writing, was undertaken in the early 1970s. The much-delayed census that has finally been scheduled for 2014 will (provided it is properly conducted and its data fully disseminated) bring forth an invaluable update on contemporary Angola. But no such information was available during the first decade of peace. Most works on Angola therefore contain an obligatory disclaimer as to the (at best) approximate knowledge about crucial dimensions of the economy and society: the exact size of the population, for instance, is the subject of intense speculation. However, the problem goes beyond mere state ignorance about the country or a faulty statistical apparatus. The authorities' secretive, at times even manipulative, approach to information means that they have routinely impeded access to data, especially those which are deemed unflattering. Access to Angola is much better now than in the war years, but the country remains amongst the most inhospitable and restrictive for the conduct of research in present-day Africa.

Chapter 1 explains the system of political and economic domination established by President dos Santos during the long years of the war. At independence in 1975, the MPLA faced dismal initial conditions as a result of the conflict, economic decline and lack of bureaucratic capacity to run the state. But the regime leveraged external resources, in the form of oil rents and military protection, to secure its hold over Angola. In the process, dos Santos used the extraordinary circumstances of the war to carve out a veritable parallel state under his personal control that came to encompass the country's revenue-handling and coercive organizations and hold extensive links with the international economy. Its centrepiece was and remains the national oil company, Sonangol, an island of competence nursed by some of the world's top consulting firms. Especially during the last decade of the war, this configuration of power also enabled the enrichment of a small number of MPLA barons, generals and leading families that revolved around the presidency. Throughout, I highlight the importance of the oil endowment as well as elite decisions in shaping this system. Why does the wartime parallel system deserve a full chapter in a work on postwar Angola? In short, because this system— the epicentre of JES's structure of power that won the war—is the key beneficiary of the peace, its domination expanding to encompass the whole political economy of the reconstruction era.

The subject of Chapter 2 is the reconstruction of Angola enabled by the post-2004 boom in oil production and price increase as well as a strategic partnership with China. I underline the extent to which the elite has been in the driver's seat throughout this process, hiring a multitude of foreigners to enact its self-defined strategy for postwar Angola. After surveying the elite's priorities—infrastructure and the reshaping of the urban environment—as well as the obvious blind spots in its reconstruction agenda, the chapter explores the regime's modernizing vision and deployment of developmental language. The dreams of peace and oil-based prosperity articulated by the MPLA are certainly shared by a majority of Angolans. However, in practice its agenda excludes large sections of the population. I argue that the regime has a discernible plan for remaking the country that is markedly shaped by elite interests and drinks from several, mostly illiberal, sources for inspiration, and that the usual donor prescriptions play a marginal role in it.

Chapter 3 continues the analysis of the regime's ambitions by exploring the ways in which it sought to consolidate its grip in the decade after the end of the conflict. Here, as throughout the book, terms such as "state", "party", "government" and "regime", distinct concepts in political science, are used somewhat interchangeably in a manner that mirrors both their usage in Angola and the elusiveness of barriers in a system entirely dominated by the MPLA.[60] I argue that, though built upon the regime's coercive might, this hegemonic drive benefited from the desire for political order by war-weary Angolans, including former UNITA supporters. After exploring the chequered history of the MPLA prior to the 2002 victory, the chapter surveys its policies in both the urban environment—the "archipelago of cities" it had always governed—and the ambitious drive to master the rural world. Policies towards urban society, I argue, are focused on the cooptation of the educated and the ambivalent fostering of a state-supported middle class, with the poor viewed as a problem and subjected to containment. In the rural setting, the state is engaged in the unprecedented takeover of large swathes of previously ungoverned territory and the taming of populations that had frequently eluded its writ during the war. While it deploys a language of inclusive nation-building and public goods provision, the state's actions in the periphery are instead focused on the achievement of control.

Chapter 4 focuses on the rise of capitalism with Angolan characteristics: that is, the postwar stabilization of Angola's economy and its takeover by a few oligarchs surrounding the presidency who monopolized the available enrichment opportunities. As Chapter 1 shows, this process was initiated during the last decade of the war via the manifold schemes of the parallel system. But the scale of accumulation in the context of the peace-era boom is of a different order of magnitude altogether, not only in terms of the benefits available to insiders but also in regard to the role of foreign capital and expatriate workers in the process of commercial expansion. The chapter studies this postwar dynamic and its main oligarchic beneficiaries, before inquiring as to the moral economy of this *sui generis* capitalism, its social influence on contemporary Angola, and its sustainability beyond oil.

Moving to the international sphere, Chapter 5 deals with the transformation of Angola's position from a disreputable war-torn state to an apparently successful African growth story. Angolan elites have used this leeway to establish new partnerships as well as recalibrate existing ones around commercial interests and away from the governance concerns that had dented the regime's image a decade ago. In continuation of the offshore strategies of the 1990s, but on a different scale and degree of sophistication, they have also been able to put the deregulated, fluid character of the world economy at their service. This shrewd engagement with the international setting has culminated in the rise of Angola's going-out strategy, the major peacetime innovation of the parallel state. With all the might of a petro-state undergoing a boom, the Angolan state has acquired assets abroad in partnership with elite private interests and become a major international player, especially in Portugal. Angola's foreign strategies in the peace era have shifted Angola's status. The MPLA is no longer fighting for survival or managing scarcity, indebtedness and insecurity; in some exalted corners, there is even talk of Angola as an emerging power. Yet I argue that this relative success is precarious. A downward turn in the price of oil, which has underpinned the unusual experience of Angola and the regime's range of choices over the last decade, can swiftly unravel them.

This book ends at a moment in time in which the MPLA remains the hegemonic force in Angola. Its leitmotif is therefore the regime's authoritarian consolidation over the span of the first decade of peace. However, I argue that, by 2012, this unproblematic era of domination, characterized by popular apathy and regime aloofness from social pressures, was coming to an end. Over the past couple of years, Angolans, especially the young for whom the war is but a distant memory, have become increasingly vocal. Scepticism about the MPLA's development rhetoric is spreading; the collective dream of modernization, so powerful a mobilizer only a few years earlier, is encountering growing cynicism. The president's standing, for long inviolable in public, has become the subject of widespread derision. In the protean context of post-postwar Angola, the unintended consequences of the MPLA's actions and inactions since 2002 are fast becoming politicized. At the time of writing, this does not yet threaten the regime but raises the costs of continued domination.

I

IN THE SHADOW OF WAR

OIL AND THE MAKING OF THE PARALLEL SYSTEM

To understand the structures of political and economic power in post-2002 Angola, we need to start with the extraordinary circumstances of the country's independence in 1975 and the subsequent drawn out conflict. These initial conditions—of war, the implosion of the non-oil economy and the state apparatus, and dependence on oil revenue for state survival—shaped the MPLA regime's approach to power. In turn, the state's stranglehold over oil came to define state-society relations, the rapport with the international economy and the sort of institutions that would be built and nurtured in postcolonial Angola.

Crucially, the war's long "state of exception" also provided the pretext for a degree of decision-making centralization that is rare even when compared with other petro-states and would certainly not have obtained in peacetime. Invoking the existential challenge of the war and the need to bypass the incompetent formal state, President José Eduardo dos Santos (JES) wrested control of the oil revenue stream and carved out a parallel state centred on the presidency and the country's opaque yet capable national oil company, Sonangol. In time, this gave rise to an oil-driven, internationalized political economy and global networks of support and patronage. These provided JES with an unprecedented degree of discretionary power, allowing him to sideline the state administration, the party apparatus and all other structures of potential influence across Angolan society.

MAGNIFICENT AND BEGGAR LAND

This chapter explores Angola's postcolonial trajectory through the prism of its foundational challenges[1] and oil endowment, and looks at the resulting institutional patterns and governance strategies. The chapter then outlines the manner in which the president's complex and adaptable system of rule became the *modus operandi* of power and never went away. This parallel state—the very stuff of Angolan post-colonial politics—while the bearer of some successes, is inextricably linked to the stunting of formal institutions, the misappropriation of public resources on an epic scale and the consolidation of JES's authoritarian rule. In telling this story, I strike a balance between the roles of structural factors, which powerfully influenced Angolan politics, and of agency. Elite decisions, especially at the formative stage of the early post-colonial years, were pivotal in shaping an original and often ingenious, if predatory, system of governance. Nor can one ignore the extent to which the system bears JES's imprint, even if it was put together on the basis of contingency and pragmatic adaptation rather than the implementation of a blueprint.

More important for the purposes of this book, the parallel system, which had defined the war, also came to define the peace. Far from being rolled back after 2002, the system was reenergized by the war victory and the meteoric rise in oil production and revenue, mutating into an ever more intricate structure of control at the centre of the *sui generis* reconstruction agenda discussed in Chapter 2. "The imperative of the postwar period," commented a prominent civil society activist in Luanda, "has been to maintain the president's power and constantly reinvent the system to achieve that".[2] The choices made in the heat of Angola's tragic early years and deepened during the chaotic 1990s had gained a life of their own, circumscribing the political economy for the long-term.

IMPLOSION AT INDEPENDENCE

In the messy history of European imperial retreat from Africa, few instances were more calamitous than the demise of Portuguese rule in Angola.[3] Following the April 1974 Carnation Revolution that toppled the dictatorship, the Portuguese armed forces vowed to end the three long-running African wars and decolonize their overseas possessions. Amidst Lisbon's revolutionary politics, not much thinking went into the form of decolonization, the political system bequeathed or the fate of European populations; on account of the leftist character of the new

Portuguese regime, it was tacitly assumed that power would be passed on to likeminded "modernist" liberation groups. In Angola, however, there was no nationalist equivalent to Guinea's PAIGC or Mozambique's FRELIMO, but rather three viscerally antagonistic movements. A Portuguese attempt at brokering a transitional government failed; the massive departure of the settlers commenced, and by mid-1975 a war for control of Angola had begun. In short order this became an international conflict with South African, Zairian and Cuban invasions on the side of the different Angolan factions while the US and the USSR played covert roles. At independence on 11 November 1975, Luanda was held by the MPLA and by early 1976, the massive Cuban support had repulsed the competing movements, momentarily expelled their foreign patrons, and earned it control of the state.

This short war changed Angola beyond recognition. Driving around the country in mid-1976, José Manuel Zenha Rela, a Portuguese civil servant who had decided to stay on and serve the new state, found a scenario of utter desolation:[4] ghost towns completely destroyed, fields where the harvest had not taken place and the bush was fast advancing, stray cattle roaming the plains, cars and agricultural equipment cast aside on the fields and roads, and abandoned industrial plants. In the cities too, streets were silent as the majority of cars had gone; the shops, although open, had empty shelves, and the few with supplies had long queues. Much of the country's infrastructure was blown to pieces. But the most serious gap lay in the departure of the vast majority of technical staff. Although exact numbers are unavailable, several interviewees who played a prominent role in this period referred to there being fewer than one hundred university graduates left in the country in 1976.[5] Things were even worse at the middle and lower levels. Whites in Angola had performed many tasks that would have been fulfilled by African workers in other colonies. With an estimated 85 per cent of illiterates, there was simply no one left to manage the economy and the state at the requisite level. As a senior official remembers with bitterness: "this was not just a matter of engineers or doctors: in 1975, everyone who knew how to turn a screw disappeared overnight [...] you must understand, in this place no one knew how to do anything".[6]

The senior MPLA leadership was at a loss in this fast-changing environment. Most had not been to Angola for a decade or more. Their limited knowledge of the country[7] and memories of the backward colony of their youth had not prepared them for the shock of returning to a fundamentally different place in 1974. Adolfo Maria, by then an MPLA dissident, remembers the "cosmopolitan" feel of the city and its "new avenues, high rises, shops": "This was another Luanda".[8] For under the shadow of war, major transformations had occurred.[9] After the start of the conflict in 1961, the Portuguese did not budge politically but enacted a series of legal and economic reforms in a belated Portuguese version of developmental colonialism.[10] The settlers cornered most of the benefits of this era but there were important improvements for the African population. Seeking to limit discontent, the colonial government repealed the detested Indigenous Statute, including its forced labour provisions, did away with compulsory crops, and created rural markets that soon boosted smallholder commercial production. Crucially, the Portuguese also welcomed additional foreign direct investment and made sustained metropolitan budgetary transfers to support infrastructure development.

As a result of steady technocratic management and a capable counterinsurgency campaign (made easier by the fact that the liberation movements fought each other), the war, though brutal, was confined to remote regions and had no impact on the vibrant and diversified economy, which posted annual real growth rates of 4.7 per cent between 1961 and 1974.[11] By 1974, in addition to a fast-growing manufacturing sector centred on consumer goods and light industry, Angola was a major exporter of sisal, maize, coffee, cotton, diamonds and iron ore, while oil, the extraction of which had started in the mid-1950s, became the major export in 1973. But the clearest proof of this prosperity was the wartime doubling of the European population to about 350,000, the second in sub-Saharan Africa after South Africa. Although this last gasp of colonialism remains understudied, there is no doubt that its long-term impact in terms of state formation was huge. Ironically, the nationalist challenge had propelled the Portuguese to create a unified Angola for the first time in history: tarmac roads crisscrossed the country, the administrative grid became denser, and the pull of the central society brought into its orbit previously detached regions.

By early 1976 all of this was gone. The eye-catching debris of settler modernity—its roads, factories and high rises—was everywhere but it had not been built for Angolans. They did not know how to make use of it any more than they could man the institutions of the state. The complex system of settler-owned rural trade was gone[12] and rural communication routes and scheduled transportation were often abandoned. The lack of supply led to absenteeism by agricultural workers, a precipitous slump in production and retreat into subsistence farming. This resulted in the dismantling of economic relations between different sectors and regions, dealing a death blow to a nationally integrated economy.[13]

In subsequent years, the MPLA blamed the war for Angola's economic involution. The war was obviously critical, but this explanation avoids the fact that the government's policies were singularly self-harming and could only have run the country into the ground, even in regions and economic sectors largely unaffected by the war. The MPLA introduced socialist management and central planning, and made unrealistic commitments to the state-led creation of heavy industry and, later on, import-substitution industrialization. Although many self-defeating policies were Angolan choices, Eastern European advisers were not helpful, especially in regard to the private sector. As Manuel Ennes Ferreira writes in his definitive analysis of MPLA economic policy until 1991, these industrial goals were pursued without relation to, and always undermined by, budgetary, monetary, financial, exchange rate, price and fiscal policies.[14] Set against this baffling record of mismanagement, the policy pronouncements of the Politburo and the relevant ministries are straight out of *Alice in Wonderland*.[15]

Other dynamics made things worse. The state apparatus was perceived as a political prize[16] and taken over by unskilled Angolans, which resulted in the demise of its capacity. Political loyalty was paramount and remaining technical staff, while sorely needed, chafed under semi-literate party bosses. The MPLA expropriated the property of departed settlers and soon hounded out most property-owning Portuguese still in the country but lacking good party contacts. Even before the re-emergence of UNITA's South African-supported challenge at end of the 1970s, the Angolan economy was in precipitous decline. "We did so many stupid things in those years", confided a senior civil servant after reviewing the major economic policies of the era.[17] The economy never returned to pre-independence productivity levels; most sectors collapsed entirely.

SONANGOL AS THE CENTREPIECE OF THE PARALLEL SYSTEM

The exception was the oil sector, then mostly based in Cabinda province and nearby waters.[18] This was carefully preserved to become the fiscal lifeline of the Angolan state. During the years of guerrilla war and exile, the MPLA had been rhetorically bellicose towards the Western oil companies that provided the colonial authorities with crucial fiscal support.[19] However, when confronted with the 1975 implosion of the Angolan economy, Agostinho Neto, the country's first president, accepted that oil would be as important for regime survival as the Eastern Bloc's military aid. In order to manage a smooth transition for the oil sector, the MPLA put together a National Commission for the Restructuring of the Petroleum Sector under the responsibility of Percy Freudenthal, a white Angolan businessman who had become close to the movement.[20] The most pressing task was to arrange the return of the main oil operator, Gulf Oil, whose subsidiary the Cabinda Gulf Oil Company (CABGOC) was responsible for the bulk of Angola's oil production. Gulf had left in November 1975 as the war raged. Through a mix of pressure from Nigeria, which hinted at retaliation against Gulf interests in the Niger Delta, and Angolan reassurances of business-minded intentions, the Commission managed to bring the company back. By March 1976, Gulf Oil had paid an outstanding share of royalties to the MPLA, thus recognizing it as the legitimate Angolan government despite US opposition. Other companies active in Angola such as Petrofina and Texaco were also encouraged to return by their apparently reliable, professional Angolan interlocutors.

Although the full nationalization of the oil sector was rejected, in accordance with the decision to expropriate settler property the Portuguese oil company ANGOL was nationalized. Behind this apparently bold measure, however, lurks a transition more typical of conservative Francophone countries than radical Angola. At a time when Portugal had not even recognized the MPLA as the government of Angola,[21] members of the Commission went to Lisbon to sign a memorandum of understanding with ANGOL's parent company to the effect that the Angolan NOC they were about to create would keep many of ANGOL's (mostly Portuguese) employees.[22] Many simply stayed on and became Sonangol employees. Once this was settled, the founding team moved into the ANGOL building in downtown Luanda and crafted the new Angolan NOC. "In no other area of the Angolan economy was there such a degree of continuity, with both structures and people kept in place," one Sonangol executive who started out in pre-1974 ANGOL said. "You see, through colonialism, foreign invasion, Marxist-Leninism and capitalism, I have not left the same building."[23]

Sonangol itself was created in June 1976 as the Angolan oil concessionaire, sector regulator, and tax-gathering agent. Although a Petroleum Ministry was later established, it was always a political lightweight and never rivalled the NOC's influence. According to a member of the founding group, the vision that animated the new company can be described as "flexibility, reliability, and pragmatism". Sonangol would not embrace the Marxist economics that shaped Angola until the end of the Cold War: its "compass was the international oil economy, not domestic policy fads".[24] In particular, it was to be insulated from the political race for a "share of the spoils", "the sheer incompetence", the anti-corporate mentality, and the disregard for the rule of law prevalent in all other sectors of the economy.[25] Sonangol executives also understood that with a Soviet- and Cuban-supported government and the overt hostility of the US, they would have to go out of their way to appear trustworthy to Western oil investors. Finally, Sonangol did not define its mission in an overambitious manner. Acutely aware of the complexity of the oil sector and the paucity of human resources in Angola, Sonangol's priority became contractual negotiations with oil firms, while the latter would remain responsible for exploration and production. In order to improve its negotiating performance, Sonangol was committed to close partnerships with the best available expertise.

An important such partnership was with the Algerian NOC, SONATRACH. In May 1976, a high-level delegation arrived in Luanda to help set up Sonangol. Algerian experts became all-purpose advisers to Sonangol in "coming to terms with the practical side of things", and helped to train a considerable number of first-generation Angolan personnel. Italy's ENI also played a role by providing technical education to many Sonangol workers at its Milan training institute. But Sonangol's rather surprising major source of apprenticeship was Arthur D. Little, the reputable US consulting firm. Arthur D. Little had been a much-appreciated oil sector consultant to the colonial government and the Commission had found some of its recommendations of increased state participation in the oil industry congenial. President Neto, it was reported, quizzed the Commission about the maintenance of such "imperialist" advisers. But he was reassured to know that the Algerians (who also worked closely with Arthur D. Little) spoke very positively of them and thus allowed the arrangement to stand.[26] Running the Angola operation out of its London office to avoid complications with the US government, this "counter-intuitive hiring"[27] provided Sonangol with an indispensible source of contractual acumen (it set up Angola's first PSA), knowledge of energy markets, and overall sector organization, getting involved in everything from seismic data and creation of offshore blocks to running road shows and bidding rounds.[28] A final partnership of Sonangol's flew even more in the face of the geopolitical fault-lines of the day and definitely set a pragmatic tone for the years to come. From 1976 until the early 1980s Marc Rich, the billionaire commodity trader soon to turn long-running fugitive from US justice, was the exclusive trader of Angolan oil.[29] Spectacularly, many of Rich's cargoes were sent directly from Angola to South Africa, though the two countries were at war.[30]

How could a self-defined Marxist-Leninist regime bring into being a company that not only flouted the basic tenets of socialism but also cavorted with American oil and consulting firms, all the while exerting the pivotal role in the otherwise stillborn postcolonial economy? To start with, it had to do with the individuals involved. The backgrounds of Sonangol's core team were bureaucratic and entrepreneurial rather than in nationalist subversion of Portuguese domination. But they quickly became well-networked MPLA members who enjoyed the confidence of President Neto. They shared the common social background of the upper ranks of the party, the exceedingly small, late colonial world of Luanda-based, mostly mixed-race educated Angolans. In this confined social circle many influential actors in government, the party and Sonangol were related by blood ties or by friendship. No matter how unorthodox their views may have sounded, their loyalty was never in doubt, an undeviating characteristic of Sonangol officials up to the present. They were also respected as technocrats at a time when Angola possessed very few university-educated cadres. More important, they enjoyed strong political support for their project. In normal conditions, a company like Sonangol would never have been allowed to operate in such a manner. But there was a perception that the oil sector was a matter of life or death, ensuring the viability of the MPLA state and paying for its Cuban protectors. Whatever the management style, it would be tolerated if it permitted the steady flow of resources. The oil sector was explicitly excluded from the domain of socialist policy-making and made to finance its follies as well as the war effort.[31]

This pragmatism met with great success. By 1983 Sonangol and its foreign partners managed to surpass late colonial oil production levels.

Sonangol Limited, a London office responsible for the direct trading of Angola's share of the oil, was established in the same year, the first of several Sonangol subsidiaries to span the globe. Sonangol also managed to diversify the number of foreign investors in Angola's upstream (primarily through Elf-Aquitaine's acquisition of block 3 in 1979), although the largest share of production remained with CABGOC, which was bought out by Chevron in 1984. Not that this dependence on one company constituted a burden. Gulf and then Chevron (their operations protected from US-backed UNITA rebels by Cuban troops and Soviet weaponry) proved to be reliable allies for the eighteen-year duration of US enmity. The hostility of the Reagan Administration did not change the thrust of Chevron's Angola engagement.

There were dangers along the way. With Neto's death in 1979, it was not obvious that the Sonangol exception would continue. The upper echelons of the party were keen on reining in the company. The marginalized Finance Ministry, always a critic of the NOC owing to its quasi-fiscal operations, engaged in "constant wars with Sonangol".[32] Even the mostly quiescent Petroleum Ministry agitated for cutting Sonangol down to size. By this stage however, Neto's successor José Eduardo dos Santos realized that Sonangol should be ring-fenced and made to report to the presidency alone. The two reasons for this remained constant for the subsequent three decades. The first is that, in the face of the challenges posed by the war and a dysfunctional public administration, Sonangol alone could be trusted with missions that were core to the preservation of the state. These missions included not only the management of the oil business but also important quasi-fiscal operations and the running of aspects of the war effort, as I will discuss below. The second reason is that by keeping Sonangol outside the purview of the party-state, JES was ensuring a remarkable degree of discretionary power over upwards of 80 per cent of government revenue. These would cascade down the power structure—on his terms.

Sonangol's aloofness from the broader dynamics of Angola's political economy was therefore safeguarded. The president's tight grip prevented any disorderly, Nigerian-style bleeding of company resources. Management remained respectful of the company's technical team and the latter stayed on, enlarged by new legal, engineering, geological and economic expertise drawn from Sonangol's many educational partnerships. By the late 1980s, a World Bank team reported "the shortage of

33

skilled and trained manpower in Angola", but went on to say that the petroleum sector was the least affected by it. "So far Sonangol's high- and medium-level management positions have been staffed with comparatively experienced and competent personnel [...] Sonangol has [also] effectively and advantageously used external consultants to supplement its capabilities in all aspects of its operations." "General government policies in the oil sector have been enlightened and thus deservedly successful," the report concluded.[33]

In a few short months in 1975, Angola's diversified economy and robust infrastructure had collapsed entirely. These initial conditions, together with the revenue-generating petroleum sector that survived, defined the country's subsequent institutional trajectory. The rump state controlled by the MPLA, with Sonangol at its core, was soon transformed into an oil-based rentier state. The outcomes of this process were unconventional. In many ways Angola was a failed state, and not just in terms of popular expectations of service delivery: it was absent from large tracts of its nominal territory until 2002, had no fiscal capacity outside the oil sector, and provided no security or regulation beyond confined urban spaces. That said, at the heart of the system resided a capable core of enclave institutions, certainly unfit for governing the population or providing territorial-administrative coverage, but remarkably capable of ensuring regime survival and the prosperity of insiders. Despite numerous external and internal challenges, the MPLA state had managed to secure a long-term flow of resources through a pragmatic, commercial link with Western oil corporations. These companies ran a physically sheltered "economic sanctuary"[34] in the coastal and offshore areas of Cabinda and Zaire provinces which, by ensuring the virtual totality of the regime's revenue and networks of international support that advanced its interests,[35] jointly sustained the MPLA's political order. Its other pillar until 1991 was the large-scale, Soviet-supported presence of a Cuban expeditionary force.

The upshot of this extraverted rapport with the Western private sector was the regime's remarkable degree of autonomy from Angolan society. As Terry Lynn Karl notes, the manner in which a state earns a living affects its pattern of institutionalization, and petro-states share broadly comparable trajectories.[36] Angola's state-society rapport reflected the state's fiscal strength and lack of need for direct taxation as well as the physical insulation of the offshore oil sector from both the war and the

Angolan masses.[37] Nor was the state interested in diversifying the economy away from oil or generating mass employment. This autonomy led not to a general strengthening of the state apparatus but to a narrower consolidation of enclaves and the president's informal control, with the war providing the excuse for the absence of any institutions of restraint. Sonangol's role as the ring-fenced conduit of the country's wealth was pivotal in this regard.

THE PARALLEL SYSTEM UNBOUND

When the MPLA buried socialism at the beginning of the 1990s and the elite enthusiastically converted to crony capitalism (see Chapter 4), Sonangol was far and away the foremost entity in Angola's political economy, and certainly the best suited for the new dispensation. At this stage, the company took the momentous step of restructuring itself into a holding company, the Sonangol Group or Sonangol EP, and broke away from the relatively restricted field in which it had thrived. This was not a matter of trying to become Exxon or Saudi Aramco, especially at a time when Angola's oil sector was turning towards ever more technologically complex tasks. The goal was rather to create a series of subsidiaries and joint ventures in related businesses where Sonangol could profit from rising opportunities. Soon Sonangol, which expanded from about 100 employees in 1976 to at least 9,000 three decades later, was active in areas verging from shipping and air transport to insurance, banking, real estate, catering, etc. By the turn of the century, this had turned Sonangol, Africa's second largest corporation, into a veritable constellation of interests whose global footprint is discussed in Chapter 5.[38]

This growth was made possible by the exponential expansion of Angola's oil sector that followed the discovery of deep and ultra-deep water oil deposits from the mid-1990s onwards, attracting dozens of oil companies from the world over, including virtually all top corporations, and tens of billions of dollars in investment.[39] The civil war onshore barely dented this upward trend. And throughout, relations with foreign oil companies remained as unproblematic and cooperative as they had been in the Cold War. Having interviewed dozens of oil company officials during the past decade in Angola and elsewhere, I have rarely found anyone expressing a negative view of their interaction with Sonangol. More than a few were enthusiastic and even admiring. A top oil executive of a major European firm with decades of involvement in Angola did not hesitate to say that Sonangol is "the Angolan miracle".[40] Some seemed never to have shaken off Idi Amin-type expectations of African leadership and were struck when they realized that they were dealing with global citizens "with a similar outlook": "when you are dealing with someone like Vicente [Angola's vice president and former head of Sonangol], you are dealing with people like you and me," noted an executive from a US oil company.[41] International bankers, whose role in the parallel system is constitutive, share the same positive view of the company's reliability. Ironically, tensions that arise between the oil companies and Sonangol reflect the NOC's hard bargaining, fostering of competition, and relative technical competence that put it in a equitable position vis-à-vis foreign partners.

There is no doubt that, from a purely technical perspective, Sonangol has been wisely managed. This atypical African corporation mostly runs according to operational principles of technical competence, stability and reliability that are entirely at odds with those of the Angolan public administration. However, it has done so for the sake of the presidency's interests, which has honed Sonangol into the central political tool of its stranglehold over Angola. By controlling oil revenue and having at his disposal such a sophisticated structure, JES possesses a rare concentration of resources and the means for their distribution that affords him a high degree of autonomy in regard to both domestic and international pressures. This personal lock over resources and all that comes with them is considerable, even when compared with other autocrats in oil-rich states. It can only be understood in terms of Angola's particular trajectory, especially the permissive atmosphere of the war, as well as the choices of the president himself over more than three decades of rule.

The key to understanding Sonangol's unusual role is that the company did more than run the oil sector; it shadowed and often replaced the state administration, first in the fiscal sphere and then in every other systemically important sphere of Angola's political economy. This started inconspicuously enough in the mid-1980s, when Angola needed to pay for oil field developments in Cabinda. Unable to make these payments amidst general mismanagement and a collapse in oil prices, the government turned to Western private banks but these, while keen on doing business with Angola, were sceptical about normal repayment arrangements. The outcome was the blueprint for the dozens of oil-backed loans that followed.

Loans mostly contracted from major Western banks were run via special purpose vehicles, which are offshore financial tools that allow lenders to benefit from safe repayment structures through oil price protection, debt service reserve accounts and an accelerated repayment mechanism, and repayments made directly in oil. Since these oil-backed loans were targeted at the oil sector, Sonangol, whose reputation and creditworthiness far exceeded those of the government itself, would run the whole operation. In context, the decision to leave Angola's financial system (including the Finance Ministry and the Central Bank) out of the loop seemed reasonable.[42] But "as more of these kinds of loans were signed, bankers grew more confident, and President dos Santos began to build on this mechanism,"[43] the scale of this opaque financial structure came to rival the above-board operations that formal organizations were aware of. These operations became invisible not just to the Angolan public administration, but to any other entity, like the IMF, with an interest in Angola's accounts. Sonangol's centrality to the parallel system as Angola's revenue generator was part of a much broader process of non- or de-institutionalization of decision-making.

A number of people with intimate knowledge of these matters insist on the contingent character of the parallel system's build-up; they say it was only after it was up and running that its usefulness for many other purposes became obvious. There is no doubt that the system emerged in a pragmatic, piecemeal and adaptive manner, and that no pre-existing model was being copied. At the same time, the agenda for side-tracking resources and power was certainly there from early on, as demonstrated by a mid-1980s stab at running a slush fund through Sonangol UK's oil trading on a scale that necessitated high-level political support.[44] As in all oil-rich polities, power holders were searching for ways to consolidate their grip over resources. The parallel financing system eventually emerged as the solution under the shadow of total war in the 1990s.

While the system was set up in the 1980s, it was during the decade after the return to war in late 1992 that the oil-backed parallel system became, in Olivier Vallée's words, "that gothic construct of wealth accumulation".[45] The structures linking the presidency and Sonangol to the international system that had been created in previous years were ideally suited for the panicked conditions of the new conflict, which amounted to as many arguments for the further consolidation of presidential power. These included the fact that UNITA initially held the upper hand, the need for a massive, breakneck reorganization and reequipping of the armed forces in the wake of the Cuban and Soviet departure, and the constant need for fresh loans to service the war effort and keep the poorly managed economy afloat. In the context of the elite's sudden embrace of wild capitalism discussed later in this book, the "leading apparatchiks [search for] ever more innovative ways of financing the war effort"[46] also proved compatible with profiteering and outright theft.

A major development here was the increasingly central role of international brokers in everything from arms sales and diamond concessions to army logistics and loan contraction.[47] Again, this started out as improvisation: in the face of a UN embargo, dos Santos turned to middlemen like Arkady Gaydamak and Pierre Falcone to secure weaponry for the regime.[48] Their success in both delivering the goods and working with political elites soon led to central roles in the negotiation of oil-backed financing with Western banking consortia and sovereign debt renegotiations crucial for the war effort. This small cast of intermediaries would also translate their newfound influence, often phrased as "friendship", into considerable business partnerships with the elite, especially in the diamond sector.[49] For the first time, this came to involve the President's own family, members of which soon acquired large fortunes. This extensive use of foreigners as emissaries of the president for matters of state survival was a further qualitative step in the de-institutionalization of decisions at the domestic level. "This was no longer a matter of the Finance Ministry or the party not knowing exactly what was going on," a journalist with knowledge of the period notes, "at this stage, only a handful of individuals had any clue about matters of life or death".[50] It was also revealing of the much broader shift in the character of war in Angola, with the international market replacing allies' military support for the regime in the form of a new cast of mercenaries and foreign "commercial" intelligence providers.[51]

The privatization of Angola's war, in addition to being a source of self-enrichment for the politico-military elite, provides telling evidence of the global power networks that arose in the 1990s and the way they fortified (indeed, enabled) the MPLA's control of the state.[52] For the underbelly of fixers just described was intimately linked up with an extensive structure of service providers—bankers, accountants, auditors, lawyers, intelligence experts—who facilitated the interests of the Angolan elite. A number of scandals that have emerged since allow us to piece the story together. The highest profile such scandal is the so-called "Ango-lagate" affair, an oil-for-arms deal with French interests that allowed well-placed individuals, mainly through over-invoicing, to collect aston-ishing side payments.[53] The corruption trials around the national oil company Elf Aquitaine, an even bigger scandal rocking France in the late 1990s, also provided extensive evidence of the operations of the Angolan parallel system.[54] The secretive 1996 renegotiation of Angola's debt to Russia, when at least US$386 million were paid to needless intermediar-ies and facilitators as well as presidential insiders, shows that even the country's debt burden could be turned into an enrichment opportu-nity in the right circumstances.[55] The huge sums UNITA managed to extract from diamonds seem paltry in comparison, even at the best of times in 1993–94.

In the last years of the war, the financial operations of the parallel state became notorious, as did its role as an offshore mechanism for the appro-priation of rents by the Angolan elite.[56] The resulting black hole in Angolan state finances, into which, according to the IMF, US$4.22 bil-lion disappeared between 1997 and 2002,[57] was dubbed the "Bermuda Triangle". According to some estimates, the Bermuda Triangle was devouring up to *half* of Angola's annual earnings at this stage.[58] The Angolan government claimed that the major discrepancies found were the product of poor accounting and lack of capacity, not theft. To this the campaigning NGO Global Witness retorted, "a government and state oil company that handle billions of dollars through complex offshore arrangements, including the use of Special Purpose Vehicles and tax havens, can certainly manage a simple balance sheet".[59] The Angolan authorities were livid at this degree of scrutiny by outsiders. As a top government figure later put it, "we knew we had enemies out there and [...] their intention was to put us in a corner".[60] As we will see in Chapter 2, these Angolan concerns were not unwarranted, as the disparagement of the parallel system did contribute towards halting reconstruction funds for Angola in the early postwar period—even though the parallel system would weather these criticisms.

Disparagement from Western campaigners notwithstanding, the par-allel system of the late war years wasn't just a corrupt conspiracy and the missing amounts must not be understood as wholly destined for elite pockets. A lot of these quasi-fiscal operations, Nicholas Shaxson writes, were related to "legitimate, or at least quasi-legitimate, construction contracts, arms purchasing deals, covert payments for Angola's extensive intelligence apparatus, and other matters".[61] As a seasoned oil expert put it, "in Angola the normal state is useless. Even in Saudi Arabia, if the king wants something done, he trusts it to Aramco. In the Angolan context, and in the middle of a war, it is entirely understandable that [JES] would trust such an important role to one of the few tools he had at his disposal."[62] But it is precisely on account of these multiple roles—the governance of core matters and the siphoning off of state treasury thoroughly enmeshed—that the system thrived. The system was so promiscuous that it became impossible to differentiate between legitimate and illegitimate purposes, *raison d'état* and personal enrichment.

Moreover, from the viewpoint of the outcome, it doesn't matter how one labels these parallel structures, for they unfailingly resulted in the privatization of power and strengthening of JES's empire over Angola. Sonangol and the control over Angola's oil revenue it affords is the centrepiece of his rule, but there is much more to the complex edifice he built around it. Indeed, a full definition of the parallel system would include not just the presidency-Sonangol nexus but also a complex web of intelligence services (Angolan state entities as well as foreign private-sector operators, especially in high-end technical surveillance), roving diplomatic emissaries (Angolan as well as foreign), business partners and international service providers (accounts, lawyers, bankers). These entities would have limited mutual knowledge and come into contact for specific purposes only, with the presidency as their sole common point.

THE PRESIDENCY AND THE PARALLEL SYSTEM

As mentioned above, Angola's oil endowment and the initial conditions that forged its postcolonial institutions are central to the country's trajectory. But without JES's long reign and the choices he has made over the years, Angola's structure of power would likely be different. The story of JES's rise is well known. Born in the Sambizanga neighbourhood of Luanda in 1942, JES was one of a small number of black students enrolled in the prestigious Liceu Salvador Correia during the 1950s. Joining the MPLA in Brazzaville in 1962 in a subsequently romanticized escape from Angola (the fishing trawler he used to make the journey now stands on a pedestal at the centre of a roundabout in Lobito), JES spent most of the liberation war in exile. This included several years in Baku, where he took a degree in Petroleum Engineering and married a Russian woman, Tatiana Kukanova, who is the mother of his eldest daughter, Isabel. He had a number of high-ranking positions from 1975 to 1979, including those of vice-prime minister and foreign minister, but real power was always vested in Agostinho Neto.

After Neto's death in 1979,[63] the different sensibilities within the MPLA cancelled out the obvious party barons as not black enough, too left or too right. JES was the typical compromise choice: young and good-looking but quiet and apparently none too smart. Intimate acquaintances from those years remember him not unkindly as a good football player and a polite figure but also as "shy", "apathetic" and "lacklustre, except in regard to women".[64] His *modus operandi* was and remains uncharismatic and backstage. It is no coincidence that while less successful African leaders, including JES's arch-rival Jonas Savimbi, are routinely endowed by the public with magical superpowers, he has never shaken off the grey, committee-man image or been credited with powerful juju. Most important, he gave the impression of "not having strong views about anything and being easy to manipulate by the *mais-velhos* [the elders]".[65] This was certainly the case of the MPLA's ideological *éminence grise*, Lúcio Lara, who was instrumental in dos Santos' accession to the presidency.

As always in such cases, the impression was false. After a quiet start, JES spent the early 1980s meticulously consolidating his grip over the MPLA and lowering the profile of the *mestiços* and whites who had surrounded Neto. (This was merely a cosmetic move: in institutions of systemic importance such as the armed forces and Sonangol, as well as in his immediate circle, whites and *mestiços* remained in key positions). As noted above, he also took great care in cordoning off Sonangol and the money side of things as his personal domains. By 1985, when a number of leading figures critical of JES were evicted from the Politburo, he was in full control of the party-state apparatus.

At this stage, the presidency, still installed in the suburban, partly Yugoslav-built Futungo de Belas palace, became the sole centre of power. In the 1990s, the presidency moved to the grander, refurbished colonial governor's palace in Luanda's Cidade Alta, but the inner circle of the President is sometimes still referred to as the "Futungo". This book uses terms such as "the palace", "Cidade Alta", and "Futungo" interchangeably, as do Angolans, to refer to the sphere of President dos Santos' formal and informal power. The major features of this system—amongst the

41

most centralized in sub-Saharan Africa—have remained consistent over the years. The presidency's structure of control goes considerably beyond a shady coterie of advisers, important as they were and remain, to encompass an extremely well resourced administration that moonlights and oversees the party-state.

This never meant doing away with the party-state or moving all functions of the state to an informal sphere. As discussed in Chapter 3, while JES jealously guards decision-making over every important aspect of policy—revenue, coercion and foreign relations—for many quotidian state tasks he needs the formal administration. His relationship with the party is equally multi-layered. Although he curbed the MPLA's authority in practice and nurtured his own personal structures of power instead,[66] "comrade" JES has always been careful to talk up the MPLA's formal role and movement party mystique. On rare occasions, this may introduce nuances to his preferred approach. The trade-offs are well worth it for dos Santos. As Chapter 3 shows, the MPLA became a solid, now-national organization, providing the president with a tool for managing elites, running in the regime's elections, distributing patronage, privileges and social status, and minimizing conflict and splits. The MPLA gives the JES system a degree of sophistication much beyond Mobutu-style autocracies. But regardless of this institutional and party-political façade, the locus of power is the presidency, and it remains absolute.

Over more than three decades in office and major political, economic and military shifts, JES has deployed a variety of tools in order to sustain this control and shown a prodigious capacity for improvisation and learning. Yet in the words of Leonardo Sciascia, he has the knack for "making every innovation serve old purposes".[67] At a human level, he developed a marked preference for "isolated men without a retinue".[68] This has included whites, *mestiços*, foreigners, Angolan descendants of Cape Verdeans and Saotomeans, former *fraccionistas* (dissidents) from the 1977 Nito faction and UNITA escapees who developed a strong loyalty to him. Organizationally, an extensive in-house presidential bureaucracy took precedence over all matters of state, with ministries hobbled by a game of musical chairs and ad hoc commissions preventing serious institutional consolidation. A variety of intelligence organizations and the loyal Presidential Guard gave the president an unmatched mastery of information and the means of coercion. The transition of the armed forces from a party-political organization overseen by commissars to a "national" outfit in the 1990s helped in cutting off direct linkages with the MPLA and establishing presidential control over them. From the 1990s onwards, as I will discuss in Chapter 3, the president even created his own "civil society" organizations to consolidate his personal grip. And crucially, the parallel state held a complete monopoly over revenue with Sonangol answerable to JES alone. Through war and peace and myriad constitutional reconfigurations and political transitions, these pillars of presidential power have been fortified up to the present day.

The presidential bureaucracy is the most visible element of this. The Casa Militar and Casa Civil, the two branches of the presidency responsible for military and civilian affairs respectively, soon outranked the relevant bodies in public administration and have the last word on all major (and many minor) policy matters. As an MPLA politician once privy to the presidency noted, "the Casa Civil and Casa Militar are the real government, they are the government of everything".[69] The presidency employs its fair share of members of the president's extended families, some of whom not particularly capable. But it also includes technically competent, knowledgeable people providing the president with an essential cadre of expertise. Many of them are talented individuals who are not from leading families but have been whisked from obscurity and nursed by the president into prominent roles.[70] Even if, like Vice President Manuel Vicente or former Minister of State Carlos Feijó and so many others currently in or outside the presidency, they acquire a belated (formal) high status in the MPLA, there is no doubt in anyone's mind that they owe everything to JES.

This means that, despite its undoubted amount of human capital, "the presidency feels like a medieval court".[71] There is a hard core of perpetual figures such as the communications advisers Aldemiro Vaz da Conceição and José Mena Abrantes, and while few are permanently ejected from the inner circle, given presidential caprice, the need for scapegoats or genuine mistakes can mean that "today you're in, tomorrow you may be out".[72] Thus the prevalent mode around the president is sycophancy; few people are comfortable presenting even mildly contradictory advice, and the reserved JES has next to no informal, friendly rapports, even in his inner circle. Unsurprisingly for someone in power for more than thirty years, JES slowly cut off the close relationships he had once had. Few if any prestigious members of his generation are left in the inner circle that can speak to him with candour (not to mention common sense). Doing so means a loss of access, as the late MPLA veteran Maria Mambo Café is said to have discovered after admonishing JES, so it was reported, to beware of his children's high profile and ostentatious behaviour.[73] He has also, in the words of an MPLA official, "brought the Sambizanga into the palace":[74] in the security services but more generally across the board, extended family and people from his old neighbourhood have been given prominent positions.

A key strategy of presidential control is the underdevelopment of the state administration. JES "likes to create an aura of indispensability, without him, or a direct connection to him, nothing works or is allowed to work", notes a prominent Angolan journalist.[75] That doesn't mean that formal institutions and their ministerial leadership don't count, although some really don't: it means that their authority comes from elsewhere. The clearest example of this is the travails of the Finance Ministry over the last decades: it has gone from super-ministry to irrelevancy more often and faster than anyone can keep track of.[76] If the minister is someone with clout at the presidency, maybe the Ministry will count for something; if the economy enters a danger zone, perhaps some leeway for eleventh-hour reforms will be allowed. But this can change overnight. The Planning, Economy or "Economic Coordination" ministries can suddenly be tasked with much of the Finance Ministry's role. Important decisions (say, the replacement of the Angolan currency in 1990) can be discussed with the ministerial staff after the fact.[77] The erstwhile influential minister can be sacked for no reason. The result is a muddle and, compounded by a lack of investment in human capital outside the parallel state, it is no wonder that the public administration is incapable of performing the most basic of tasks—itself an argument for the continuation of non-institutional policy strategies.

Another of the president's recurrent ways of undermining institutions is the creation of ad hoc commissions to "resolve urgent problems", manage prestige projects and high-profile events, or run foreign credit lines— tasks the public administration "cannot cope with".[78] These commissions are directly answerable to JES; they may have civil service and ministerial personnel but are run by unelected persons whom the president trusts. The presidency gives these commissions total financial independence from the government and they can invoke presidential power at every turn. The commissions are known as a site for the accumulation of resources and nomination to them is often perceived as an "opportunity to do well for oneself,"[79] but they also wield considerable power. Few moments in Angolan political life reveal more of the real order of things than a presidential commission in full swing. As an Angolan journalist put it,

> Do you know what [a commission] means? It means everything. They can walk into any public or private institution in Angola and do as they see fit. As long as people think you come from the presidency, and no one would even dream of asking if you really do, you are all-powerful. ... The GRN [the Office for National Reconstruction, discussed in Chapter 2] for instance: those Chinese people walked around with the halo of the Casa Militar around their heads. People are scared shitless, and there are no limits to what they can do.[80]

In addition to their near-divine status, the ad hoc commissions are also typical of the JES system precisely for being ad hoc; they fold and disappear from one day to the next, their duties reassigned or extinguished. It is noteworthy that, in addition to working through a multiplicity of structures, the president sustains his grip over the system by keeping everything and everyone on the move, allowing no one to consolidate their hold over a crucial policy area and no politician of any standing to become cosy in his or her seat. As Shaxson points out, this strategy of fragmentation explicitly pushes the different structures of the JES system into a competitive logic that results in a "built-in bias against coherent, unified policymaking".[81]

Lastly, a pivotal dimension of JES's rule is his personal control of the means of violence. He used the 1991–92 transition, which entailed the transformation of the one-party state's armed forces, the FAPLA, into a national institution, the FAA, to sever any connections between the military and the MPLA. But the result was not the creation of armed forces above politics: as the commander-in-chief, JES saw his dominance of the armed forces significantly strengthened by this move. The FAA's reorganization by General João de Matos, the architect of the government's victory in the war, further consolidated JES's grip. Here too, the principles of the parallel state applied. There was a formal FAA structure bringing together the MPLA's old, often ragged FAPLA units and bits of dissident UNITA, which did not matter much. And then there was "an operational structure that really fought the war, where resources and power resided".[82] Studded with mercenaries, foreign consultants, and state-of-the-art equipment, this operational structure was mostly composed of Special Forces and run by trustworthy generals like the Faceira brothers and Matos himself; they were "answerable directly to the president and overseen from the Casa Militar".[83] Mostly *mestiço* (or white) and therefore with limited political ambitions, these officers were typical of JES's choice of competent, outsider characters.[84] Dos Santos' post-2002 hold over the armed forces, whose ranks of about 120,000 men remained at wartime levels more than a decade later, has only got stronger. General João de Matos was let go just before the end of the war.[85] His successors, including the current head of the FAA and former UNITA general Geraldo Sachipengo Nunda, are political lightweights and beholden to JES.[86] Other security outfits are equally loyal to the president, including the presidential guard, the "Ninja" PIR riot police and the internal and external intelligence services, the SINFO and the SIE. Yet other secret units are rumoured to exist, with fast-mutating acronyms that convey the impression of the President's omnipotence.[87]

Despite the occasional attempt at pushback, the president's concentration of power went largely unimpeded by a quiescent party-state apparatus. The dynamics that apply here are similar to those that enabled the rise of Sonangol. In both instances we see a pragmatic acceptance by internal factions and party barons, in the face of a fight for regime survival against UNITA, of solutions to structural weaknesses in formal state capacity that in turn concentrated resources and power at the very top. But this permissive "elite protection pact"[88] was based on more than a simple wartime assessment of common threats, pivotal though this was. Dos Santos was careful throughout, and especially from the early 1990s onwards, in satisfying the material and status interests of sensitive constituencies. The small scale of distribution during the war years fell short of a genuinely clientelistic system: the beneficiaries of a "Christmas bonus" in the late 1990s mentioned by Tony Hodges,[89] which probably did not go beyond a few thousand, delineate the narrow boundaries of this constituency. Yet the system cajoled, bought off and satiated (and, on rare occasions, effectively marginalized) those that might have constituted a threat to JES's rule.

Concessions to key constituencies did not detract from the fact that real decisions resided exclusively with the president. Indeed, the smooth running of the system may well have been (and continues to be) a function of JES's long incumbency and unitary management. In exercising his mastery, JES shows a penchant for byzantine lines of reporting and decision-making that prevent the clarification of roles and the institutionalization of offices. He instead seeks to keep direct communication between state bodies to a minimum. This renders the governance of Angola an ever-shifting process whose only certainty lies in the president's overarching power. JES's overlapping strategies—surrounding himself with both technocrats and thuggish musclemen, entertaining influential groups while preferring men without too many social attachments—jointly constitute his complex approach to the exercise of power. In the words of Pepetela, one of Angola's best-known novelists, they reveal "the thinking of the great chess-player that he is".[90]

Perhaps this is a bit of an exaggeration. Because he is so elusive—eschewing, for instance, interaction with most other African heads of state, avoiding as much as possible the continent's summitry, and barely giving any interviews for twenty years—interpreting JES amounts to the Angolan equivalent of Sovietology. If in the old days JES was consistently underestimated, in time everything he did became invested with meaning and is assumed to be part of a master plan.

THE PARALLEL SYSTEM AND THE PEACE

To sum up, the historical genesis of institutions is key to making sense of their subsequent trajectory. Once established, institutions gain a life of their own and are extremely difficult to bypass.[91] Postcolonial Angola's were forged in a critical juncture bringing together independence, civil war, a settler exodus, foreign invasions and a population unprepared for self-governance. In such circumstances, the oil endowment proved defining for the political economy as well as the pattern of international relations and the character of nascent institutions. Far from a curse, oil was first the lifeline for the embattled MPLA regime and then the principal factor in its resounding defeat of the UNITA insurgency. In a classic instance of extraversion, the regime established a durable commercial relationship with outside entities and redeployed the rewards of that relationship—ample oil revenue and the possibilities of the offshore system—to strengthen its domestic position. The insulation of Sonangol, which could not have happened outside the extraordinary circumstances that obtained until 2002, was instrumental to this success.

Throughout the war years, Angola was managed via an innovative configuration of power that matched formal state attributes with informal, discretionary control over extensive revenue. In rentier states in Africa and elsewhere, it is not uncommon for formal institutions to be less important than partly hidden structures,[92] but the Angolan parallel system seems to be an extreme example of this. Though the purposes it served were equally narrow, it was very different from the "shadow states" of West Africa that consisted of relatively informal structures of plunder.[93] The Angolan parallel state was highly capable and contained important rational-legal aspects. Dos Santos managed this array of power structures astutely, making use of co-optation and never fully eclipsing formal state institutions or the party. This said, his grip over the system was unambiguous and went unchallenged. Some decisions were ad hoc and the product of circumscribed choices, but the overall shape of Angola's real government—in particular, the decision to tip state capacity building towards enclave units controlled by JES—is elective. It grew to have its own logic of self-perpetuation, and became a major contributor to the weaknesses in formal state capacity it had been born to compensate.

The question of what would happen to the parallel system was a frequent one at war's end, with press coverage full of innuendo about the president's desire for "retirement"[94] at the height of his glory as "the Architect of Peace", and international financial institutions pushing for the "normalization" of economic management. Some hoped the advent of peace might constitute yet another critical juncture in which choices would be made to durably reconfigure institutions in the direction of more open governance. If that had been the case, the parallel system's legacy would still have weighed heavily. But there was never any chance of this happening. A perceptive International Crisis Group report noted that genuine reform would threaten the power of the presidency, the diversion of revenue, "and the patronage networks and private accounts supported by that diversion [...] the choice is up to the government, and particularly President dos Santos."[95]

In the context of a total victory and the prospect of a tremendously profitable peacetime economy, this was not a choice the Futungo agonized over. JES never left. By 2010, he had solidified his grip even further through the adoption of one of the most presidentialist constitutions in Africa. This new constitution eliminated the need for direct elections for the presidency and, in theory, allows JES to stay in power until 2022.[96] As we shall see in the next chapters, the president and the people around him understood that many aspects of wartime management had to be reconfigured. But their goal was to preserve the parallel system's grip over Angola's political economy.

With peace and the spectacular reconstruction that ensued, the parallel system didn't merely survive in very different circumstances: it was recalibrated, diversified and grew out of all recognition into a giant web of privileges and resource extraction. Avenues of undreamed-of elite enrichment were created in the new, more complex economy, with compulsory joint ventures with foreign firms providing the basis for the growth of Angolan-owned business groups. In the guise of reconstruction, oil-backed structures and partnerships were created that again went around formal institutions, but on a larger scale than ever before. Sonangol became a de facto sovereign wealth fund, using billions of dollars to pursue an increasingly ambitious external investment policy. All of these structures were tightly run by an unconstrained presidency, which further consolidated its role as distributor of the oil wealth to chosen constituencies and articulator of the country's relationship with the international economy. Oil, which had allowed the MPLA regime's survival, would now finance the building of a new Angola.

2

THE SPECTACLE OF RECONSTRUCTION

*"[Angolans] are special. Therefore, despite the size and complexity of the task of national reconstruc-
tion, now that we are at peace we shall [find the way], so that in the next ten, fifteen, twenty or
thirty years we can radically change the situation of Angola and guarantee that each Angolan will
have a better life."*

José Eduardo dos Santos, 2005[1]

*"Backward countries seeking to break through to modernity are normally derivative and unoriginal
in their ideas, though necessarily not so in their practice."*

Eric Hobsbawm[2]

After months on the run, death came to Jonas Savimbi on 22 February
2002 in an ambush in the easternmost province of Moxico. Myths about
his demise—who amongst his closest had betrayed him, whether the
Israelis had tracked him down—continue till this day. The last stretch of
the war, which the government had restarted in late 1998, saw the
deployment of scorched-earth tactics and the large-scale removal of
populations to deny UNITA support. It lasted much longer than
expected, with a weaker UNITA adapting once again to the guerrilla
methods it excelled at. Eventually the overwhelming advantages of the
government—an oil income stream 50 times superior to what UNITA
had at its disposal[3]—had kicked in.

Their leader gone, UNITA forces nonetheless maintained the chain
of command and dutifully laid down their weapons. On 4 April 2002, a
peace agreement was signed in Luena, with the commander-in-chief of

51

UNITA forces and the head of the FAA embracing and the latter referring to "the start of the reunion of the Angolan family".[4] This was not the sort of peace the international community had promoted twice in Angola and countless times elsewhere in Africa: it was a clear-cut military victory. After four decades fighting the Portuguese, foreign invasions, and two competing liberation movements, the MPLA's control of Angola was now complete.

On a visit to Luanda two weeks after the killing, I was struck by the fact that many people were still darkly questioning whether Savimbi was really dead (the government broadcast images of his bullet-ridden, fly-infested body; this assuaged some but not others). But intellectuals and politicians were already talking about the new world to come. In some ways, it sounded suspiciously like the old world that the war had destroyed; in others, a project without precedent. Was the MPLA's agenda for Angola about "reconstruction" or about the building of a new society? Where did they get their inspiration? And what, and whom, was left out? The extraordinary decade that ensued, bringing together an ambitious programme of national reconstruction with the unique opportunity provided by a sustained oil boom, saw choices that will shape the lives of Angolans for a very long time.

Crucially, Angolan decision-makers alone made these choices. The MPLA had an almost unique degree of autonomy from the society it ruled: victorious and cash-rich, it hovered above a demobilized population exhausted by four decades of war and in no position to make claims over the direction of reconstruction policy. From 2004 onwards the MPLA was also able to diversify foreign relations, maximize the external resources at the service of its reconstruction agenda, and distance itself from foreign pressures over the sort of Angola it should seek to rebuild. Its initial focus on infrastructure was not contentious; but it was only a segment of a wider set of commitments whose centrepiece was the transformation of Angola in the MPLA's own image of an urban, civilized and modern country. To this effect, the party-state deployed an ambitious language of state activism promising everything from welfare provision to industrialization, and engaged in a veritable orgy of spending, ostensibly in order to achieve these goals. In his review of international attempts at saving failed states, Christopher Cramer dubs the standard mix of donor reconstruction policies the "great post-conflict make-over fantasy".[5] Angola would be rebuilt on the basis of a fantasy—but it would be the MPLA's own.

FINANCING RECONSTRUCTION

Angola did not shift smoothly into reconstruction gear. The general elation at the coming of peace was soon tempered by the parlous state of Angola's finances and the looming humanitarian crisis threatening millions of lives. Whatever the reconstruction fantasies of Luandan statebuilders, for the subsequent two years there was little space for long-term thinking. In addition to the 450,000 Angolan refugees in neighbouring countries, an extraordinary four million people—an estimated one third of Angola's 2002 population—were internally displaced; most faced acute food shortages and the threat of epidemic outbreaks. The UN system agencies would play a crucial role in this regard for years, daily feeding an estimated one million Angolans as late as 2006.

The humanitarian emergency of the early postwar period came on top of the process of disarmament and demobilization of an estimated 105,000 UNITA soldiers (and more than 300,000 dependents) who rapidly converged on 27 quartering areas distributed around the country.[6] This process, which the government insisted on masterminding through MINARS,[7] was protracted and extremely partisan, with big food provision and "reintegration kit" contracts dished out amongst presidential insiders, and did not meet basic needs.[8] Disarmament in particular would never fully occur; though some weapons were collected, many merely disappeared into society, leaving Angola heavily armed until today. Reintegration, admittedly difficult to define in the context of four decades of conflict and with little "normalcy" to return to,[9] also fell short of expectations. UNITA cadres were well treated, comfortably accommodated in Luanda and the provincial capitals, and quickly given a stake in postwar society.[10] Senior military officers were either integrated into the FAA and the police or comfortably retired with a pension fitting of their UNITA rank. But the numerous rank-and-file were forgotten in dusty cantonments for the subsequent three years. Some of the thorniest problems of early postwar Angola eventually resolved themselves on account of "acute conflict fatigue",[11] as in the extraordinary case of the resettlement of IDPs. But this owed much more to the work of NGOs, churches, family and local community networks of support than to the actions of government. The latter's callousness in dealing with former UNITA soldiers gave rise to lasting resentment.

Perhaps more important for the Angolan government at this stage, the country's financial situation was exceedingly precarious. In 2002 and

2003, the exponential increase in oil production and the price of oil had not yet occurred, and a series of quickly maturing oil-backed loans meant that Angola found itself, in the words of Vice-Prime Minister Aguinaldo Jaime, on the verge of a "severe financial crisis".[12] Angola's leaders knew well that they could not put the country back together without a major foreign input and repeatedly called for a donors' conference to help them mobilize financial resources. But this need for foreign money never translated into a willingness to accommodate any degree of conditionality. The government's objective was to maximize the international contribution towards reconstruction while subordinating these resources to its political agenda.

The major Western donors were less than forthcoming. Concerns about egregious siphoning off of oil revenue and myriad insider deals had plagued international perceptions of Angola in the last years of the war. High-profile campaigns by organizations such as Global Witness, Human Rights Watch and the Open Society Institute, among others, shed light on corrupt practices in the oil sector and self-enrichment by the Angolan elite. The increased influence of activist agendas on transparency and the role of the extractive industries in armed conflict further dented the Angolan government's reputation.[13] For its part, the IMF had become an implacable critic of the opaqueness of Angola's oil accounts and the Fund's leaked documents pointed towards the routine disappearance of billions of dollars.[14] Finally, there was scepticism in some quarters that an oil-rich country such as Angola should need a major external financial commitment towards reconstruction, with the resident UN coordinator calling on the government to share "a greater part of the burden".[15]

It is important not to overstate the extent to which Western donors took on board these concerns.[16] Even at the 2001–4 height of international criticism of oil sector corruption in Angola, the enthusiasm of foreign oil investors and banks, as well as their home governments, never wavered. Angola's woes rarely surfaced in the mainstream international media. Yet there was enough momentary unease with the quality of Angola's governance to create a quasi-consensus amongst prominent Western states and the Bretton Woods institutions that a donors' conference should be postponed until the government could explain the whereabouts of missing oil revenue and commit itself to implementing some of the reforms put forward by the IMF.[17] Potential donors also wanted to know that the government intended to spend its considerable resources in a developmental direction rather than expect foreigners alone to foot the reconstruction bill.

Prominent Angolan decision-makers described the reaction to this refusal in terms of "shock", "huge pain" and a "sense of betrayal": "once again," one of them remarked, "we were backstabbed by the West".[18] The sovereignty-conscious Angolan leadership was unlikely to concede when faced with perceived international bullying. More to the point, the measures on the table were aimed at the very heart of JES's parallel system and especially his discretionary hold over oil revenue. If taken on board these "economically risky and politically suicidal"[19] measures would cancel out his grip over the orientation of reconstruction and ultimately the levers of political power in postwar Angola.

The government's problems at this stage were serious enough to compel officials, with a sinking heart, into a sort of passive-aggressive engagement with some international critics. This included far-fetched episodes that would be impossible a couple of years later. In late 2003, for instance, Aryeh Neier, the veteran human rights campaigner and then President of the Open Society Institute, travelled to Luanda and began "negotiating directly with the Angolan government in an effort to encourage transparency in the oil- and diamond-rich country".[20] But this self-described "phony dialogue"[21] brought no tangible reforms. Unsurprisingly, the donors' conference was postponed on numerous occasions from 2002 to 2004. In 2004, during a visit to the USA, President dos Santos apparently raised the issue with President George W. Bush, to no effect. In fact, the donors' conference would never take place and, by early 2005, it was the Angolan president himself who postponed it indefinitely.

What had changed in the meantime was the appearance of a major international partner, China, willing to deal with the Angolan government with none of the preconditions set forth by Western donors. Out went the dialogue with the likes of OSI and any pretence at fulfilling Western transparency requirements. After months of negotiations, the Chinese government extended credit lines to Angola in March 2004, and very soon Chinese companies staffed by tens of thousands of imported labourers were deeply involved in the reconstruction of the country's infrastructure. By 2009, public and private Chinese loans to Angola amounted to at least US$13.4 billion (according to some estimates, US$19.7 billion),[22] and bilateral trade had grown thirty-five times in the eight years up to 2008.[23] "China exploited a void created by the

West itself", noted Ambassador Ismael Gaspar Martins, Angola's Permanent Representative to the UN, almost a decade later.[24]

Soon enough, references to a so-called "Angola model" became ubiquitous.[25] Simply put, this Angola model is a resources-for-infrastructure deal, whereby the Angolan government pledges oil cargoes in exchange for Chinese credit lines to help finance its reconstruction. In turn, 70 per cent of the contracts would be attributed to Chinese corporations. In many ways this has been a mutually beneficial rapport and its contribution to Angolan infrastructure reconstruction very substantial. I will not review this in unnecessary detail as the existing research is of high quality, but some matters deserve clarification. As Deborah Brautigam notes, the assumption that China's oil-backed deal with Angola was unprecedented is wrong: by the time the deal with China's Exim Bank was signed, Angola had contracted no fewer than forty-eight oil-backed loans amounting to many billions of dollars, predominantly with Western banks and governments.[26] Indeed, the mortgaging of oil had been the key revenue generator for the parallel system as described in the previous chapter. Nor was this an innovative deal from China's perspective.

That said, there is no doubt that the size and timing of the deal changed the nature of the reconstruction process. Some experts point to factors other than the Chinese connection that better explain the increasing Angolan leeway as the decade progressed, with emphasis on the growth in oil production (from 1 to almost 2 million barrels per day), the rise of the oil price,[27] and the availability of other credit lines. These points are valid, but one cannot underestimate the extent to which the Chinese credit lines mattered at a time when Angola "hadn't yet paid its Paris Club debts and therefore had no access to normal credit"[28] or the symbolism of China's role in the broader transformation of Angolan external relations discussed in Chapter 5.

However, when assessed from the vantage point of 2014, the impact of this partnership seems more limited than assumed at the time. On the face of it, the Chinese presence is quite dissimilar from the familiar Western role in Angola. But far from having destabilized the time-honored way of doing things, the Chinese adapted very quickly to the nature of Angolan business and firm-state relations. The Chinese presence was easily and willingly instrumentalized by the Angolan elite and put at the service of its agenda. As the senior MPLA politician Lopo do Nascimento remarks, the Chinese made Angolan reconstruction viable but "they did not influence the model itself, which was defined by the Angolans [...] the Chinese merely delivered on the basis of Angolan priorities".[29] Unsurprisingly, this included taking JES's parallel system for granted and working through it. This didn't just give a new lease of life to the parallel system, which the president, as we have seen, had no intention of unwinding with the coming of peace. The Chinese partnership allowed the exponential increase, diversification and further internationalization of the parallel state.

Nothing illustrates this better than the establishment in short order, alongside the Eximbank arrangements,[30] of a deal with an opaque Hong Kong-based consortium, CIF, to which I will return in Chapter 5. While the Exim Bank credit lines remained under the control of the Finance Ministry, the president decreed that the CIF monies were to be run out of the Presidency by a mysterious Office for National Reconstruction (GRN) headed by General Kopelipa. The GRN, which essentially took over much of the functions of the Ministry of Public Works, was shrouded in secrecy for the five years of its existence, despite the fact that some of the highest profile (and also most dubious and worst performing) reconstruction projects—the urban folly at Kilamba Kiaxi, the early attempt at revamping the railways, the ZEE industrial park—were run by it. At the time, the creation of the GRN was said to have been in response to Chinese concerns about the misappropriation of Exim Bank monies, and direct presidential control an attempt at keeping the reconstruction process "honest". But this makes no sense, as the public credit lines remain with the MINFIN till the present day (and were much better managed than the CIF monies).

Instead, the CIF connection, bringing together new Chinese interests with powerful Angolan politicians and the cast of Western middlemen familiar to the reader from the multiple shenanigans of the 1990s, is an instance of mutual "assimilation"[31] whereby Angolan reconstruction builds on rather than unsettles the existing networks of the parallel state, and is channelled towards the private enrichment of power-holders. CIF has garnered some attention on account of a high-profile US government investigation,[32] its global footprint, and John Le Carré-type conspiratorial contours. Although on an impressive scale, it is but one of several circuits through which money flows in the reconstruction era have allowed the continuation of the parallel state. Only now it could thrive on an utterly different and more diversified scale, permitted by reconstruction and the unexpected multiplication of Angola's oil revenue.

RECONSTRUCTION: INFRASTRUCTURE
AND "EVERYTHING ELSE"

With rising oil revenue and credit lines finally at its disposal, the MPLA was now able to tackle the vast enterprise of reconstructing Angola. Reconstruction itself can be conceived of as a two-phase process. The first phase, simply put, amounts to rebuilding the physical infrastructure of Angola. The second phase could be dubbed "everything else", as it pertains to the more complex creation of quotidian governance across the country, the provision of public goods, and the diversification of the oil-based economy, all of which are central to the party-state's rhetoric for a new Angola. There is no straightforward chronological sequence here—big talk about economic diversification started as early as 2002, while the physical reconstruction of even the most basic infrastructure is still ongoing in 2014—but for analytical purposes it is useful to differentiate between the two, and think of phase two as necessarily building upon the newly minted or repaired infrastructure.

The extent of the physical task ahead cannot be overstated.[33] Large cities such as Huambo and Kuito had practically been obliterated. 98 per cent of bridges (amounting to more than 300) were destroyed, as were 80 per cent of factories, 60 per cent of hospitals, 80 per cent of schools and most of the country's roads.[34] The three major railways were unusable. The damaged electricity system intermittently covered only a small part of the country[35] while piped water was a rare luxury even in cities. An estimated 10–12 million landmines scarred the landscape. Even in the few areas that had not seen much combat, such as Luanda, the state of disrepair of the mostly colonial-era infrastructure was considerable. The cost of war damage to the country's infrastructure alone was an estimated US$60 billion.[36] With almost every piece of infrastructure in tatters, Angola was simply not a place for the small-is-beautiful approach to reconstruction: large-scale rehabilitation was both necessary and entirely legitimate. The subsequent commitment has been on a scale rarely seen in sub-Saharan Africa. According to a 2011 World Bank assessment of Angola's infrastructure, the government invested an estimated US$4.3 billion, or 14 per cent of GDP, *every year* in ports, railways, roads and power generation.[37]

Of these, the priority has been the road system. The past decade saw the rehabilitation of some 8,000 km of asphalted roads, with US$2.8 billion spent annually from 2005 to 2009.[38] This is easily the single most important government contribution to the country's wellbeing since the end of the conflict. Although the quality of some stretches is uneven, the major roads linking Luanda with Malanje, Huambo and Benguela have been repaired to a mostly acceptable standard and changed the lives of many within their reach. The economic consequences, while positive, are fewer than expected, primarily because of lack of investment in the interior, the continuing malfunctioning or absence of rural markets, and well-organized protection rackets by police that cream off much of the surplus of struggling farmers trying to reach markets on the coast.[39] But there is no doubt that road infrastructure is a prerequisite for further development and that the population welcomes it.

The renovation of the railway system has also been a priority, at the cost of an estimated US$3 billion by 2012.[40] The government's promise of having Angola's three main railway lines rebuilt by 2008 was not feasible and many unanswered questions remain about the CIF role in these projects, including the virtual disappearance of Chinese contractors during the financial crisis of 2009–10. By 2012, the Malanje railway was functional and the Benguela and Namibe railways were scheduled to reach their terminuses within a year. Yet there was a significant gap between the building of the infrastructure and its smooth running. Inaugurations were frequently followed by extended periods of closure. Luena station, opened with alacrity by the president on the eve of the 2012 elections, was shut immediately afterwards as the stretch between Kuito and Luena "wasn't actually ready, and we don't really have the people to run the train system yet".[41] When trains started to run, the railway operators did not have enough qualified personnel and services were slow and infrequent. At its best, the pricy Luanda-Malanje train runs about three times a week, and despite the fact that the equipment is spanking new (it even includes personal television systems in first class), it takes more than 8 hours at about 40 km per hour to reach its destination; the road trip takes about 5 hours. The Lobito to Huambo train runs about once a week and has few passengers, although the segments beyond Huambo get more passengers on account of the parlous condition of eastern roads. The halting of services for long periods has also been reported. A visit to Malanje in early September 2012 showed that the train hadn't arrived for more than a month; no one knew why, or when it would return.

In addition to the complications of railway management, broader issues pertaining to the economic viability of the railways have been raised. Some critics argue that the railway rehabilitation projects are a prime example of "colonial fetishism", "rebuilt because they were there" rather than on account of a thought-out strategy, and that the costs exceed even the more optimistic prospects of profitability. The most elaborate plan, the Lobito Corridor along the 1344 km-long Benguela railway, is dependent on the extent to which the mineral-rich central African economies of Katanga and Zambia reconnect with it as well as the revamping of agricultural activity along the route. By 2014, these had not occurred and physical reconstruction of the railway had not yet fulfilled "its potential for generating domestic economic linkages or multiplier effects".[42] For the time being, officials acknowledge that the railway system will need massive subsidies to keep going, with the CEO of the Luanda-Malanje railway admitting that monthly revenue covered only 10 per cent of its operational expenditure.[43] Already there is talk of "privatization into capable hands" and of public-private partnerships. Be it as it may, the slow return of trains to the Angolan hinterland is a reality, and at its best the railway system can be an invaluable tool for national development.

The road and railway segment of the reconstruction agenda, while not without its problems, did partly materialize. There are projects that have experienced serious delays such as road building in the north and east,[44] which mirror the government's sense of geographical priority as well as the fiscal collapse of 2009. But there is reason to expect Angola to have fully functioning primary road and railway systems by 2015. These aspects of physical reconstruction, which are coterminous with the state's development of the "logistics of control" discussed in Chapter 3, advanced relatively fast. Other dimensions of physical reconstruction such as electrification and the provision of drinkable water, whose benefits accrue to the population, have been slow. This is partly because of the state's genuine incompetence in managing complex structures that necessitate long time horizons. In the electricity sector, expanded capacity was not matched by the requisite transmission systems and the gap between supply and demand was actually wider in 2011 than at the end of the war.[45] In water provision, a cacophony of local, provincial and national bodies (helped and hindered by a large number of foreign donors and consultants in a sector where the government has welcomed their role) prevented any integrated agenda from developing. But the key logic for the sort of infrastructure projects the party-state prioritized during this period was twofold. It showed a marked preference for infra-structure that was ambitious, spectacular and, in one word, *big*-exemplary projects of its successful stewardship of the country; and for infrastruc-ture that would increase its capacity to project power across space.

These communication infrastructure projects were a significant part of the building craze of the postwar years, but the government's rush to alter the physical landscape of Angola went much beyond them. The list of huge-but-useless projects is almost too long to engage with. There were the many football stadia built for the 2010 African Cup of Nations, most of which now lie abandoned. There were the expensive airports such as the one in Ndalatando, a provincial capital barely 200km from Luanda. The airport cost US$40 million but by 2013 no commercial airline, not even the national carrier TAAG, was considering scheduled flights to it. Other remote airports in places like Cunene are suffering a similar fate. And there are of course the three airports built or refur-bished within 30km of each other in Lobito, Benguela and Catumbela, the latter costing an estimated US$250 million. This gigantism fits the sensibility of decision-makers but the motivations for these capital-intensive projects go further: as an Angolan journalist puts it, "the bigger the better, the more expensive the better, because the bigger [the insid-ers'] take will be".[46]

Key to all of this is the ubiquitous and much-criticized construction industry, one of the major beneficiaries of the last decade. Despite the considerable size and profitability of the sector, there is hardly any com-petition, with a small number of mostly Portuguese, Brazilian and Chinese companies (as well as a handful of Israeli, South Korean and Lebanese firms) cornering the major contracts. All have close relations with the presidency that ensures their market share, keeps other contrac-tors out and costs high. The fast pace of reconstruction permits plenty of opportunities for corruption, especially through over-pricing of mate-rials, fake invoicing and transfer pricing.[47] The fact that powerful Angolans are in business with these companies means that state institu-tions (mostly weak and incapable of performing a supervisory role any-way) are not encouraged to look into their accounts. The lack of a func-tioning central Procurement Office makes it impossible to track the myriad projects taking place at any one time. This opaqueness is increased by the fact that the biggest contracts have been directly adjudi-cated, often by the presidency and organizations such as GRN. To top it all, many infrastructure projects have no cost estimates "prior to the start of planning, or even to the start of construction".[48] It is not surprising that cases of impossibly expensive and/or bad quality works abound. A much-discussed example is the Chinese-built Luanda Central Hospital which had to be vacated after two years of occupancy because it threatened to collapse. But there are many others. "The costs of reconstruction in Angola are astronomical, the highest in the world", notes a senior international official.[49]

In sum, the infrastructure reconstruction agenda resulted in significant financial leakage and there were major blind spots in the government's sense of priority, with some sectors and some regions (with emphasis on Luanda) getting the lion's share of spending. But the benefits for the population of having major provincial roads rebuilt are considerable. Angolans overwhelmingly approved of this focus on infrastructure and want more, if not to the detriment of social expenditure. Not all low-lying fruit has been picked. Impressive improvements in popular welfare could be achieved if the electrification and water and sanitation agendas were implemented. The same applies to the rebuilding of secondary roads, and in particular the dirt roads that connect villages to communes and municipal centres. Such structures are crucial for the functioning of rural markets yet remain neglected. But even critics of the regime admit that when it comes to infrastructure, the record is partly positive, and certainly puts the infrastructure rebuilding record of the UN and the Western donors in places like Kosovo and East Timor to shame.

Still, with money to pay for it and a long line of contractors waiting to do business, infrastructure is not the most complicated aspect of reconstruction. The difficult stuff—phase two of reconstruction, tying reconstruction to a coherent vision for the country's development, the implementation of developmental policies and the sustained delivery of public goods—takes more than hard cash. At these more ambitious tasks the party-state falters, despite the fact that the MPLA 2008 Manifesto was an unbridled wish list of phase two items. The pattern is similar across many areas of public policy verging from social housing to the diversification of the economy and the pursuit of industrialization. The party-state claims the central role in delivering these results in the form of a large-scale, signature project. Every policy area has one. For agriculture there is Aldeia Nova; for wholesale and retail rural trade, PRESILD/Nosso Super; for schooling, the Campus Universitário and its counterparts in provincial capitals; for housing, the Kilamba Kiaxi complex and other large-scale projects; and for industrialization, the ZEE. The state puts forward considerable amounts of public money but subcontracts the building of the projects to the private sector (with emphasis on the handful of construction firms already mentioned), always at great cost and with minimal oversight. When finished, these projects often do not work or will work at a loss, for there are no management systems, educated personnel, time horizons or "planning", despite the 2025 Plan discussed below.

The purest manifestation of this high-modernism is the Zona Económica Especial (ZEE) established near Viana, 20 km east of Luanda, and presented as a model for industrial development elsewhere in the country. Covering 50 km2, the ZEE was started by General Kopelipa's GRN in 2006 and then passed on to an especially created Sonangol subsidiary, SIIND, in 2010.[50] (This is a poisoned chalice that Sonangol wasn't enthusiastic about assuming responsibility for.) The ZEE is not Angola's only industrial project; other unrelated schemes are being pursued. For instance, a 2013 conference hosted by the Ministry of Industry in Talatona talked up the industrialization of the Brazilian state of Paraná as a model for Angola.[51] While a bevy of Paraná consultants were ecstatic at the prospect of business, two Sonangol officials in the audience claimed not to know about the Ministry's industrial plans.[52]

Nonetheless the ZEE dwarfs all other projects. The ZEE development plan is in two phases, the first exclusively state-owned and managed, the second meant to attract private sector industries at "some later stage".[53] The first phase involves establishing 73 state industries run by Sonangol executives seconded for this purpose. The ZEE's blueprint is a big half moon meticulously divided into 73 plots, each inscribed with the output of a projected factory: shoes, painting and varnish, carpentry, electric materials, hardware/ironmonger's, detergents, mattresses, cement, pasta, bread, bicycles, hygiene products, bathroom suites, mortar, plastic, optic fibre, wire fences, PVC plastic, electric cables, medium and low voltage switchgears, etc. The best way to describe the ZEE is as a sort of theme park of import substitution industrialization that "ideally brings together everything that the Angolan economy needs".[54]

Under the Cabinet for National Reconstruction's stewardship, the ZEE was secured by the army and virtually inaccessible, even to ministerial figures. A euphoric throng of job seekers roaming the gates was beaten back on occasion during 2011. Although access had improved by

2012, security remained tight and the site impossible to get into without an authorization that was difficult to obtain. But the arresting images taken from the air of enormous (mostly empty) warehouses lined up in neat rows were endlessly replayed on TV and reproduced in the regime's glossy publications and slick roadshows. Opening ceremonies and official visits by foreign dignitaries have multiplied since 2011, with a carefully choreographed "blessing" by Angola's Catholic bishops a highlight.[55] In order to convey the image of Angolan industrial modernity, some tinkering at the edges is necessary. In my visit to the ZEE, though the offices were over-staffed with Angolans, I rarely saw any involved in technical tasks. But, in the words of an Angolan journalist, "when there are official visits to the ZEE, they get rid of the Brazilians, Chinese and Portuguese that really run the place, gear up Angolan workers with the latest technology, and there is the photo-up: Angolans managing factories and operating complex machinery!"[56] In fact, the factories remain under the de facto management of foreign "industrial promoters" who sold them as "'turn-key' projects to Angola with everything already in place".[57]

Driving around the massive ZEE area, it is impossible not to think of failed import substitution projects the world over and of the cost for Angola of all the unlearnt lessons.[58] There are many reasons why the ZEE is headed for failure. First, the energy supply—the bane of Angolan reconstruction—is erratic; the eight factories at work during my March 2012 visit were dependent on expensive generators. Second, most inputs for the factories need to be imported at great cost. Although the foreigners who run the factories were initially tasked with "the identification of supply chains and sources of inputs and primary commodities",[59] either this has not taken place or the results are not cost-effective. In the case of the optic fibre factory, a favourite of the regime, the real costs of the finished product are estimated to be somewhere between three and five times the cost of commercially available optic fibre.[60] Third, products were chosen not with a market in mind, but for prestige reasons. The paint factory, for instance, was initially geared up by GRN to produce an expensive varnish that is not popular with Angolans.

And finally, no one involved has any notion of what the total costs of the ZEE or of individual enterprises within it amount to. In mid-2012, the products of the several factories were still in storage, as no one knew how to price them. A senior official noted that "we wanted to do market studies to see [which products were commercially viable] but we actually have no idea [and neither did the people who set up the ZEE]".[61] Costs that are known are exorbitant and far above those of imports. Some form of protection would always be needed to jumpstart local industry and an initial financial loss is entirely justifiable. But the ZEE feels more like a money pit than an operation in need of nurturing. For the ZEE to work, it would simply have to become something else. Amidst the crisis of 2009, it was not clear if the ZEE would ever become fully operative. The return of high oil prices is again enabling it. As things stand, the subsidies needed to keep it up will be enormous. "And then," a critic notes, "one day a fiscal crisis comes and someone will pull the plug".[62]

That the Angolan state can be seriously tasked with accomplishing assignments as complex and elusive as industrialization is something that needs explaining. Some of it is down to the centrality of the state for the MPLA's development vision discussed below, but there is more to it. The ZEE illustrates the two steps typical of many Angolan development schemes. The first step is the myriad contracts entailed by the building of the ZEE itself. Before it produces anything, it is already a success for insiders. According to a senior MPLA figure, "this is not just a matter of the GRN having built it in its usual secretive way". In addition "many of the factories were bought second-hand, already obsolete" and not only were they "extremely expensive" but they came "tied to equally expensive management contracts as we can't run them ourselves".[63]

The second step is more circuitous, and amounts to a major form of elite appropriation of state assets simultaneously taking place across large swathes of the Angolan economy. In brief, the state makes a major investment "in the national interest", such as the ZEE, often through a public-private partnership. That investment eventually is passed on from the private sector builder to the state but soon fails at enormous cost. Subsequently, the government privatizes to regime interests (or those of its foreign allies) the hulk of the initial capital investment at highly favourable prices. This privatization often explicitly favours the private entity that built the project in the first place, deemed "the people who can make this work again".[64] Interviews on the subject of ZEE brought out the wish to "pass this on to Angolan businessmen when it is all up and running".[65] Something like this has already played out in regard to three high-profile projects of the reconstruction era: the Chinese-built "new municipalities", the Aldeia Nova agricultural project and the PRESILD/Nosso Super network of state-owned supermarkets. A witty foreign consultant to the government dubbed these Public-Private Partnerships "Public-to-Private Partnerships".[66] Many Angolans who are savvy to the logic behind these projects aptly refer to them not as stupid money-losing ventures but as elite rackets.

Increasing the housing stock is one of those areas where popular aspirations resonate with MPLA priorities. During the 2008 electoral campaign, JES went as far as announcing the tantalizing commitment to build one million houses by 2012, an impossible goal even without the 2009 economic crisis and general mismanagement. Although building sites have appeared on the outskirts of most provincial capitals, it is on the outskirts of Luanda that many of these projects have materialized. Cidade do Kilamba, the first and highest profile of a projected 36 satellite cities to be built nationwide, was meant to be "the jewel in Angola's reconstruction crown".[67] In the spectacle of reconstruction, Kilamba is the housing counterpart to the ZEE's industrial miracle. With typical hyperbole, President dos Santos inaugurated the unfinished and empty Kilamba by boasting of "the biggest residential project ever built in Angola, constituting, *at a global level*, a profound example of the social policy pursued in this country to resolve its housing [shortage]".[68] That Kilamba was not meant as social housing was scarcely a secret, but the trajectory of the project came as a shock even to cynics.

Built by the China International Trust and Investment Corporation (CITIC) in less than three years for US$3.5 billion, this urban transplant of some 750 high-rises about 30 km southeast of Luanda briefly captured the imagination of Angolans, with its lawns, cleanliness and sheer newness. From the start, a number of vocal Angolan urban experts criticized the unacceptably steep costs of Kilamba and the high-maintenance model as unfit for Angolan habits. They argued that in new as well as old buildings and condos in Luanda, even amongst the better off, there is typically no willingness to pay for collective costs and all shared infrastructure (joint generators, water provision, elevators, green spaces) is derelict within a few months. They pushed instead for much cheaper, more accessible, and self-standing housing developments that would be easier to maintain and a better fit for Angolan mores. But their urgings could not compete with the "thirst for bigness"[69] of government planners, or the baser personal gains expected from the project.

When the GRN, which had masterminded the project and kept all details under wraps, mysteriously faded away in 2010, Sonangol (again) got to carry this burden via its purposely-created subsidiary, SONIP.[70] SONIP then subcontracted the sale of Kilamba apartments to Delta Imobiliária, a private company whose owners included Manuel Vicente and General Kopelipa, which received the sales contract without a public tender.[71] Surprisingly in view of the centrality of Kilamba for the government's rhetoric about social housing, Delta Imobiliária announced for-profit prices so out of reach for more than 95 per cent of Angolans that the public mood instantly went sour: US$120,000 for the cheapest flats, with the top end going for US$200,000 (amongst the few who could afford such housing, living in distant Kilamba was out of the question). Private banks were uninterested in providing credit for this, so buyers were scarce. By mid-2012, only about 300 flats had been sold out of the initial offering of 3,180, and Kilamba—often facetiously brought up in Luanda conversations in the same breath as the 2008 one-million houses utopia—had become something of an embarrassment. Faced with the upcoming elections, the government decided to dish out 43 apartments to every ministry and major government body, with orders that they be distributed internally to senior civil servants on acquisition terms unavailable to other Angolans. This did not prevent the MPLA from peddling imagery of Kilamba and of the happy families who didn't actually live there as electoral campaign evidence of its social housing commitment.[72] Even in its own terms, the government's urge for modern cityscapes is improvisational. It had no clue what to do with the whole project.

Less talked about than Kilamba, but of equal scale and greater folly, is the new municipality of Dundo in Lunda Norte, the diamond-rich, lawless eastern province. One of the four GRN satellite cities, this "Kilamba do Dundo" was built in utmost secrecy, its perimeter secured by Angolan police, an Angolan private security company, and a Chinese security company responsible for the 3,000 Chinese workers. The ragged appearance and squalid living quarters of the non-technical Chinese staff—and prohibition from circulating outside the project site—gave rise to predictable Angolan rumours as to their prisoner status. Phase one of the Dundo project, which was nearly finished when I visited in November 2011, is meant to house 30,000 people and includes five-, seven-, and nine-storey buildings, with a centrepiece of four 18-storey towers, some of the tallest structures in central Africa. The development, reported to be modelled on an existing one in China, is fitted for the Chinese taste, with wooden floors entirely inappropriate for the climate, tiny kitchens unfit for Angolan conviviality and, as an Angolan technician pointed out, "no place for people to dry their manioc", the local staple.[73]

The project is meant to house 120,000 people, or a full third of the population of this large and essentially rural province.[74] Amidst this sparsely populated and underdeveloped region, 1,100km away from Luanda, the visual impact of finding a large, empty city amidst the bush is unsettling. Dundo is a byword for Angolan remoteness, with travel to Luanda estimated at some 20 hours by road in good weather (and much longer in the rainy season) and a decommissioned airstrip allowing the landing of only a precarious ten-seat plane until late 2012. Who is going to live in this new municipality? How are water and electricity going to be connected to it? And where will people work? In the annals of Angolan reconstruction, Kilamba do Dundo will be the white elephant par excellence.

Even the otherwise mostly neglected agricultural sector got its own improvement scheme. The eccentric premise of the US$70 million Aldeia Nova project was the exportation of the Israeli kibbutz model to Angola, simultaneously producing agricultural development and the reintegration of former combatants. The government provided the money but the project itself was outsourced to the LR Group, the Israeli defence contractor that had played a crucial role in the FAA war effort and was, on the strength of its insider status, carving out a business empire in Angola much beyond that initial lucrative niche.[75] That the LR Group was not primarily known for agricultural development suggested from the outset that Aldeia Nova was a project blessed by the powers that be. "The LR Group were [practically] running the army", a senior Angolan official involved in the project argued, and for them "Aldeia Nova was a transition from military affairs to business".[76] Besides scepticism towards the appropriateness of the kibbutz model, a further source of concern was the ominous location for the first Aldeia Nova, in Waku Kungo, Kwanza Sul province. This region, known as Cela in colonial times, had endured the largest and costliest Portuguese attempt at building a white peasant utopia, with settlers imported for the purpose and untold millions sunk into it. Although productivity had finally improved in the last years of colonialism, Cela had never proved as fertile as expected. This failed Portuguese attempt at rural engineering was followed by a much worse Bulgarian post-1975 collectivization plan; the

Bulgarians plus the war eventually brought the region to utter ruin. No wonder that experts with even a basic sense of the past faced this new Israeli master plan with trepidation.[77]

The project revolved around the establishment of seven villages whose inhabitants would work on poultry farming, cattle rearing and milk production as well as crop production. Stewardship of this vast project from 2004 to 2008 was beset with a wide range of problems, ranging from poor implementation of irrigation and crop management to cultural incomprehension vis-à-vis Angolan workers. The knowledge base of the project was Israeli, and Angolans didn't have the capacity to run it by themselves.[78] Moreover, the costs were far in excess of predictions, and the Aldeia Nova experiment needed constant injections of cash to keep running. In particular, the energy needs of Aldeia Nova were entirely dependent on expensive generators consuming 90,000 litres of diesel per week, making the whole enterprise (especially of milk production) commercially unpromising to say the least.[79] By the time the Angolan state took it over in 2008, all of this was known and yet little if anything was done to put the project back on a sounder footing. Subsequent indifferent local management, collapse in time discipline and the unavailability of basic inputs, as well as the government's increasing unwillingness to pay for the whole thing, meant that the end was only a matter of time. As early as 2009, even José Cerqueira, the government-appointed CEO, conceded that the Aldeia Nova model was too expensive a solution for the small number of people it had settled, a mere 600 families.[80] By 2011, Aldeia Nova was bankrupt, and the families hadn't been paid for months. There was no production whatsoever. The solution? Establish a public private partnership between the Angolan state and another Israeli company, the Mitrelli Group.

This failure did not lead the government to revisit the kibbutz model: several more Aldeia Nova-style projects are in the process of being built all over Angola, at an estimated cost of US$400 million. I had the opportunity to visit one of these, the US$24 million Cacanda project outside Dundo in Lunda Norte, just before its inauguration in November 2011. As in Waku Kungo, Cacanda is built upon a colonial-era agricultural estate, once ran by the all-powerful diamond company, Diamang; and like Waku Kungo as late as 2010, it looks state-of-the-art under deft Israeli management. According to two interviewees involved in the project, that is precisely the problem.[81] There was only a handful of Angolan technical staff with the requisite expertise and the families of veterans attached to Cacanda were not capable of playing a meaning-ful role. Inauguration was only two days later, with the Angolans soon taking over the whole project; there was little time for training. Added to this are all the problems of Aldeia Nova's first incarnation, but with the burdens of Lunda Norte's remoteness piled on top. Cacanda is but a few miles away from Dundo's Chinese-built "Kilamba" described above. Gazing at both, one can but be sceptical as to the fate of these investments or Lunda Norte's dubious honour at being burdened with them. One insider had a clear explanation for this throwing of good money after bad, the pursuit of the kibbutz model against common sense and economic viability alike:

> You see, such projects [in Angola] are overpriced; a private company moves in on a fat contract to implement them, lots of money to go around from the very start. The big plan is of course to use public money to build farms [which won't work] and then give it out to a private entity. ... The same thing applies to Nosso Super: they get it built, they ruin it, and then it has to be passed on to private management for next to nothing; and they give it to those close to them, who even come across as saviours of the public interest![82]

If Aldeia Nova is the most prominent government attempt at restart-ing agriculture, PRESILD/Nosso Super is the equivalent for the rebuild-ing of the trade network. Ever since the 1975 collapse of rural markets, Angola has spent lots of time and money rejigging them, but markets remain empty or even non-existent in remote locations. The postwar policy for addressing this was a national scheme called PRESILD that cost US$600 million in its first two years alone.[83] It aimed at building the structures for acquiring staple produce from farmers, storing it, and channeling it to consumers across the country. The idea seemed worthy, even if it was pursued to the detriment of more obvious incentives for stimulating rural commerce and overestimated the state's capacity to run a very complex structure. In practice, the focus was on building physical infrastructure and on the expensive acquisition of stocks, with manage-ment systems, training, and local-level structures neglected. The Nosso Super retail network was created in 2008, but the 31 supermarkets soon emptied out their goods and these were not replenished. The supermar-kets failed and closed down; years of inaction ensued. By 2012, NRSA, a private company owned by Angolan investors in partnership with Odebrecht, the Brazilian company that had built the network, took over Nosso Super for 10 years on concessional terms.[84] Far from prioritizing small and medium farmers, a lot of Nosso Super's produce is imported, with local products acquired from "reliable" (that is, large-scale) producers. The construction of networks for acquisition of local produce was neglected, even in provinces, such as Malange, with extensive local production.[85] Indeed, Nosso Super was "selling [many] of the same [mostly imported] products as Jumbo or Shop-Rite", two prominent foreign supermarket chains.[86] The process was complete.

This chapter could be burdened further with many examples of capital-intensive, state-sponsored projects that ended up failing or in private hands. The cases discussed above are not exhaustive but provide a representative sample across different sectors of the government's approach to important dimensions of reconstruction. And their number keeps on rising. Energized by the post-2010 economic recovery, projects such as these are now coming up throughout Angola (the occasional Dundo satellite city excepted, mostly on the coast). But most expenditure and political attention remains firmly stuck in the capital. The culmination of the gigantism of these projects is of course the transformation of Luanda itself into a mirror of the elite's aspirations for the new Angola. Although it was barely affected by the war, a case can be made for tackling Luanda's woes. Population pressure (with perhaps six million inhabitants, the city expanded fifteen-fold in less than 40 years) compounded by neglect until 2002 means that Luanda's infrastructure is either a mess or doesn't exist, as in the case of the farther-off *musseques* (the local term for the slums outside the cement city, where most Luandans live). But the party-state's focus on Luanda is only obliquely a matter of popular welfare. Similarly to other oil-rich states' buildup of glitzy new capital cities, greater Luanda is to be the showcase for Angola's economic miracle, the centre stage for the spectacle of reconstruction.

The physical transformation of Luanda that this entailed has come to fascinate scholars and journalists. While it is fully in line with trends in many metropolises of the developing world—Luanda is scarcely the only megacity shaping itself to fit elite and middle class lifestyles—Angola's available resources have meant a scale of ambition that has few parallels over the last decade.[87] The most evident sign of this is the changing skyline, with high-rises popping up all over the city amidst the rubble of old Luanda. Many of these buildings are for commercial purposes such as offices and shopping centres. In addition to the Latin American-style chasm between the poor and the rich who flaunt their material culture without qualms, the city is festooned with an overkill of consumer-oriented publicity advertising the wealth of the new Angola. Central to this vision of Luanda as a modern, sophisticated city is the revamping of the 3km-long Luanda bay waterfront through a 700,000m² land reclamation and landscaping project. This is the first step of an ambitious drive to reinvent the Luandan coastline that includes the Island of Luanda and the Nova Marginal area around Praia do Bispo. The first part of the project, conservatively estimated to have cost US$200 million, is dotted with more than 3000 palm trees "mostly brought in from Miami" and luxury restaurants and outdoor cafes.[88] The manicured lawn, prohibitively expensive to keep up in Luanda's dry climate, was laid out by SIS, an Irish company that specializes in football stadium lawns and had already received the contract for the African football championship of 2010. "The 3D photographs of the Bay project are futuristic, but this is not a virtual world, like in a video game. The future is happening in full view for everyone [to see]," gushed an enthusiastic Luandan magazine; "It seems virtual in 2011, but the technical experts guarantee that it will be real in 2012."[89]

The unavoidable counterpoint to this modernizing frenzy lies in the exclusion of the poor. In distant Luena, I witnessed a top civil servant shooing off five cleaning ladies and their small children, who were briefly resting on the stairs leading up to the just-inaugurated but inoperative train station: "Get out of there, [your presence here] is ugly".[90] On a vastly grander scale, this mindset—that poverty is unsightly and mustn't distract from the achievements of national reconstruction—presides over much of the reorganization of the capital. It also offers insights into the leadership's thinking more generally. The urban geography of Luanda is such that while there is, broadly speaking, a European city and "native" quarters, the social pattern of habitation is historically very mixed.[91] Prosperous neighbourhoods such as Alvalade, Maianga and Miramar are only minutes' walk from bad slums, and in some cases slums exist at the very centre of town. This is incompatible with the modern aspirations of the MPLA leadership. So a great deal of this modernizing agenda has entailed the demolition of inconveniently located slums, often without warning, a process well documented by Angolan NGOs.[92]

These extensive demolitions occur not only for the sake of prestige public works but also for the advancement of private urban projects, especially the building of luxury condominiums. For the eviction of the unfortunately placed poor is paralleled by the retreat of the better off to gated communities and more socially homogeneous settings. This is particularly the case in Luanda Sul and Talatona, the new suburbs where many foreign businesses increasingly prefer to be based. This major hub of gated communities and corporate offices now provides a nowhereland experience for the rich and the expats, with the poor kept at bay by high walls and barbed wire. The poor don't always go without a fight: evictions from prime agricultural land in Camama for the building of the unselfconsciously named Garden of Eden luxury complex, for instance, resulted in violent protest. But state authority invariably weighs in on the side of the wealthy.

The irony behind the showmanship of Luanda's gaudy remake and skyscraper and condominium craze lies in its utter neglect of foundations—and this is meant quite literally. Architects agonize over the safety and viability of these large structures, especially in the sandy and watery lands of downtown Luanda. But the lack of concern for foundations is much more extensive and encompasses the neglect of sewage systems, water provision and electrical supply. Some of Luanda's signature buildings have had to build separate systems, including enormous, noisy and expensive generators, and are veritable self-sustaining islands.[93] The elite prioritizes the build up of everything visible and status enhancing: the façade of modernity, and to hell with the plumbing.

THE ROLE OF FOREIGNERS

At the centre of the reconstruction era lies the expatriate labour force. A massive inflow of Western and East Asian expatriates quickly descended on Angola as soon as the country settled into reconstruction mode from 2004 onwards. Angola's stress on national sovereignty and distrust of external involvement, itself typical of many postcolonial states, is heightened by a history of foreign intervention and the more recent undermining of the government's reputation by anti-corruption campaigners. Yet decision-makers understood that Angola did not have the management systems and technical capacity to reconstruct its infrastructure or to run the more elaborate postwar economy. As a result, Angolan reconstruction came to include as much international input as in states with multilateral, UN-directed efforts.

However, there are crucial differences. This external involvement occurs within a political context defined by the Angolan government;

the key foreign role is played by the private sector and state-owned corporations rather than by international organizations or NGOs; and their
involvement is premised on non-negotiable financial rewards to members of the elite who are unavoidable partners in expatriate entrepreneurial activities. The Angolan government has thus tapped into external expertise in order to advance reconstruction, but on its own terms.

The Angolan economy has for decades presupposed a key role for
non-Angolans, as there are insufficient skilled Angolans to man the state
and the economy at the requisite level. As we saw in Chapter 1, the
departure of more than 300,000 Portuguese settlers in 1975 destroyed
the non-oil economy. The post-independence state only managed to
limp along because of the presence of tens of thousands of Eastern Bloc
advisers who included anything from respected Cuban doctors and
teachers to less reputable Soviet GOSPLAN advisers, Bulgarian agricultural technicians and East German secret police experts. After the Cold
War, these were replaced by a large number of foreign workers, UN
agencies, NGOs and church charities. This scarcity of human resources
applied to the oil industry, which remains dependent on expatriate technical expertise, and to the running of the war effort, on account of which
a sinister cast of international "technical advisers" made considerable
fortunes until 2002. Other things that worked satisfactorily in the last
years of the war did so because they were under management contracts
with foreign firms. This was the case of areas as varied as the water supply
in Soyo and Caxito, solid waste collection and port operations in Luanda,
and ground handling services at Luanda airport.[94] As we have seen, there
are islands of excellence within Angola's political economy such as
Sonangol but they serve purposes other than day-to-day management of
the country.

The postwar period witnessed an explosion in demand for foreign
labour in all areas, verging from reconstruction proper to the manifold
services sector in the major cities. The key difference between the current
period and earlier decades is that this external presence, while useful, had
previously circumscribed Angola's autonomy. In the past decade, however, the expatriate contingent was orchestrated, and its political leverage
curbed, by the Angolan elite. The Portuguese in particular have returned
to Angola in great numbers, reaching 80,000 in 2008[95] and an estimated 130–150,000 in 2012,[96] in tandem with the growing importance
of postwar Angola for the Portuguese economy discussed in Chapter 5.

While some are Angola-born, many are simply looking for business or employment opportunities, as are some 40,000 Brazilian citizens. The number of Chinese workers in the country is the subject of considerable debate with 50,000–75,000 a conservative figure,[97] while the *Financial Times* mentioned an estimate of 260,000 by mid-2012.[98] Smaller but visible presences include Malians, Lebanese, Indians and Spaniards, as well as assorted northern Europeans, North Americans, Israelis and South Africans. In truth, no one knows how many foreigners are currently in Angola and estimates that include migrants from other African countries well exceed half a million.

This massive influx of expatriates, particularly Western ones, has changed the face of Luanda. Look around as you sit in the traffic anywhere in the cement city, the southern suburbs of Luanda Sul and Talatona, or the road in between, and the faces of the occupants of the other cars will give you an intimation of this transformation: the city has been partly re-Europeanized.[99] The Brazilian-inspired, fashion-world tale *Windeck*, the country's most popular soap opera in 2012, even included Portuguese and Italian characters trying to cope with life in Luanda. The more discreet Chinese mostly stay on the capital's outskirts, but occasionally venture into the fancier parts of Luanda, where they patronize in large numbers gambling haunts like Talatona's Golden Lion casino and the Tivoli Hotel.

This expat life is increasingly comfortable, the terrible traffic excepted. A well-paid foreign worker in today's Luanda can stroll through glitzy shopping malls, attend fashion shows (often peddling the wares of down-and-out Portuguese couturiers in search of a fresh market), enjoy frequent concerts by renowned stars and hip Ibiza DJs, go for drinks in a five-star hotel with a bay view, eat at scores of luxury restaurants dotting the Ilha and the better quarters, and access their home countries via the constant (and frequently overbooked) flights by many international airlines. While the 1990s expatriate cast was made of mercenaries, oilmen and relief workers, today's range of foreign presences spans every conceivable field and economic activity.

And the whole place works because of them. Of course, the expatriates come from very diverse backgrounds. Within the highly diverse Portuguese community, for instance, one can find anything from top managerial staff in leading corporations to mid-level construction types and fly-by-night, unskilled opportunists. It is undeniable that a sizeable portion of the expatriate crowd is no asset for Angolan development. But too much focus on the lower end of the spectrum obscures the fact that the skills base of the Angolan economy is once again mostly foreign. Like the French and Lebanese in Côte d'Ivoire back in the day (and once again) or ethnic Chinese minorities in much of Southeast Asia, it is this motley group of expats that makes Angola go round. One could conceivably have run the simpler war economy without them, but even then foreigners played an important role. In the new Angola they are indispensible.

The direct role of foreigners in reconstruction is well known. But the same applies to almost every other major sector of the Angolan economy. The government's incapacity to achieve its ambitions single-handedly and a desire for overnight results lead it to splurge on all the consultants and subcontractors that oil money can buy. The resulting rampant "culture of consultancy" means that even where there is the illusion of an Angolan role, the actual tasks are being performed by KPMG, Ernst & Young, McKinsey, Deloitte and lesser international providers of myriad services handsomely paid by the Angolans. This major role for foreign consultants, as well as their proximity to elite Angolans, can also create conflicts of interest: in 2010, for instance, KPMG closed down its Angolan operation for as yet unexplained reasons, fired everyone, and reopened with a new team brought in from Portugal.[100] Worryingly, the Angolan side of these arrangements seldom seems interested in "concrete, technical learning" or transfer of knowledge, a matter I will return to in Chapter 4. For their part, foreigners are in no hurry to making themselves redundant. As one executive put it, the lack of capacity and, arguably, willingness to learn, on the Angolan side means "big business and endless business" for him and his competitors.[101]

The Angolan elite is not only unconcerned by this presence which it controls so well, but has encouraged it. It sees foreigners as essential both for the short term needs of reconstruction and for the longer term running of a complex economy. Powerful Angolans also prize these foreigners as steady managers of their own business interests, for behind every Angolan tycoon there is often a mostly Portuguese managerial team. This is frequently coupled with suspicion about the capacities, work ethic and honesty of other Angolans, to the extent that a number of Angolan wealthy are known to dislike hiring their countrymen, even for relatively minor tasks.

Feelings in less moneyed corners of Angolan society are different. Other than the consistent mistreatment of the Congolese, whom no one protects or cares about,[102] little by way of overt anti-foreigner agitation has transpired in recent years. There is some distrust towards the Chinese, who have brought in a large and often non- or semi-skilled labour force to work on the construction projects.[103] Contrary to other African countries, however, few Angolans envy the low pay and often menial tasks associated with the Chinese. Yet resentment against white expatriates is brewing amongst Angola's aspiring middle classes, in what one of the MPLA's senior politicians did not hesitate to describe as a "time bomb".[104] Fresh out of mostly low-quality universities and brimming with a mixed sense of entitlement and insecurity, they see foreigners in key positions as an impediment to social mobility. Conversations about employment almost invariably converge on the perceived advantages given to expatriates and the over-representation of "Angolan" whites and *mestiços* in the filling of Angolan jobs (the quotation marks are ubiquitous as many are assumed to have only recently received their Angolan passports).[105] There are also persistent complaints by young (non-elite) Luandans that the door policies of luxury nightclubs in the Ilha are discriminatory and even racist, with white patrons breezing through on the assumption that they can afford the high prices.[106] The whole matter is refracted through the prism of Angolan history and unavoidably racialized.

The result of this deep ambivalence towards a large-scale foreign presence is an erratic visa regime and recurrent expulsions of illegal foreign workers. Amongst the most memorable images of recent years are the near-monthly televised deportations of glum-looking foreign workers (many of them Portuguese), followed by spirited commentator debates on the pros and cons of mass immigration and its impact on Angolan jobs and "national culture" that uncannily mirror their counterparts in the Western world. It doesn't take a very pessimistic assessment of the Angolan economy to realize that this over-dependence on outsiders is brittle and will not sustain major economic shocks or populist reactions. Some foreigners are aware of the precariousness of their status and seek "to get rich quick and leave this place".[107] But many others, especially amongst the Portuguese, seem oblivious to the complexities of Angolan society and are settling in for the long haul. As a foreign diplomat noted with dismay, "they are amoral about the internal politics, and the fact that this is an extraordinary place doesn't register with them".[108]

As in the Gulf oil monarchies, this politically apathetic stance is a prerequisite for foreigners' presence in Angola. Foreigners are spoken of, and refer to themselves as, "service providers" to the authorities, implementing whatever they are asked to do and benefiting from whatever opportunities come their way. Foreigners are not in Angola to change the Angolan way of doing things, something they could not do even if they wanted to; and they don't, as the present system is highly lucrative for them. The sole and implausible exception came from BP in 2001 when, in a brief flirtation with the transparency agenda, it unilaterally published the value of the signature bonus it had paid Angola. The government's brutal reaction came in the form of a threat of expulsion. A bruised BP retreated back into oil *realpolitik*, and foreign investors have never strayed from this path since.

By far the most frequent outcome is for foreign companies, including prominent global firms, to "quickly adapt to local mores to the point of going native".[109] The business activities of foreigners are subject to overt or covert partnerships with Angolan insiders, without which they cannot enter the Angolan market or thrive in it. While essential for the reconstruction effort, the foreign private sector is not collectively organized. Opportunities for individual companies depend on the discretionary power of a handful of Angolan decision-makers and the complex and arbitrary visa regime results in an insecure presence on the ground. This makes foreigners both crucial to the reconstruction effort and marginal individuals without much political clout. Even high-profile players such as the major Brazilian and Portuguese construction companies, which are particularly close to the presidential palace, are better thought of as resilient courtiers than as consequential actors in their own right.

This political marginality also applies to international organizations (IOs) and NGOs. This is partly due to their meagre financial resources when compared with the revenue stream of the Angolan government: in the past five years the *combined* total of World Bank, United Nations and European Union resources for Angola was about 1 per cent of the Angolan annual budget, an amount that doesn't buy them much influence. But the key factor is the Angolan strategy of strictly defining the contours of any external entity's role and guaranteeing that it advances the government's agenda. This doesn't just mean wanting IOs to play the role of mere service providers; it also means confining IOs within narrow and apolitical fields to prevent them from arrogating governance matters. As an IO staffer commented with deep frustration, "we could provide them with plenty of assistance on management systems, budgetary tools or procurement arrangements, but these are precisely the areas where they don't want any assistance".[110]

The government's message for the past decade is clear: international development organizations must either adapt to the new balance of power, or decamp. Many of the estimated 100 international NGOs active in Angola around 2003 did the latter and closed their Angolan operations. In the fulness of time, the remaining donors, IOs and most NGOs ended up obliging the authorities and now stress their obsequiousness towards the government's agenda. A vital element of this relationship is that the internationals should not be seen to cast doubts over the government's reconstruction storyline. As an international official remarked:

> good UN relations with the government are kept by underlining the positive and leaving other matters on the side. Social indicators and governance matters are out of bounds. [For instance] in a normal country the UNDP has a decisive role to play in areas such as budget support. But development strategy is beyond our remit as the government treats this as a sovereign issue.[111]

The result of having to play a "constructive role that does not embarrass the authorities"[112] is a considerable abridgement of the scope for critical involvement. It is also in marked contrast to the 2002 UN blueprint for Angola's reconstruction, a sort of "Peacebuilding 101" that did not shy away from criticizing "the deeper institutional problems concerning the nature of governance in Angola".[113] None of this talk is to be heard today. Having interviewed UN staffers and management in Angola throughout the last decade, I have seen it undergo a transition from an assertive stance in the years immediately after the war to a quietist and placatory partner of the government's agenda for niche issues. For in regard to "the big questions, there are no opportunities for engagement".[114] Despite a still-important presence in Angola, then, the foreign development agencies have played a minimal role in defining the reconstruction agenda or influencing the government's own plans. But if the traditional Western donor package proved so peripheral to Angolan reconstruction designs, which models have mattered, and where do they come from?

THE DEVELOPMENT VISION

In hindsight, the party-state's swift adoption of a grandiose vision of state-led reconstruction was fully in character. As we have just seen, this did not preclude a central role for the foreign private sector but defined unambiguously who was in charge. The language of state-directed reconstruction was partly the product of the increase in oil revenue, which has always emboldened resource-rich states to think and talk big. Angolan elites also have a natural affinity for whichever language maximizes power and influence and keeps them at the centre of the political economy—formerly the nationalist vanguard and the centralized economy, now the national bourgeoisie and other MPLA tropes.

For all that, the welfare language of Angola's rulers will come as a surprise to anyone who gleans their knowledge of Angola from occasional news items about oil and corruption. With the end of hostilities, Angola's grinding poverty and social neglect were retrospectively blamed on the war, and the MPLA resurrected a vocabulary of state-building and social concern for "average" Angolans. Since then, every government statement and MPLA electoral manifesto is laced with commitments to development and runaway progress: from public goods provision and HIV/AIDS awareness to women's rights, there is scarcely a progressive agenda that the government doesn't pay allegiance to. This is of course smart politics as it resonates with popular "modern" aspirations for improvement. In a typical 2006 address, President dos Santos noted that "it is necessary that the population feel that there are constant improvements in medical assistance, education, commerce, transportation, water and electricity supply and in the respect for their rights".[115] Far from being objectionable, much of the party-state's public discourse is premised on shared ambitions for the country; from the opposition to the NGOs and the media no one could possibly disagree with them.

Where does this relentless developmental rhetoric come from? The MPLA does not have a penchant for producing exotic political philosophies. What it has instead is a long mimetic tradition of absorbing anything that claims to be modern and rhetorically converging with prevalent ideas of progress, if divorced from reality, whether socialism until 1991 or democracy now. As a somewhat estranged technocrat and MPLA member admits, the party:

> likes to occupy the [rhetorical] terrain: if the MPLA doesn't talk development, there may be some guy, some organization—the Catholic Church, the opposition—picking it up. So any [progressive] agenda that comes up, the MPLA picks it up, swears allegiance to it, and does nothing—but it manages to crowd out others saying the same thing.[116]

This leads the MPLA to embrace a wide variety of pro-poor measures to the extent of turning them into legislation, yet consistently eschew implementation.[117] The best way to understand the MPLA's emphasis on development is as a discourse of the party about itself and its legitimate authority over contemporary Angola. As Béatrice Hibou noted in regard to Ben Ali's Tunisia, an exalted vision of state-driven progress and modernity is inherently elitist, presupposing a population that is "ignorant, easily influenced [and] living in obscurantism" but enlightened by a party-state that is "rational [and] cultivated".[118] The focus of the MPLA is less on specific reforms than on reformism itself whose definition it alone provides.[119] The result is that this modernizing language is strong but not really about results: it is about the party looking at itself in the mirror and liking what it sees.

A prime example of this is the vaunted yet undisclosed 2025 Long-Term Development Strategy, the importance of which has increased with its top-secret status.[120] The Strategy is a serious disappointment once you get to read it. It is certainly long, at 700 pages, and initially gives the impression of a fairly comprehensive document, despite being written in the bland language of a global consultancy mindful of liberal buzzwords ("civil society", "good and transparent governance", "public-private partnerships" etc. recur). The initial chapters, of a more diagnostic character, provide accurate sector portraits and make use of the scarce available data. But the remainder is a wish list of developmental outcomes almost wholly unconcerned with process and making unrealistic assumptions about state capacity and political will. It is symptomatic that details of the Strategy rarely get mentioned by the powerful; the reason for this is that practically no one has read it or knows its contents, if one excepts the handful of policy intellectuals and foreign consultants who wrote it.[121] The Strategy does not inform day-to-day government business in Angola and actual policies over the past decade reflect it obliquely, if at all. To understand the developmental outlook of the leadership, we have to search elsewhere.

There is in fact an absolute dissonance between the developmental rhetoric and the MPLA agenda. Beyond the specificities of its historical trajectory, the MPLA's reconstruction vision can be understood in terms of a high-modernist mindset[122] fired up by the resources, and sense of endless possibility, of an oil-rich economy, with which students of oil boom-era follies of the 1970s will be familiar.[123] Its aim is to transform

Angola into a self-styled modern country with an emphasis on infra-structure and other inanimate objects.[124] Investment in people and institution building are secondary in this vision. Upon close inspection, there is no sustained attempt to build up the management systems of the complex technology that is the modern state. Like the oil sheikhs of old, powerful Angolans assume that skilled foreign expertise (as with luxury consumer goods) can be acquired to do the technical heavy lifting: they can be the beneficiaries of the end-product.

It is unsurprising that this Angolan-style reconstruction agenda, though phrased in universalistic terms, fully reflects the regime's geographical and social biases. In spite of recurrent references to agricultural development, and belated incentives for private investment in non-oil sectors and the provinces, public expenditure remains overwhelmingly focused on the cities. In this vision, modernity is intrinsically coastal and urban, and Luanda is the pinnacle of Angolan modernity, as discussed above. Even in the city environment, reconstruction means prioritizing the things that, for the elite, represent the modern, and the urban spaces where they dwell. They happen to coincide with what the elite wants from life: shopping malls, skyscrapers, private condominiums, marinas and other "visible badges of being an important oil state".[125]

Socially, the target of government policy is not the poor majority. The elite appropriates the lion's share of the benefits of the reconstruction era. But since the end of the war, the MPLA has favoured the expansion of a broader constituency of beneficiaries, normally dubbed the "national bourgeoisie". This phrase, whose recurrence in this book mirrors the MPLA's constant usage, has been subjected to numerous interpretations since it entered the Angolan mainstream after the demise of socialism. The most expansive interpretation is that of a postwar "middle class" of some half million people out of an estimated 20 million Angolans that includes civil servants, members of the security apparatus, and educated urbanites. (Confusingly, the expression can also be used in reference to Angolan entrepreneurs, a much smaller group, as discussed in Chapter 4.) The regime perceives the creation and nurturing of this national bourgeoisie as the essential backbone of MPLA support for the long term and has therefore targeted many postwar improvements at it. These verge from the provision of housing, car ownership and retirement pensions to the expansion of the civil service from 200,000 to 400,000 (with salaries greatly increasing in value and mostly paid in a timely fashion) in the decade following 2002, as well as many other status enhancing opportunities. The bourgeoisie's newfound disposable income is in turn crucial for the development of Angola's urban consumer culture best seen in the massive expansion of supermarkets and shopping malls. It is undeniable that this segment of the Angolan population substantially benefited from the improvements of the last decade.

This middle class agenda is, incidentally, a step up from the MPLA's micro-sphere of concern of the war years, and shows the regime's understanding that it cannot sustain its dominance without expanding benefits to wider constituencies. Two aspects of this agenda are noteworthy. The first is that the MPLA wants to internalize the process of class formation: through a limited distribution of the oil rent, it seeks to engineer the rise of a loyal and dependent state class rather than create the conditions for the spontaneous emergence of an unattached and unreliable middle class. The second point about this agenda is that "there is little room [in it] for the poor, who are often seen as an obstacle to, rather than the primary focus of, development".[126] The World Bank notes that "public delivery of social services is [...] skewed in favor of the urban rich"[127] and the same applies to most public expenditure. While the data are patchy, it is clear that war victims and the poor have not benefited much from the economic growth and that poverty reduction is not part of the postwar story. More generally, while the universe of beneficiaries of state largesse has been steadily expanding over the past decade, it remains a minute percentage of the Angolan population. It certainly falls short of the distributive systems that other petro-states have sought to build, which tend to include at least a plurality of their citizens.

The disparity between the developmental claims and the real focus of government attention is such that some observers interpret it as evidence of an outdated and wrong-headed but "sincere" view of the state as strong and interventionist. According to this view, the MPLA simply doesn't have the managerial means to live up to its ambitions. Yet this is to underestimate how easily the MPLA adapted to what James Ferguson called a "nongovernmental state" during the 1990s.[128] During those years, far from being wedded to the big, socially responsible state, the elite thoroughly privatized important state functions and got itself out of any sort of commitments towards popular welfare, which were passed on to the churches, the NGOs and the UN system. It is hard to avoid the conclusion that the "big state" choices made in the decade of reconstruction were much more a matter of elite preferences for policies that would benefit it than of concern for the real problems of Angolan society.

Informing the government's reconstruction agenda is a not altogether coherent mix of past and present experiences. The late colonial set-up that collapsed in 1975—Angola's only major period of conventional stateness—has had a strangely influential afterlife. For the subsequent quarter-century, urban Angolans inhabited an architectural time warp infused with the promise of modernity of the early 1970s. An insidious "1973 nostalgia" took root, with many technocrats and intellectuals distinguishing between "the bad politics of the [Portuguese] regime and the extraordinary achievements of the [late colonial] period".[129] The contributions of a small cadre of "admirable and selfless" Portuguese civil servants is even acknowledged by Angolan officials, to the extent that the memoirs of the late colonial Finance Secretary, Eduardo Costa Oliveira, could be flatteringly prefaced by his Angolan counterpart, José Pedro de Morais, three decades later.[130] At war's end, the success of late colonial Angola and some of its signal projects—the coffee sector, the railways, light manufacturing, Diamang—were irresistibly the focus of renewed interest.[131] Rebuilding Angola came to mean the literal rebuilding of what had been destroyed, even if some of that had been rendered obsolete in the intervening decades. As an Angolan intellectual acerbically put it, "the elites believe in this [late colonial model]; for them, the problem [was that] the Portuguese were running it, but the model itself they like".[132]

Of course, as I explain in subsequent chapters, the Angola that materialized in the last decade is not a return to the colonial era. It is rather at the rhetorical level that the impact of the late colonial model is clearest. Ambitious settler imaginings of Angola as a "new Brazil" have become central to the aspirations of the inheritors of the state, if now mixed with a brash oil-fuelled nationalism. As mentioned in the Introduction, the dominant strands of the MPLA differ from the elites of the defeated liberation movements, who were mostly mission-educated and only marginally related to the colonial state and Portuguese culture. The MPLA attracted urbanites who were intensely "Portugalized"[133] and often employed in the lower and middle ranks of the colonial civil service. Confusingly, this social group spawned the MPLA while many of its members were beneficiaries of the late colonial attempt to bring Angolans into the fold of Portuguese rule. It is not surprising that those settler aspirations would appeal to them as well.

Despite these occasional throwbacks, many contemporary experiences speak to the sensibility of the Angolan elite as they pursue their reconstruction drive. Brazil, discussed in more detail in Chapter 5, is a key provider of models, lifestyles and manifold consultancy services and represents, in many ways, the ideal society for elite Angolans.[134] China is also influential, if in a more circuitous way. Angola is not unique among states of the developing world in having a superficial elective affinity with the Chinese political-economic model. China provides the example of a reform process that strengthens, rather than weakens, the status quo. Interviews with politicians of a certain age with memories of Maoist China bring out their baffled admiration for the Chinese accomplishment. When placed in the context of China's role in present-day Angola, this has occasionally given rise to simplistic accounts of pervasive Chinese influence and Angolan emulation of its partner's structures. The engagement with the actual Chinese experience of economic reform and social transformation is in fact very shallow. Little by way of detail is known or understood by the Angolans, and few if any specific lessons are taken on board. The role of agrarian reform as a major contributor to Chinese GDP growth and popular welfare from 1978 to 1991, for instance, is ignored by the urban-minded MPLA. Perhaps the Angolan elite believes that, rhetoric aside, the nuts and bolts of the Chinese experience are of limited relevance for a rentier state with scarce human resources.

The same applies to references to Luanda as "Africa's Dubai" in the media, and in private and public statements by politicians.[135] The Angolan elite (like, say, Venezuelan elites in 1970s Miami) is enamoured of the modernity of Dubai's built environment, and the speed with which it was achieved. Since the 2008 inauguration of an Emirates flight to Luanda, Dubai is thronging with Angolan shoppers, the back offices of Angolan companies and businessmen keen on the city's "amazing open access, without bureaucracy or taxes".[136] But there is no serious engagement with the political economy of that city or willingness to emulate it beyond the hiring of expats who can be jettisoned at will. Alternatively, Dubai is a stand-in for a generic global modernity of cleanliness, efficiency, and consumer-centred urban experience. While superficial, this fascination has serious consequences, with shiny modern buildings mushrooming all over Luanda, and scarce electricity supplies being rerouted to satiate their nightly consumption.

The MPLA's sources of ideological inspiration highlighted thus far are to a large extent authoritarian. But its approach to the West is not outright negative, and at this moment in time at least, the regime styles itself as a market-friendly democracy. Its approach towards the West is therefore ambivalent and selective. Appreciation of the West's material culture and lifestyles, essentially interiorized as their own by the Angolan elite, is boundless. The elite is able to think highly of these in oblivion of the West's history and of the institutions that have produced them. On the other hand, a track record of Western undermining of the MPLA, the illiberal character of the regime, and an emphasis on non-interference in Angola's internal affairs result in loathing towards Western normative activism. Moreover, a Western-style liberal state is not a desirable end goal for anyone of any consequence in Angolan decision-making. This said, at its most lucid the Angolan elite discerns the fact that the West is not a unitary actor bent on democracy promotion and poverty alleviation, and that "there is a huge difference between Deloitte and Amnesty International".[137] They believe that many commercial players in the West have valuable lessons to impart as well as the pragmatism to deal with Angola on the regime's terms. Shorn of pesky politics, the presence of Western management consultants, bankers, asset managers and lawyers is both welcome and influential.

The baroque list of influences on the MPLA's development vision is virtually endless. Any given week in Luanda may simultaneously see the embrace of Third Worldist solidarity on the occasion of a visit by a Cuban Communist Party delegation, the adoption of a boilerplate urban planning report by a Western global consultancy, the extolling of the Israeli kibbutz, and the praising of Brazilian industrialization. Because even a cursory visit will allow observers to notice these parallels, there is a tendency to forget that the foreign models are refracted through the prism of Angolan sensibilities and priorities. These outside references are prestigious. But whatever doesn't fit, powerful Angolans discard, in a highly original exercise in "*bricolage*". They manage a wide set of contemporary and historical experiences for their own purposes, with half-learnt lessons, distortions and lip-service more frequent than genuine attempts at emulation. It is thus unsurprising that Angola's reconstruction turned out to be an original mix of familiar models digested and made unrecognizable at the ground level; the result is Angolan through and through.[138]

THE SPECTACLE OF RECONSTRUCTION

A POTEMKIN RECONSTRUCTION?

The macro-economic story of what the Angolan economist Manuel Alves da Rocha calls "the golden years" was remarkable, with 15.5 per cent yearly average growth between 2002 and 2008, or eight times the average for the period between 1980 and 2002 (2.1 per cent).[139] It is no wonder that the MPLA got to the 2008 elections in buoyant mood, or that it would abandon its studiously vague rhetoric to promise concrete deliverables for the subsequent four years. The MPLA electoral manifesto made pledges that a capable state would have taken a generation to achieve with difficulty. Of particular resonance for the population was the promised 100 per cent electrical coverage in the cities, 60 per cent in peri-urban areas and 30 per cent in rural areas; the 100 per cent water access in urban areas, and 80 per cent in rural and peri-urban areas alike, and the later much-decried promise of building one million houses, half of them in the provinces.[140]

But only a few months after the elections, the 2008–09 financial crisis and consequent drop in oil prices exposed the fact that these costly illusions were entirely premised on oil money, despite the government's stated goal to diversify the economy. A 32.4 per cent slump in oil revenue led to a 75.1 per cent drop in public investment. The subsequent attempts to keep up the kwanza resulted in a sharp decline in hard currency reserves. Most important for the reconstruction effort, there were serious payment delays to contractors, especially in the construction sector,[141] which by mid-2010 had resulted in debt estimated at US$9 billion.[142] Many of the country's signature building projects came to a standstill; thousands of Chinese workers simply disappeared back where they had come from. As in the 1990s, public administration salaries went unpaid.[143] Shockingly, the government even had to call upon that old foe the IMF, as discussed in Chapter 5. The official narrative was shaken to the core and the foundations of reconstruction were suddenly deemed fragile, even fraudulent.

By mid-2010, the macro-economic situation had again improved and by 2011 it was business as usual. The IMF Stand-by Arrangement brought in needed reforms, some of them of note, but in the context of shoring up the existing system rather than moving away from it. The limitations of the government's plan to transform the country through public expenditure without reforming the public administration, curbing corruption, diversifying the economy or improving education and other social indicators had been exposed.[144] The crisis had also revealed that the fiscal threat to the status quo didn't just come from an "end of oil" doomsday scenario. The train of life the MPLA had concocted by 2008 became unaffordable when the barrel went below US$60, and immediately painful adjustments were needed. Yet the crisis proved to be a mere blip. By 2013, the government was more careful, its foreign exchange reserves increasing to about US$34 billion. But the policy mindset was the same, as shown by the swift return to intemperate projects like the ZEE, Kilamba Kiaxi, the Luanda bay refurbishment, Aldeia Nova, PRESILD, and so many other ambitions that the 2009 crisis had mercifully brought to a halt. The apparently infinite possibilities of Angola's petro-capitalism for both capital-intensive extravaganza and personal gain had again emboldened power-holders.

For anyone who knew the Angola of a decade ago, significant improvements are undeniable. Two key dimensions—infrastructure reconstruction and macro-economic stabilization (see Chapter 4)—have seen genuine progress and there are others where the record is positive. This said, the overall benefits of reconstruction were scarce, disappointing and unevenly distributed, making Angolan society one of the "most unequal in the world", with a GINI coefficient of 0.586 in 2009.[145] A reconstruction project phrased in inclusive terms hid an urban and "bourgeois" agenda with extensive geographical and social blind spots. As we have seen, the winners of this period were again the small elite around the presidency, the upper reaches of the party and the armed forces. Having already benefited from the last decade of the war, they were able to turn the peace into a limitless business opportunity. The outcome is also clear for the minority of urbanites and civil servants who took advantage of the economic opportunities and social enhancement of the reconstruction era: they have never had it better. The same can't be said for the majority of the population in the slums and the countryside. The poor benefited from one overwhelming fact: the end of the war, guaranteeing they would no longer be preyed upon by UNITA or by a merciless, poorly fed army. But they have not been the target of significant public expenditure and survive by relying on their own efforts.

The guiding theme running through the myriad attempts at rebuilding is the urban and modern aspiration of the MPLA leadership and the desire to make the country fit that mould. Yet reconstruction itself proved a capricious mash of disparate influences and played out as an oil-fuelled spectacle of excess, with "signs of material development masquerading as its substance",[146] more Imelda Marcos than Lee Kuan Yew. Symbols of state potency and authority were given primacy over sustainable improvements. The high-modernist language of state-led development, at odds with the really existing party-state, was incongruously attached to a crowd of private-sector expatriates paid for by oil money.

Yet the absence of a vision for broad-based development did not mean a lack of strategic orientation on the part of President dos Santos and the MPLA leadership. For at the centre of this decade's political agenda lay an elite project that transcended physical rebuilding. It had two overlapping goals: the MPLA's imperative of remaining in control of Angola for the next generation, and the perpetuation of JES's rule through the parallel system's lock over reconstruction. In this agenda, and regardless of the inclusive language, Angolan reconstruction was to be channelled towards the benefit of the powerful. From the perspective of the regime, then, the reconstruction era proved a success.

3

THE CONSOLIDATION OF THE
MPLA PARTY-STATE

As the fog of war dissipated, the MPLA found itself in a position rarely attained by African regimes: the rebels had been crushed, many of their former supporters were running for cover or joining the winning side, and the remaining opposition was helpless. Unchallenged, cash-rich, and infused with the legitimacy bestowed by the war victory, the MPLA now had a virtual monopoly over Angola, even where it had no actual presence. The MPLA's generational hold became a given for party officials who gleefully invoked analogies with Mexico's PRI and with other long-lived regimes.[1] In the story the party tells about itself, this outcome was preordained, yet the decades-long route to becoming Angola's hegemonic political force was anything but obvious. It was also a far cry from the MPLA's complex, narrow origins and fractious internal culture.

This chapter explores the different ways in which the MPLA sought to consolidate its grip over Angola in the decade after the end of the conflict. This dynamic went beyond the MPLA's coercive strength, its hegemonic drive matched, at least initially, by a strong desire for inclusion in the party-state order by Angolans of all backgrounds. I begin by looking back at the party's historical trajectory, which is pivotal for understanding its worldview, relations with society, and approaches to the state apparatus. I explain that the MPLA's rule is better conceived as a party-state structure of domination in which conventional boundaries between party, state and public administration are virtually meaningless.

Since Angola's transition towards a multiparty system, one of the MPLA's acts of apparent reinvention, the enmeshment of party and state has been dissimulated, but is no less real for that. The following section explores relations between the party-state and the urban society it has long presided over. Its focus is on the strategies for co-opting social forces that it deems consequential (the media, civil society organizations, professional guilds, the opposition, and more generally the educated segment of the population), as well as the limits of this process.

The MPLA's approach to the hinterland has a different character altogether. Ensconced in the cities and absent from most of its nominal territory until the end of the war, the party-state is now engaged in a large-scale takeover of the rural world. The final section explores the strategies pursued by the MPLA in Angola's vast periphery. The official state-building agenda consists of reconstructing infrastructure and the administrative grid to provide quotidian governance across the country; it also includes vague nation-building aspirations of "bringing Angolans together" and ubiquitous commitments to public goods provision. Yet the real process of MPLA expansion is focused on the often-draconian consolidation of state authority, the co-optation of local elites and elimination of rivals, the violent extraction of resources, and the locking in of electoral dominance for the long haul.

Throughout this exceptional decade, the MPLA's "peace dividend" materialized as tight control over an exhausted population and the party-state was relatively unconstrained as to the shaping of postwar Angola. Yet as this quietist period of unhindered domination came to a close around 2012, and societal claims became louder, the contradictions, exclusions and unintended consequences of the MPLA's choices have started to surface.

THE MPLA PARTY-STATE

Though constitutionally welded together during the socialist years, the MPLA and the Angolan state have had no formal connection since the end of the Cold War. The existence and dominance of the party-state are carefully camouflaged.[2] The Angolan state is presented in reliably conventional ways: a brand new constitution with a clear-cut division of power between the different branches of government, ministries, an ombudsman, a court of auditors, an electoral commission, a justice system. In the official account, the MPLA, the former single party, simply happens to be the political party that won the 1992, 2008 and 2012 legislative elections. You will find many prominent people able to say this with a straight face. The relationship between the state and the party is in fact so deep, multilevel, and enduring that no one knows where one ends and the other begins.

Angola's real structure of power is only obliquely related to this formal edifice. To simplify somewhat, in actuality the state administration is subordinate to the party; both are subordinate to the president's diktat. MPLA structures double and frequently eclipse governmental bodies; no one of consequence in government can do without party membership; presidential protégés without a robust MPLA background will be fast-tracked up the party ranks to bring their party status into line with their influence at the presidential palace. The MPLA penetrates the administration and society at all significant levels. Inheriting the colonial apparatus in 1975, the MPLA has imbibed this legacy and moulded every aspect of Angola's public life since. At the same time, it has revealed a protean capacity for adaptation and even reinvention. Far from destabilizing it, the partial liberalization of the last decades gave the old MPLA a new lease of life. In the years after 2002 the MPLA became, more than ever, a national organization, providing the president with a tool for managing elites, distributing patronage, privileges and social status, and minimizing conflict and splits. This is an amazingly resilient and competent machine, if not at governing, then at keeping itself in power.

Origins

Who would have foreseen it, in view of the MPLA's messy, inauspicious beginnings?

As mentioned in the Introduction, its social origins lay in the remnants of the Creole bourgeoisie that held strong memories of pre-scramble domination but had been marginalized by the transformation of Angola into a white settlement colony.[3] As the first generation having access to university education in the metropolis, future leaders like Mário Pinto de Andrade, Agostinho Neto and Lúcio Lara cut their teeth in the Portuguese leftist politics of the late 1940s and were durably influenced by the culture of the illegal Portuguese Communist Party. Years of inconclusive micro-activism ensued, much of it outside Angola itself, but a bridge between the Portuguese-speaking and mostly urban activists and the Angolan masses was never established. The small groups that would later coalesce in the founding of the MPLA paid formal allegiance to modern ideas and an inclusive pan-Angolan discourse, but were from the outset constrained by the asymmetries that characterized late colonial Angola. These included mutually reinforcing chasms between *assimilados* and other Africans; between descendants of the old families and *mestiços* and "new" *assimilados*; between whites and *mestiços* and blacks; and between culturally Portuguese members of the central society and others. These divisions over race, ethnicity and status—the very fault-lines of Angolan society—were imbibed by the MPLA at inception. They would recur and on occasion almost destroy the party. They were never solved and endure under the surface of today's apparently more cohesive and tranquil party. The tension between the universalist aspirations of the MPLA's nationalist project and its very narrow social roots would forever mark the party.

This goes some way to explain why, even compared with other liberation movements, the MPLA's progress between its foundation and the Portuguese revolution of 1974 was unusually "tortuous and fragmented".[4] This is true about its actions as an anti-colonial movement—its belated recognition by the Organization of African Unity, its lack of operational capacity and insurgent success—but even more so when it came to the internal politics. The MPLA's first Congress in 1962 resulted in the marginalization of its founder, Viriato da Cruz, on account of his being *mestiço* (Neto, who was black, got the top position instead). The subsequent decade saw violent schisms on matters such as the monopoly of leadership positions by coastal Angolans and the overweening role of "intellectuals" in the movement's structure, all of which were coded references to the prominence of *mestiços* (and some whites) in the movement. Most of these enmities were fuelled by baser disputes having to do with personality, rank, control over resources, and women. Accounts of life in the Congolese and Zambian exile bases are consistent in their portraits of the despotic behaviour of guerrilla leaders. Disturbingly in view of the MPLA's modernist claims, accounts have also emerged of its use of witchcraft accusations and the "reign of terror" it unleashed upon populations in liberated areas.[5]

More important, the war effort never thrived. In addition to the debilitating rivalry with other movements and the success of Portuguese counter-insurgency, the MPLA failed to galvanize the peasantry (which mostly saw the MPLA as an alien presence)[6] or create a clandestine organization within colonial Angola itself. There were some brief and limited successes in the east but these had mostly been reversed by the early 1970s. To top it all, a string of dissensions culminated in two spectacular revolts against Neto's authoritarian leadership: the Revolta Activa, which was led by intellectuals and involved a good segment of the party's cadres; and the defection of a top official, Daniel Chipenda, who carried away about a third of the MPLA's guerrillas. By the time the Portuguese regime imploded in April 1974, the MPLA was practically spent as a fighting organization.

What followed is one of the most spectacular turnarounds in liberation politics. Angolan towns underwent an explosion in urban political activism that attached itself to the MPLA and the figure of Agostinho Neto. These new groups knew nothing about the actual MPLA, whose leaders had not been to Angola for more than a decade, its internal repression or its poor war record. Far from being an impediment, this ignorance allowed these fledgling groups to "project their dreams of national combat or revolutionary struggle" onto a distant image of a brave liberation movement.[7] By the time exiled MPLA officials got to Luanda in late 1974, the city had given birth to a cacophony of extreme-left organizations with Albanian, Trotskyist, Maoist, Marxist-Leninist and Stalinist tags as well as trigger-happy shantytown youth groups, each of which claimed to be *the* rightful embodiment of the movement. MPLA officials were both happily surprised at this enthusiasm—which rescued the movement from the internal crises earlier in the year—and suspicious of its overly ideological and undisciplined character. With civil war approaching, the leadership was perceptive enough to accommodate and even push forward these groups, which would prove instrumental in the urban mobilizing against UNITA and the FNLA, the defence of Luanda against foreign invasion and the MPLA's capture of state power at independence in late 1975.

This case of tragic misunderstanding sorted itself out soon afterwards as Neto started to repress and jail the wayward, and no longer useful, factions. It is impossible to do justice here to the complexity of internal MPLA politics during these years of flux.[8] Its culmination was the Nito Alves coup against Neto on 27 May 1977. Apparently encouraged by the Soviets and foiled by the Cubans, this is doubtless the key event in the early history of the MPLA. Its failure unleashed a countrywide campaign of retribution during which an undisclosed number of people, sometimes estimated to be in the tens of thousands, were executed.[9] Although the factions were unrelated to Nito's coup (in fact, Nito Alves had led the early repression against them before falling out with President Neto), the destruction of the *Nitistas* provided the pretext to mop up leftist dissenters. The aftermath of the coup also marked the end of the MPLA dalliance with "the people". Later that year the MPLA formally embraced Marxism-Leninism and turned itself into a vanguard party with a purged membership of only about 30,000 loyalists, a format the party would maintain until the end of the Cold War.

By this stage, however, something crucial had happened: the makeshift liberation movement had taken over the state. The Angolan civil servants of the late colonial apparatus rallied to the MPLA as soon as it came to the towns, mainly because of family and cultural proximity with the leadership rather than the Marxist ideals that had enthralled the educated youth.[10] But Marxism, with its emphasis on state control and intervention, was an enabling language for those wanting to take over,[11] whether it was Creoles at the summit of the state finally establishing themselves as the new power class or barely literate Angolans in the lower ranks of the civil service. This new state inherited the disrupted but surviving mores of the colonial state and manifested the Portuguese-speaking, urban mind-set of the central society that disproportionately took it over. It is noteworthy that the immediate post-independence period, while an economic and institutional downward slide as described in Chapter 1, also allowed tens of thousands of people to experience an extraordinary degree of social promotion. But for Angolans from peripheral societies, the new state remained an alien entity not unlike the old state. As before, accepting the state's behavioural codes and outlook became a prerequisite for gaining a foothold in it.[12] The state was also infused with the MPLA's febrile, conspiratorial culture of exile and guerrilla war and the police state routines of its external sponsors.[13] This, together with the recurrent South African attacks and ongoing civil war, gave the party-state a suffocating national security culture that is one of its perennial traits.

Authoritarian learning

This inflexible culture makes the 1991–92 apparent reinvention of the MPLA surprising. In response to the global geopolitical shift and the

UN-mediated peace process, the MPLA stripped away its "socialist ready-to-wear"[14] and reluctantly claimed to embrace democracy and markets. This was done in a moment of weakness for the regime, with its major external sponsors gone and UNITA at the height of international respectability. But the MPLA pragmatically adapted to the new dispensation. This feat of what Anne Pitcher called "transformative preservation", whereby the MPLA managed to navigate unscathed through a world-historical shift, reveals a machine that had become sturdier and more sophisticated than most analysts ever thought possible.[15]

In order to reproduce domination in a changed context, the MPLA went through a steep learning curve, in what the Middle East expert Steven Heydemann calls "upgrading authoritarianism":[16] the reorganization of strategies of governance to fit new circumstances, including selective engagements with electoral processes and market liberalization that paradoxically strengthen the regime. These significant changes happened at the level of organization, strategies of co-optation, and image management. When it came to the party structure, the post-socialist era necessitated a change of scale. In order to reenergize the party apparatus for the 1992 elections, the MPLA readopted the model of the mass party as per membership. Even in the lean years of elite membership, the MPLA had preserved lower mass organizations such as the OMA and JMPLA, but the reopening to mass membership brought in millions of new members. By election time in 1992, the membership had expanded to close to 2 million, and by 2012, the party claimed about 5 million members, an estimated 25 per cent of the Angolan population. (As we shall see, the inner sanctum of power remained undisturbed. These extraordinary numbers say much about the party's national footprint but also diminish the benefits to be gained from membership.)

With mass expansion, the MPLA also recast itself as a catchall party. In the period between mid-1991 and the 1992 elections, and again since 2002, the MPLA expended a huge effort in developing a national infrastructure that would contradict UNITA's caricature of the MPLA as a coastal and urban party. Much of this strategy had to do with the recruitment of influential or potentially influential actors across society from diverse ethnic and regional backgrounds. The first step of the strategy for broadening the party's support base was the *"Grande Família do MPLA"*, a co-optation drive that gave the impression of reaching out to former dissidents and estranged progressives and emphasized the party-state's modern and urban identity.[17] Although the *Grande Família* was aimed at the sociological world of the MPLA, the party's offer to include repenting rivals was in subsequent years extended to any prominent members of the opposition (UNITA, the Cabindan factions, and others) who would accept the MPLA's terms. This subordinate co-optation excluded the sharing of political power but was and remains generous and reliable in terms of material benefits.[18]

As part of its recasting as a democratic party, the MPLA also developed a canny penchant for self-presentation. The embrace of a market economy was key in this regard. With the demise of Marxism off went the poorly cut uniform and in came Savile Row suits. As Chapter 4 shows, Angolan "capitalism" was really a byword for the party-state's fostering of elite accumulation. To be on the safe side, the MPLA also seized a sizeable chunk of state assets for itself: just a week before the elections of September 1992, it created GEFI, a party holding company with controlling shares in at least 64 businesses, including banking, aviation, fisheries, breweries, car importation, industry, hotels and, crucially, the media.[19] This revamping of the party-state's image was aided by the hiring of deft Brazilian political marketing firms to manage the 1992 electoral campaign (the work of the celebrated Geraldão), the "war for peace" media onslaught of 1998–99 run by media consultant Sérgio Guerra's M'Link[20] and the peacetime election campaigns of 2008 and 2012. From the mid-1990s, lobbyists and image consultants would also be hired in the major Western capitals to advance the view of the regime as a respectable post-socialist interlocutor.[21] Not the least of the party-state's PR feats has been to present itself after 2002 as the party of order and progress, while UNITA is labelled the party of *confusão*.

How did this unusually fractious party manage to pull itself together? The abundant oil money and capacity to feed every key constituency was and remains a significant factor, as does the inhibiting role of JES's leadership for would-be factionalisms. But a major explanation lies in the existence and character of the party itself. Other countries in the region that are oil-rich have far more rickety political structures and a much lower degree of elite cohesion. Nigerian politics never cohered around strong parties; Congo-Brazzaville, Cameroon and Gabon are traditional autocracies with different degrees of horse-trading and ad hoc coalition-building amongst factions, while Equatorial Guinea is in essence a family tyranny.[22] Surveying the divergent paths of authoritarian states engaged in electoral practices, Jason Brownlee concludes that the regimes that best navigated the challenges of partial liberalization and came out stronger are those founded upon capable organizations that generate "political power and long-term security" for insiders while increasing the costs of dissent.[23] This fits the MPLA trajectory like a glove, for the party performs functions that are crucial for JES and the party elite alike.

For the president, it is an essential vehicle for the exercise of power. It provides JES with a liberation movement mystique—a story about origins and a sense of legitimacy—and a national apparatus, and is a reliable mechanism for regulating elite conflict, distributing patronage, and getting out the vote. Like other smart autocrats, JES has always known that governing through a dominant party is much preferable to crude, exposed personal rule. Outside the policy areas that he controls directly (revenue, the coercive apparatus and foreign relations) JES delegates many quotidian dimensions of Angolan life to the party-state: it is the face of power that average Angolans most frequently encounter.

The MPLA is equally advantageous for the party elite. The elite did not consciously acquiesce in JES's power grab during the 1980s and beyond. But a pact of sorts tacitly emerged whereby the president kept the reins of ultimate power while allowing regime notables to exercise authority through the party-state in non-core areas. Above all, he created a consistent and predictable arrangement whereby senior personnel of the party-state are allowed to grow extremely rich. In effect, the party elite has "traded money for power".[24] This stabilized relations between the party and the presidency and between different MPLA persuasions, all of which accepted the established order. When the tremendous and reliable advantages of staying inside the party-state are compared with the uncertain and cash-poor existence of the dissident or challenger, it is to be expected that the elite identifies a collective interest in staying united.

This was facilitated by the fact that the internal life of the party has grown mellower with the years, even if the dividing lines present at inception still run under the surface. Like other vanguard parties with an early history of chaos, the MPLA settled down, created the mechanisms to arbitrate elite disputes and the incentives for long-term elite cooperation that Brownlee refers to. Central to this is the fact that internal bloodletting was taken out of the picture. Since the coming to power of JES in 1979, no senior official has been killed. One could be thrown in jail, like the poet Ndunduma after satirizing the still-weak president in

1983, or General Fernando Miala, the external intelligence chief who lost out in a complex internal dispute over Chinese monies in 2006.[25] One could also be humiliatingly ejected from a position of authority when the need for a scapegoat arose, as Prime Minister Marcolino Moco found out when he was sacked in 1996. But permanent exclusion became a rarity resulting from personal estrangement or unwillingness to look suitably chastised. After a period in the (increasingly comfortable) political wilderness, wayward notables mostly get readmitted into the ruling clique. And even when they don't, they can still do very well for themselves. Lopo do Nascimento is one of the most senior MPLA politicians and a perpetual "social-democratic" alternative for those dissatisfied with JES. Sacked from the Politburo in 1998 after falling out with the president, he lost influence inside the party. Yet this had limited consequences for his personal wellbeing and he remains a wealthy man. All of this amounts to a great improvement over MPLA conflict management in the 1960s and 1970s.

Continuity at the core

With the end of the war, the MPLA's hegemony was extended across space and came to encompass the whole of Angolan society, including the former "povo da UNITA". For many Angolans, the "confusion between party, state and administration", in manners both symbolic and material,[26] resulted in an engagement with the party-state order, most often through party membership. Popular views on this are mixed, but the emphasis is on the transactional and the compulsory.[27] Interviewees mentioned that "you need to be a member" of the MPLA to access bank loans, jobs, university places, a hospital bed, promotions, etc. Others emphasized peer pressure, especially amongst civil servants and outside Luanda, where party membership is essential for career advancement. A particular postwar phenomenon is the mass adhesion of populations in areas of former rebel supremacy: according to Vidal, in 2004 alone 12,000 erstwhile UNITA members joined the MPLA.[28] In the frustrated telling of a former UNITA official, these populations "became confused after [the] defeat and tried to seek protection by converging towards the victors".[29]

Yet virtually all interviewees who are not upper-ranking party members played down the value of MPLA membership and even sounded a cynical note: "Look, by now everyone is a member: being a party member brings you nothing; it is still the big ones [os graúdos] that pocket the opportunities; it's rather that you can't get by if you are not a member." This ambivalent tone partly explains why the MPLA has so much difficulty in voluntarily mobilizing members for party chores and needs the president's "uncivil society" organizations discussed in the next section. It also underlines the seasonal aspect of party mobilization. It is really election time that energizes the national structure of the party, providing the MPLA with an incentive to dish out patronage to a broader set of beneficiaries in hopes of a brief spurt of enthusiasm. On an everyday basis, however, this faux-mass party closes in on itself and the serious business takes place at the confined level of the very few.

For deep inside the party things remain as they have been for decades. One of the key aspects of continuity has to do with the Eastern Bloc institutional legacy.[30] I am referring here to the impact of Soviet blueprints on MPLA structures.[31] As Richard McGregor points out in the case of the Chinese Communist Party, the MPLA still runs on "Soviet hardware":[32] a Politburo, a Central Committee, a Praesidium, and other recognizably Leninist structures. The masses are nowhere to be found.

In addition to this crucial element of institutional continuity, there are many aspects of personnel continuity, for the metamorphoses of the party-state have not much affected the top spheres. Many members of the Central Committee and the Politburo are familiar faces; there are of course younger additions, but they are beholden to JES and have been carefully safe-checked through the system. Even where there has been some turnover in personnel, the social provenance of the top leadership remains fairly restrictive. At the lower levels, the MPLA is assimilative, but its upper reaches are caste-like and the social distance from the masses remains huge. The MPLA elite is bound together by their trajectories of common socialization rather than primordial identities. But in a society as divided as Angola's, most people who have been socialized into this rarefied atmosphere happen to share a great deal in ethno-regional terms. This means that, though every region and ethnicity is represented in the MPLA higher echelons, there is an over-representation of those from the Mbundu and coastal heartland of the party. The role of Ovimbundu cadres in particular is limited and there is a sense that the few top MPLA politicians from the highlands are used as "window dressing".[33]

There are other ways in which things have not moved on: scratch the surface and you find the same tensions and unhealed wounds, and the MPLA's prickliness about the national narrative. Its worldview remains identifiably that of an illiberal political organization. With so many skeletons in the closet and authoritarian influences converging on it, it comes as no surprise that the MPLA is both secretive and deeply concerned with the proper reading of the Angolan trajectory since the late colonial era. The party's early weakness, ineffectiveness and extremely agitated history are poor material for mythmaking. The result is that sizeable parts of its past need to be sanitized and made fit for the party's epic narrative about itself. The other nationalist movements are delegitimized as ethnic chauvinists in the pay of imperialist powers; the struggle against the Portuguese is portrayed as the producer of mass mobilization, heroic and successful; the internal history of party conflict manicured; the losers in those disputes deleted.

This presupposes much obfuscation, some distortion and, most of all, incessant vigilance. The party convened conferences on Angolan history to come up with a final take on these matters, while the government put together commissions on national heroes and the national liberation struggle.[34] And beware those who slay its sacred cows. An example will suffice here. Christine Messiant, perhaps the leading analyst of Angola until her death in 2006, was shouted down at a Luanda event in 1997 for daring to suggest that the MPLA had been created in 1960 (and was barely organized until 1962) as opposed to the party's official 1956 claim.[35] The reason for this is that the MPLA does not want to give the other major nationalist organization of the time (UPA/FNLA) the credit for having jump-started anti-colonial politics or the liberation war in 1961. Even now this is no arcane matter in party circles. A "first international colloquium on the history of the MPLA" held in late 2011 still highlighted as a key goal the reaffirmation "of the historical truth of the Manifesto and Foundation of the MPLA on 10 December 1956".[36]

The same obfuscation characterizes the MPLA's dealings with memories of the war. As mentioned above, the 2002 signing of a blanket amnesty for war crimes cancelled out the judicial route. Softer options such as a peace and reconciliation commission were also frowned upon. As part of the savagery theme, the MPLA likes to remind Angolans of UNITA's brutality and Savimbi's "responsibility for the war", but always in vague terms lest this awaken a general curiosity towards the track record of both belligerents. In regard to its own brutality, the MPLA exhibits near-complete amnesia. This applies to the civil war (especially the Luanda massacre of 1992 and the large-scale removal of populations in the last years of the war) as well as other events such as the aftermath of the 1977 Nito Alves coup, the pogrom against Bakongo traders in 1993, and the post-2002 violence in Cabinda and Lunda Norte. Standing in for any coming to terms with the past is the commemoration of key moments in history that are either disembodied from their context or significantly simplified or reinvented to provide the MPLA with valiant feats against foreign and domestic foes. Events such as the 1976 repelling of the South African invasion, the 1988 battle of Cuito Cuanavale and the Kuito siege of 1992–94 are sublimated into paeans of MPLA fierceness, with the centrality of Cuba's role in the first two carefully downplayed.

Many people know these are fantasies but their reaction is often jaded rather than offended. This is a more complex matter than one might think. Angolans are sometimes willing to follow Ernest Renan's dictum that a nation is defined by joint forgetfulness, and even historical error, as much as by remembrance. In the aftermath of the war, there was a genuine desire to move on, exemplified by the TV programme *Ponto de Reencontro* where long-lost family members met again in tearful embraces; the somewhat saccharine official mantra of "enemy brothers" finally coming together was widely accepted, with no appetite left for digging into painful experiences. For their part, young people have little interest in what is for them the distant past. But as time goes by, people's attempts to cope with war trauma, especially by speaking up about their often horrific experiences, are finding the official narrative ossified with no space allowed for the airing of contrasting views.

The mirror image of this fastidious patrolling of the past is the arch-pragmatism about the present, especially the dishing out of spoils. No skeletons in the closet have been allowed to ruin the MPLA's incessant adaptation to the possibilities of the market. Although intimations of a national project were discussed in the previous chapter, the shaping force behind MPLA actions is the goal of staying in power forever, meaning the lifetimes of decision-makers in the party. Having done away with the party's historic rivals, politics in Angola in the decade after 2002 amounted to MPLA intra-party politics. The fissiparous nature of the MPLA means that there is plenty of that. Old disputes are blurred but endure. *Sotto voce* complaining about the power of *mestiços*, for instance, lies just below the surface although, to his credit, JES has never tolerated the politicisation of race. Moreover, stormy years are ahead as the eventual demise of JES is bound to deepen existing rivalries. But much of this internal strife is not ideological and pertains to access to patronage and perceptions of exclusion from it. Material disputes have not yet created durable factions inside the party, perhaps because there is so much money that there are never any true losers at the top. The party's cohesion without oil has never been tested. But for now there seems to be a cool-headed realism toning down squabbles that might jeopardize the MPLA's preservation of the ship of state. The war victory, the oil money and the party's historic belief in its own mission have jointly given the MPLA leadership a shot at enduring control—if they can keep it.

THE MPLA AND URBAN SOCIETY

By 2002, the MPLA had therefore already mastered many of the arts of the hybrid regime. Gone was the 1991 panic about the dangers of democracy and the market. The party-state had tightened its stranglehold over the economy through privatization for the benefit of insiders and distributed the spoils of state to a somewhat larger constituency, in the process consolidating some support beyond the elite, as discussed in Chapter 4. It had done away with its constitutional role as the single party and created the illusion of a mass democratic party. But the new era of peace, while primarily perceived as an opportunity to cement MPLA hegemony for the long haul, was also understood to hold dangers. Some of the latter pertained to the capacity of the MPLA party-state to digest the debris of the UNITA society and the hinterland world more generally, that is, those who had never been part of the MPLA ecosystem. But the enemy had after all been vanquished and was now dependent on the victors. More insidiously, the MPLA was concerned with the impact of peace in the MPLA society it had controlled since independence. As discussed earlier, the existential threat of UNITA had kept this society together by default, including the elements that were not supportive of the MPLA in any way. The removal of that threat would require a deliberate strategy by the party-state with the aim of consolidating, and indeed, deepening, its hegemonic status.

Co-opting civil society

Amongst other dimensions, this related to the shaping and restricting of the "civil society" nominally outside the party-state. There is in Angola little by way of a conventional civil society on account of a past of unmitigated repression by the colonial and early post-colonial governments. There is also such a disparity of material and organizational resources between a strong state and a weak and divided society that the very idea of an autonomous civil society space needs to be questioned. In the inauspicious conditions of the 1990s a civil society of sorts nonetheless had began to emerge.[37] Fronted by members of the Catholic and mainline Protestant churches and Luanda intellectuals, a peace movement challenged the government's 1998 uncompromising decision to wage "war for peace"[38] and pushed instead for negotiations with UNITA. The reaction of the MPLA towards this "alleged civil society" that tried to deny it an outright victory was furious. Although the peace campaign was brave, its impact was limited even before the killing of Savimbi ended the war, and quickly fizzled out afterwards.

As a formerly senior, but no longer politically active, MPLA member noted, "in the early 1990s the party had a choice between repression or tolerance of [civil society] movements" but ended up with a hybrid solution: non-state actors would be accepted in theory but the social space would be filled with "*our* civil society organizations, *our* opposition political parties" that would be politically and materially supported by the state itself.[39] The result is of course not uncommon in authoritarian regimes that have gone through the moves of apparent liberalization: polish off a patina of civil society and you often find the MPLA. This occupation of civil society space also means that the government's approach grew much more supple over the years.[40] One no longer shoots a prominent critic of the regime, especially if he is English-speaking and with access to the foreign media. He or she is instead seduced into a well-remunerated position. In a regime that, at least superficially, gives great status to the educated, there are plenty of ways of bringing young and estranged talent back into the fold. And it is the individuals more likely to rally against the system that the system takes greater care in co-opting.

Take the case of intellectuals and artists. There is a generous policy of arts sponsorship both in Angola and abroad, with barely any cultural activity not partly or wholly paid for by the government, Sonangol or, in the visual arts, the major banks, parastatals such as the national insurer ENSA and JES's son-in-law's Dokolo Foundation. There are also many well-endowed prizes and formal occasions where officials of the party-state show appreciation for artistic accomplishment.[41] This is almost never content-related. The MPLA doesn't manifest much concern about the output unless it is blatantly disparaging of the regime, but it has a broad interest in having intellectuals and artists play a conformist role on the right side of history. It also places great importance on having intellectuals circumscribed within the União de Escritores Angolanos (UEA), the writer's guild where many of Angola's cultural disputes play out. Visual artists have their own União Nacional de Artistas Plásticos (UNAP) while the music industry congregates around the União Nacional dos Artistas e Compositores (UNAC). Even when quarrels between members get vicious—notably on the over-representation in the UEA of whites and *mestiços*—they take place within an MPLA-maintained ecosystem. Many intellectuals are party men anyway. And only a few have achieved financial independence, say, by writing books that actually sell: most others depend to different degrees on regime patronage.

This corporatist strategy of managing professional groups through dedicated structures happens in most other areas of public life. All non-state organizations are permanently screened and their activities vouched and circumscribed in countless ways. Professional organizations like the Ordem dos Advogados (OAA, the Angolan Bar Association) and the Ordem dos Médicos are headed by senior MPLA members and those who aren't yet so are often co-opted into the party.[42] Eerily, the MPLA Central Committee even has additional "special cadre committees" that parallel the activities of each professional group in society, and the membership of both sets of bodies is frequently similar. The MPLA Luanda Provincial Committee, for instance, has no less than fourteen such special cadre committees covering every activity: there is even a "special committee for environmentalists and ecologists".[43]

The media are also kept within tight boundaries mostly defined by the Ministry of Social Communication, which was headed until 2012 by a former journalist who is a member of the Politburo.[44] State media outlets such as the country's only daily newspaper *Jornal de Angola*, and TPA, the public television, follow an unsophisticated pro-government line and do not allow the airing of critical views. There were hopes that the increase in private media outlets would make a difference but regime barons own almost all of them and carefully police the boundaries of the acceptable. A small number such as *Novo Jornal* and *Expansão* try to do a good job, but there are limits to what they can get away with; most others toe the party line without qualms. Moreover, private newspapers are almost unavailable outside Luanda. Yet the life of the Angolan journalist is not merely a matter of red lines that cannot be crossed. As with other sensitive professions, the party-state puts much emphasis on their co-optation into uncritical and well-remunerated jobs. And there is always the ultimate sweetener of the US$100,000 yearly Maboque journalism prize sponsored by Grupo César & Filhos, a business conglomerate close to the MPLA.[45]

The work of NGOs faces the same problems as many other forms of civil society life, including the narrowness of their social base, over-concentration in Luanda, the competition from government NGOs and the sustained attempts at co-optation, including the constant absorption into the party-state of NGO officials. They also have to deal with additional challenges. External financial support is perceived with suspicion and carefully vetoed by the government[46] which alone grants them the capricious license to operate. While many civil society organizations are simply MPLA creations, even those that aren't are domesticated by these constraints that place considerable limits on their actions. Shying away from overly "political" concerns of course excludes much that really matters in the country. Beyond the party-state's effective control, civil society activity faces obstacles of a more devious nature. There are fearless, civic-spirited activists in Angola. But even people who have crossed over into more critical public positions are often pinned down by petty compromises, whether professional or having to do with their networks of sociability. For in the minuscule world of the Luandan educated classes, "civil society" is a misnomer for individuals who are childhood friends, blood relatives or spouses of regime insiders.

Uncivil society

In addition to the MPLA's steady infiltration and neutering of civil society, JES went to great lengths to establish his own "civil society" infrastructure as a way of consolidating personal rule.[47] Because these organizations circumvent the party, they are better conceived as pieces of the JES system discussed in Chapter 1. But their instrumentality for MPLA electoral success, social footprint and capacity to crowd out the "good" civil society justify their inclusion here. The highest profile such organization is the Eduardo dos Santos Foundation (FESA), created in 1996 and lavishly financed by de facto compulsory donations from the private sector and Sonangol. In a remarkable study of FESA, Christine Messiant explained the way the foundation colonized every major social arena, turning JES into "the number one leader of civil society" through high-profile bread and circus jamborees such as the 28 August presidential birthday celebration, while distancing him from the failures of the party-state.[48]

Joining FESA is a sprawling number of organizations also centred on the president. These include the Movimento Nacional Espontâneo, AJAPRAZ, Fundação Fundanga, Fundação Lwini (presided over by the First Lady), the Fundação Africana de Inovação (co-founded by JES's eldest son) and the Kangamba cluster of organizations discussed below. Most of these organizations have the coveted status of "public utility", which affords them access to the state budget (genuinely charitable organizations rarely benefit from this), in addition to other money flows. These organizations, different as they are, serve one or several of three main functions. The first can only be described as a cult of personality around the president. The second is a charity show, with goods and services bestowed upon the poorer population in orchestrated, endlessly televised ceremonies of gift giving. In many ways, these organizations are the prime interface between the urban poor and the party-state. The third dimension is that of providing boots on the ground, whether for demonstrations in favour of the status quo or for punitive actions against perceived enemies. While delivering the crowds, this last aspect of their work underlines the transactional, even ironic nature of mobilization. Young people show up bereft of fervour, with an eye to free booze, partying, and on occasion cash handouts or presents such as motorcycles.

The consummate example of the president's civil society is the so-called "empresário da juventude",[49] Bento dos Santos Kangamba. Hailing from Moxico, Kangamba's name emerged a decade ago as that of a brigadier in FAA logistics twice imprisoned for fraud.[50] He is now perceived as one of the richest men in the country, though few profitable businesses bear his name. His picaresque rise in the years since, while spectacular, speaks of the way ambitious opportunists have thrived in the unsettled social conditions of postwar Angola. Attaining national prominence as the owner of Kabuscorp (Kangamba Business Corporation), the tough football club of Luanda's Palanca neighbourhood, Kangamba has married into the president's extended family and is now variously described as the MPLA's "firefighter" and electoral "war horse". Kangamba and his people are tireless. When a civil service strike threatens the hapless governor of Benguela, Kangamba is flown in to keep the peace.[51] When a handful of critics march against the president, men allegedly associated with him show up to give them a good thrashing, and overnight will put together a "spontaneous" counter-demonstration of thousands of people. At week's end, Kangamba will throw a gigantic party for Palanca youth with free beer, cash gifts and live concerts of the latest, most outrageous *kuduro* performers.

Conversations with senior MPLA members about Kangamba and the activities of other presidential outfits reveal a marked ambivalence. No one will criticize them in public, as "doing so is tantamount to criticizing the president himself".[52] And many admit the usefulness of characters that mix Boss Tweed tactics with street muscle. "Frankly, most people in the upper spheres [of the MPLA] no longer know how to move in the *musseques*: Kangamba brings out the vote and everything else."[53] But even this rational take is tinged with the fear of unpredictable lumpen youth that harks back to the turmoil of 1975–77: "They are sons of bitches but they are ours; and if we don't [use] them, someone else will."[54] Created for specific purposes, these potentially volatile groups have developed their own priorities and entertain complicated connections with not only the police and the intelligence apparatus, but also with increasingly sophisticated criminal syndicates. As a disaffected party member warned, "people at the top think they are in control, but the long-term costs will be huge: already the party is having to accommodate types like Bento Raimundo, Bento Bento and Job Capapinha," the leaders of these move- ments.[55] Their brash manners are a world away from the cosmopolitan style of Luanda's upper classes. But they remain the party-state's formi- dable and politically dependable tools—for now.

The opposition

The legal opposition to the MPLA plays a key role in the established order. Without the dramaturgy of a pluralist electoral system, the party- state's claim that Angola is a democracy would be difficult to sustain. From its unassailable perch in the decade from 2002 to 2012, the MPLA can even be said to have fostered the conditions for harmless opposition activity. This doesn't mean that the MPLA has gone soft. The crushing of UNITA in 2002, the ongoing repression of Cabindan separatists and the violent reaction against the small activist demonstrations discussed below are all reminders of what it can do when challenged. The party-state is thus intimately involved in the functioning of the opposition parties. Complaints about the intelligence services infiltrating the opposition are rife; they are also often true, but the mere rumour adds to a sense of MPLA ubiquity.

Until the 2013 extinction of sixty-seven parties on account of their inactivity or residual voting,[56] the party system was a cacophony of mostly meaningless acronyms, many the MPLA's mischievous creations or Bakongo vanity projects, or both. Only UNITA, the PRS and, more recently, CASA-CE are real political parties with electoral support that seek to express recognizably different views from those of the MPLA (the rump of the old FNLA is still around but scores a measly 1 per cent of votes; the Bloco Democrático is articulate and occasionally influential but received few votes in 2008 and didn't run in 2012).

Both UNITA and the PRS rail against the party-state's corruption. As they have historical support bases elsewhere, it makes sense for them to complain about rural underdevelopment and the concentration of government expenditure in the MPLA heartland. But their internal cultures remain authoritarian and are only occasionally focused on policy. Visitors to party branches will be confronted with leaders' outsized portraits (in UNITA's case, those of Savimbi are ubiquitous) and an extremely hierarchical rapport between officials. Debates on political ideas are poor to non-existent. Most important, having to endure in the MPLA world means that both parties have grown accommodated to the culture of the party-state, including their own carefully rehearsed role in it.[57] They often sound uncompromisingly critical yet keen on (material) inclusion in the system, something that, within limits, the MPLA is happy to provide. In sum, they are often equivocal about their alternative political projects and the extent to which they share with the ruling party assumptions about the political economy.

Their origins are of course very different. The PRS, which emerged as the third party in the 1992 and 2008 elections, draws support almost exclusively from the diamond-rich Lundas and articulates dismay at eastern marginalization as well as what amounts to a pro-autonomy agenda. The MPLA frequently labels it "tribalist" for its mostly Lunda-Chokwe ethnic support base, but the PRS is a reassuring player in the electoral and institutional game, and its prominence channels much dissatisfaction that could have gone the way of Cabinda even if, as PRS president

Eduardo Kangwana ruefully noted, the threat of arms has also made the government more responsive to Cabindan concerns.[58]

As to UNITA, it is unsurprising that it would struggle with the consequences of military defeat. As a co-signatory of the ceasefire its continued existence was never at stake. But the shadow of the MPLA's domination, dependence on the party-state's funding, and the legacy of Savimbi's rule made its conversion from an armed movement into a political party slow and difficult. The party's vague claim to represent "real Africans" against the coastal elite is belied by its mostly Ovimbundu leadership and base of support as well as by the MPLA's now-national footprint. This void was initially filled neither with a coherent policy discourse nor with a pan-Angolan populist appeal. For its part, the MPLA has continued to use UNITA's historic support base to present it as an uncouth, even savage entity that misunderstands the urban setting and is just not modern enough. An unfortunate 2011 event whereby a UNITA senior official was beaten up within hearing distance of the party leadership was given ample publicity by the MPLA media as evidence of the backwardness and authoritarianism of the former rebels.[59]

A major problem for UNITA is funding, not just for the party but for its individual leaders as well. At the end of the war, Lukamba Paulo Gato, UNITA's interim leader until June 2003, allegedly wrote to JES to request inclusion in the economic opportunities of the peace.[60] The MPLA obliged by taking care of co-opting UNITA cadres into comfortable positions the moment they arrived from the bush and were installed in the plush Hotel Trópico in May 2002. In time, this included "expenses accounts", "a Luanda installation fee", integration in the state apparatus (including ambassadorial posts), generous pensions, a house (often in the Nova Vida condominium in Luanda Sul) and business partnerships.[61] These opportunities were available to cadres who remained with UNITA, but the best prizes were reserved for anyone who would jump fence and join the MPLA. The crudeness of these *aliciamento* (literally, "enticement") tactics—the transaction is always monetary, and the amounts involved usually transpire—underlined the dominance of the MPLA. On the eve of the 2012 elections, the MPLA was still doing this, trumpeting the defection of General Black Power and other prominent UNITA members into its ranks.[62]   Some critics argue that under Isaías Samakuva, Savimbi's friendly but somewhat anodyne former Paris representative who has led UNITA since 2003, the former rebels became settled in a role of "eternal opposition playing the MPLA's game of democracy... they have lost faith that they could ever defeat the MPLA and want to sort out their individual lives."[63] This is perhaps excessively harsh a judgement. But there is no doubt that UNITA's first postwar decade was spent on the defensive, trying to cope with the political rules dictated by its former enemy and not to cross any red lines, especially anything that could label it the "party of chaos and confusion".[64] As discussed in the Conclusion, UNITA's improved electoral performance in 2012 and the frequency of street protests in Luanda would in time embolden the party to pursue more contrarian forms of political activity, with the MPLA reacting in kind.

A long-announced divorce between UNITA's postwar leadership and the party's most charismatic figure, Abel Chivukuvuku, heralded the key party-political development since the end of the war. Chivukuvuku, a sort of *enfant terrible* who in UNITA's court managed to create a reputation for independence of mind,[65] finally broke away after again failing to secure the party leadership in early 2012. Shortly afterwards, he created a new party, CASA-CE. Chivukuvuku quickly elicited independent adhesions as well as bringing with him a few hundred members of UNITA. But the real prize was Admiral Mendes de Carvalho "Miau", a member of one of the MPLA's historic families who would run as CASA-CE's number two in the August 2012 elections. Chivukuvuku is an impressive operator who has decided to move beyond the Ovimbundu heartland and compete for urban votes, according to him the only arena "where real politics is possible in Angola".[66] He knows how to rouse the crowds and speak to their concerns. The obstacles to the emergence of a new party, both political and in terms of funding, are only too obvious but this is a political movement to watch in coming years.

For the time being CASA-CE, UNITA and the PRS have few chances of upsetting the MPLA's domination of Angolan politics. Of course, it is easy to overstate the comprehensiveness of the regime's clout. The apparently sturdy approach to co-opting and neutering civil society and the opposition parties outlined in this section is in fact full of cracks. This much was revealed by the decline in MPLA urban support in the 2012 elections, which I discuss below. But the MPLA's inventive tactics, especially in the manner in which they transcend mere coercion to include "enticement", should not be underestimated.

Despite the constraints on genuinely challenging opposition activity, not all critics have been co-opted or silenced. From 2011, a series of demonstrations against the regime, and dos Santos in particular, were convened through social media and irregularly held in Luanda. These produced angry echoes on the Internet, especially amongst Angolans abroad, and facile Arab Spring analogies. The demonstrations should have been only a minor nuisance in view of the modest number of demonstrators (usually only a few dozen people), the state media blackout, and the fact that most opposition parties were too scared to join. But the government's overreaction in beating up and arresting the demonstrators gave them a resonance they would have otherwise lacked. The MPLA's real concern was not the Facebook activists but the possibility that the shantytowns would join them. If the MPLA derived a lesson from the Arab Spring, it is this: threats come not from the official opposition "machines" which, in the words of the writer Pepetela, can be easily "controlled, manoeuvred, weakened",[67] as they have for the past decade, but from volatile social movements, especially where they seem not to exist.

Matters came to a head with the injuring of Filomeno Vieira Lopes, one of the leaders of the tiny Bloco Democrático opposition party, during a peaceful demonstration against the government on 11 March 2012. This galvanized critical segments of the MPLA to complain about state brutality, but even this apparently civic-minded sense of outrage contained a more parochial coda. In many of the conversations I held on the subject in the week following the demonstration, shocked MPLA supporters invariably slipped into "they can't do that, not to Filomeno".[68] Filomeno Vieira Lopes, despite his critical take on the party-state, is a scion of one of Luanda's leading families and a cousin of many people in government and the summit of the party. His party has no parliamentary seat and, while angrily anti-MPLA, is sometimes perceived, like Filomeno himself, as a stray relative emanating from the MPLA's own *assimilado* world, the *Grande Família*.[69] (General Kopelipa is said to have been furious at the treatment meted out to his cousin.) In a way, it was the violation of Filomeno's membership of what could be deemed Angola's post-Cold War "non-torturable classes", and not state brutality per se, that incensed his wider social circle.

Listening to activists from the Bloco Democrático—which was prevented from running in the 2012 elections on a technicality—one cannot but admire their courage and agree with their sophisticated and reasoned critique of the system, yet understand why they have little hold over the imagination of average Angolans. Like Egyptian Facebook activists, they earnestly resort to a rights-based language because it is theirs. But in the world of Angolan politics, where politicians are denounced not for failing an abstract test of honesty but for failing to perform the *"paí grande"*[70] distributional role of popular expectations, the Bloco Democrático's principled language has limited traction.

Handling the musseques

A major MPLA concern since independence has been the political moods of the *musseques* (shantytowns) where an estimated 90 per cent of Luandans live, and of youth in particular on account of its troublemaking potential. The *musseques* are not homogeneous in their ethnic composition or the social status of their inhabitants, and the less pejorative designation of *"baírros"* (neighbourhoods) is increasingly deployed. But the chasm with the cement city is still a defining feature of the urban environment in Angola, with the inhabitants of the *musseques* holding a lesser status than the residents of the city core. The party-state is attentive to this sphere of the urban poor but in a very instrumental manner. Its focus is twofold: the provision of bread and circuses, especially through the "uncivil society" organizations described above, and the thwarting of social unrest.

These dimensions are overlapping and in order to tackle them the party uses diverse strategies. Via the National Institute for Religious Affairs (INAR), it invests strongly in relations with churches ranging from the Catholic and mainline Protestant churches to the many African, evangelical (often of Brazilian origin) and charismatic churches that proliferate in Angola. These are national strategies that transcend the *musseques* but are particularly convenient for the party-state's engagement with the latter. The MPLA infiltrates the informal structures of local urban governance, the *comissões de moradores*.[71] OMA, the party's women's organization, and the JMPLA, its youth wing, are also present. Moreover, the MPLA lavishes huge resources on sporting events, and football clubs in particular.[72] At the other end of the spectrum lies the hedonistic *kuduro* (literally, "hard-ass") music scene, a byword for Angola's youth culture over the last decade. *Kuduro* is thoroughly penetrated by the MPLA, with the whole production line (talent scouting, recording, distributing, the booking of shows and television appearances) run by one of the President's sons, Córeon Du.[73] Popular singers such as Presidente

Gasolina, Própria Lixa, Noite e Dia and Vaca Louca do Kuduro are either apolitical or reliable supporters of the status quo. Angolan rap is more difficult to control. Some of the most articulate social criticism of the last decade emerged in the form of punchy rap lyrics, but even in the rap world the party-state has ended up buying off important voices.[74]

At the rhetorical level, the MPLA addresses the poor majority in the same developmental terms it uses with other constituencies, and the promises of oil-driven improvement are central to this. But the MPLA operating mode amongst the masses is entirely different from that deployed with the educated, middle class core. Its approach is more akin to containment and riot control, as the *musseques* are intermittently feared as the source of anti-regime agitation and, in the worst projections, outright revolt. The experience of the Nito Alves coup of 1977 looms large in this regard. JES himself has repeatedly expressed concerns about the MPLA's capacity to mobilize at the ground level, complaining that the central structure of the party has not kept up with local organizations and "community vigilance structures", thus "allowing empty spaces that are filled, with some impact, with lies and calumny by [the MPLA]'s adversaries."[75] However, in the absence of actual anti-MPLA mass mobilization in the decade after 2002, the regime has had no incentive for meaningfully expanding distribution, let alone public goods provision, to the poor in the peripheral neighbourhoods.

The MPLA's soft power

The fact that the benefits of the MPLA order mostly bypass the poor doesn't impact on the willingness of Angolans from all walks of life to get involved with it. As Jon Schubert remarks in a notable paper, "people consciously and actively seek affiliation with the regime as a strategy of social mobility, to increase their relative power, wealth and status".[76] Even the distant prospect of minor rewards fosters conformity. Yet beyond this opportunistic engagement lies something more complicated: the culture of the party-state holds a strong appeal for Angolan urbanites. As the next section shows, MPLA power in the countryside may be new and unfamiliar. But in the urban heartland, there is an unmistakable intimacy to the MPLA's rapport with influential segments of society. In the cities, the party-state is coterminous with the postcolonial era, its rules "internalized and negotiated" and often lived as "normality".[77]

This is linked to the MPLA's virtual monopoly over what it means to be modern in Angola. UNITA detests the manner in which it is carica- tured by the MPLA as a barbarous bush army, for it too has modern aspirations. But UNITA could never count on the support of more than a small fraction of educated Angolans and its years in the maquis really did make its soldiery and leadership uncomfortable in the cities and even more incompetent than the MPLA in managing them. Conversely, the MPLA has long been the party of the educated, the urban and the state- employed, having nurtured and promoted, particularly over the past decade, a sizeable minority that owes its social status, material opportuni- ties and worldview to the party-state. If it were to fall apart, it would have to be put together again because, as Richard Macgregor notes in the case of China, "its members alone have the skills, experience and networks to run the country".[78]

As discussed in Chapter 2, the MPLA brand of modernity particularly dovetails with the bourgeoisie's yearnings for progress, especially their own. (Problematically for those arguing for a chasm between the men- talities of the better off and the poor, it also appeals to the masses, though the benefits of the party-state are not for them.) The bourgeoisie's sup- port for the MPLA on account of both this comfortable stake in Angolan society and mounting fear of the poor cannot be underestimated. It goes without saying that some Angolans in the MPLA's "natural constituency" are ambivalent or even hostile towards the party, as is the case with age- ing, embittered idealists who supported the "real MPLA before it became corrupt" or the young and educated demonstrators mentioned above. They know its ruses intimately and can treat one to dark-humoured deconstructions of the MPLA's lying and double talk. But the party- state's role in shaping the world they know, as well as the perceived absence of alternatives, most commonly translates into passive tolerance or even support for the MPLA "in the last instance".[79]

THE PARTY-STATE TAKES OVER THE PERIPHERY

For the duration of the civil war, beyond the control of the state was up to 80 per cent of its nominal territory. Since 2002, however, the MPLA has enthusiastically embraced the commitment to build a self-styled "modern state" across Angola. The resulting effort to break out of the enclaves it long held and occupy the huge and sparsely populated hinterland, extend civil administration and rebuild infrastructure is a key political dynamic in present-day Angola. In order to do so, the MPLA deploys a dizzying array of strategies ranging from high-modernist, pseudo-developmental state activism to extensive subcontracting to non-state actors used to expand the writ of the state from the political centre and provincial capitals to the remotest regions. The control over Angola's hinterland had always been a problem for the colonial state; only in the late colonial years had comprehensive territorial coverage been achieved.[80] But after 1975, the MPLA state had been no more than an "archipelago of cities". Beyond the impact of the conflict, there was a strong element of neglect that owed partly to the urban and coastal character of the MPLA and its awkward and distant relationship with the rural world.

The end of the civil war was, therefore, a beginning of sorts, for the state in rural areas had to be established anew.[81] The official narrative presented UNITA as a challenger to the legitimate order, but there were entire regions from which the MPLA had been absent and where the rebels had created state-like governance structures ruling over, at times, hundreds of thousands of Angolans.[82] Even as UNITA steadily lost territorial control, the government was unable to establish rural administrative structures. By the government's own optimistic admission, 40 percent of the territory was not under its administration by 2002.[83] While it controlled all provincial governments, many municipalities (the second-tier administrative unit) were empty, as were most communes (the third tier).[84] This was not merely a problem in remote regions: in Bengo province, just outside Luanda, three out of eight municipalities were inoperative.[85]

In contrast with the absent state of the 1990s, the MPLA framed this challenge in the relentlessly modernizing version of statebuilding: the country would be occupied, administered, systematized. As we saw in Chapter 2, the first step in this regard was the rebuilding of communications infrastructure, which has proceeded steadily over the last decade. The party-state's goal of enabling the broadcasting of power across space—the logistical prerequisite for effective control of the hinterland— has decisively advanced.[86] The process of state expansion itself differs across regions with historically dissimilar relations with the centre and unequal resource endowments. In resource-rich areas such as Cabinda and the Lundas, for instance, the motivation for this effort is strongly related to their extractive potential, but the state is no longer exclusively focused on "useful spaces".

The overall motivations for this enterprise, which has been compared with the Portuguese "effective occupation" of a century ago, are the consolidation of MPLA hegemony through territorial occupation, the cooptation of local elites and the subjection of the majority. This project was bundled up with the customary rhetoric of inclusive nation building. But this was about projecting power, and in specific locations capturing resources, rather than creating a service-delivery state. There was a marked concern with symbols of party-state potency and conveying the impression of ubiquity, particularly in areas of former UNITA support. As an Angolan activist noted, "the state tries to create in the collective imagination the idea that it can intervene everywhere at all times to defend its interests."[87] This emphasis on political order and authority contained few hints of a social contract, with the MPLA's sense of legitimacy emanating primarily from the war victory. In its bid for domination the party-state cuts deals with local powerbrokers, but the overarching demand is that of obedience.

Early administration

After the end of the war, the priority was sending out the police. This was not a matter of security as the disciplined demobilization of UNITA meant that banditry was not a major issue.[88] The government wanted instead to convey in an unambiguous, visible way that it was now the highest authority, and that it could "crush its enemies, at any time, anywhere".[89] Following the police came the MPLA party apparatus. Only much later did the aptly designated "state peripheral administration" [sic] show up; when it did, it was often a virtual affair, with many remote municipalities lacking basic infrastructure till this day. But by the 2008 elections many accessible ones had an administrator's villa; a post office; a health centre; a courthouse; a primary school. The stage set of stateness was in place; but the buildings were often empty and many remained so in 2012, some already degraded. Courthouses are particularly inactive, with judges unavailable below the provincial capital and an extraordinary 96 per cent of Angolan lawyers based in Luanda.[90] After the brief 2008 and 2012 electoral splurges, the central and provincial governments never provided the financial or human resources to man local institutions and these remain weak and incompetent, if they exist at all.

For the real face of the party-state in the rural areas is the party not the state, and the profile of the former is invariably privileged over that of the administration. This does not debase the status of senior provincial or municipal officials because they are often the senior provincial and municipal MPLA officials as well. There is a concerted effort to shift resource distribution to the "second office".[91] As an NGO official noted, "you rarely see the municipal administrator doing anything, he gives nothing to people *in that capacity*; the hand-outs and generosity always come from the party or party-related organizations"; populations see the private distribution of goods via MPLA structures as more reliable and are likelier to "reclaim privileges through the party branch than try [to secure] rights as citizens".[92] With peace, the hope of receiving MPLA support led many to join, including in traditional UNITA areas. Partly to counter UNITA's influence, the MPLA's rural clout became a vital matter in the years leading to the first postwar elections, but this was about co-opting influential local actors rather than providing popular benefits or expanding political participation. Abel Chivukuvuku, the former UNITA leader, went as far as suggesting that only in the cities could one find "free electorates and the possibility to engage in opposition politics": though MPLA domination of the rural world is very recent, its populations are now "more tightly controlled and dependent" on the party-state.[93] In order to create and consolidate this rural footprint, the party-state has pursued three major strategies: decentralization; the co-optation of traditional authorities; and the discharge of state responsibilities to non-state entities.

Decentralization

The colonial and pre-1991 legacies of administration were hyper-centralist. Talk of decentralization and local government began two decades ago and culminated in the 1999 Local Administration Decree. After 2002, decentralization was trumpeted as the key postwar policy in the Angolan periphery, but as late as 2007, the statistics were sobering: 79 per cent of "local government" civil servants were in provincial government headquarters, with only 19 per cent in municipalities and 1 per cent in communes.[94] Just before the 2008 elections, 68 municipalities were chosen to receive US$5 million from the state budget. This was officially extended to all municipalities the following year but disbursement was erratic. The government then used complaints about the mishandling of the 2008 monies, which had certainly not been a concern at the time, to argue that municipalities were unprepared, and by 2010, Angola had returned to direct expenditure by the central government.[95] A similar process ensued for the 2012 election season, but the record remains dismal, especially when it comes to investment in local capacity.

Interviews with Ministry of Territorial Administration (MAT) officials mostly put these delays and contradictions down to lack of human resources, and point to the optimistic goal of the National Plan for Administrative De-concentration and Decentralization: to "gradually" proceed towards a model of local governance that pulls together elected municipal governments, traditional authorities and "civil society".[96] At the forefront of this agenda since 2008 is a respected technocrat and Politburo member, Bornito de Sousa. In reality, it is the provincial governors calling the shots, and they answer exclusively to the president who nominates them. In turn, outside the core matters he controls directly, JES allows governors plenty of latitude to build what the late Angolan writer Ruy Duarte de Carvalho called "provincial principalities",[97] especially in regard to the political economy. They can, within limits, embezzle state money and run their provinces like fiefdoms. As discussed below, in this real world of provincial governance, traditional authorities are powerless and the Conselhos de Auscultação e Concertação Social (CACS), the consultative organs for engagement with "social forces", are either MPLA vehicles or peripheral for decision-making.[98]

Most important, political decentralization through municipal elections has been cautiously delayed. Though technical reasons are strenuously invoked (former Minister of State Carlos Feijó mentioned the lack of local capacity as a reason for postponement),[99] the regional disparities in MPLA support make it reluctant to provide rivals with locally legitimate platforms. Even the more limited focus on "de-concentration" is faced with hesitation by Luanda, all the while embracing its language. And in parallel to this pseudo-decentralized state structure one finds a party apparatus where the real power resides. As Bowerbank notes, the mislabelled process of "decentralization" is in fact a strategy of administrative occupation designed to "extend the state apparatus, increase the size and support of the party" and, in resource-rich areas, "guard access to valuable natural resources that fund the activities of the party-state".[100]

THE CONSOLIDATION OF THE MPLA PARTY-STATE

Traditional authorities

A second dimension in the strategy of occupation is the co-optation of traditional authorities. As of May 2012, 41,554 recognized traditional authorities out of an estimated total of 50,000 were on the government's payroll, a cost of some 8 billion kwanzas per month.[101] This strategy is as ambivalent as the legacy it builds on. Contrary to the British emphasis on indirect rule, which preserved or invented a regal status for indigenous leaders and often had them perform many of the daily tasks of imperial administration, the Portuguese afforded them little authority or social deference. Governing Angola through a European administrative grid, the Portuguese nonetheless utilized often-reconstituted "traditional" chiefs, or *sobas*,[102] as agents for fiscal extraction and the organization of compulsory labour. As a modernizing liberation movement, the MPLA shared many Portuguese assumptions about the backwardness of traditional society, and as a vanguard party, it had no patience for other sources of authority. But policy towards the *sobas*, in consonance with its approach to the rural world generally, was more about neglect than Mozambique-style relentless repression.[103] This made a shift of gear relatively feasible as the MPLA came to understand the usefulness of traditional authorities. This strategy of engagement is not a neo-traditional turn infused with sudden respect for "authentic" structures; it is part and parcel of the broader party-state strategy for reinforcing its presence in the periphery.[104]

Implicit in this vision is that *sobas* are not popular representatives or even-handed intermediaries between the authorities and the populations, but disseminators and enforcers of state directives at the local level where the state is otherwise absent. Information that flows upwards, including intelligence about opposition activity or the presence of Congolese illegal migrants, pertains exclusively to the interests of the state rather than those of populations. As in all dimensions of postwar rural life, borders between party and state are almost meaningless, so it is unsurprising that these salaried *sobas* have also acted as electoral agents for the MPLA, not only delivering community votes but also often preventing opposition groups from campaigning at the local level.[105] *Sobas* who are given state support are assumed to be MPLA party members. At any rate, membership of AATA (the Associação Angolana de Autoridades Tradicionais, a de facto wing of the party for controlling and institutionalizing domination of traditional authorities) mostly requires a party membership card.

Despite relentless instrumentalization, the *soba*-state rapport is more complicated than meets the eye. It is hard to generalize about traditional authorities in view of the very different degrees of social legitimacy they enjoy according to locality, the impact of the war, and the extensive social transformation of the last decades that saw the multiplication of competing claims and many *sobas* moving to Luanda.[106] However, in most areas, the state-*soba* relationship is as much about the state seeking out the *sobas* as the *sobas* actively soliciting state patronage. Pacheco notes that, from the perspective of the *sobas*, "there are certain advantages to "being" State, in terms of capacity to impose, prestige and security".[107] A high official complained, "we now have more *sobas* than population: there has been an explosion of traditional authorities [and as everyone thinks that] the state is their father, they want a piece of the cake".[108] In this regard, most *sobas* fall very much in the same category as other regional elites and not a few opposition politicians: their most pressing concern is personal inclusion in the circle of regime beneficiaries.[109]

One can interpret the postwar *sobas*-state relationship as entailing a bifurcation of Angolan nation building: contrary to the modernizing discourse, the MPLA is in effect building an archaic rural bubble.[110] The doctoral thesis of Carlos Feijó, until 2012 one of the President's key advisers and a major architect of the state's peripheral policy, is a sustained defence of this approach, if argued in terms of "legal pluralism".[111] However, the binary assumptions about two different spheres, urban and rural, the latter of which can be durably tamed, are belied by the degree of social change, including the ongoing rural exodus, and by the MPLA's own uncompromising modernism. The state resorts to the *sobas* and other tactically adequate means insofar as they allow it to expand its writ. But rather than fossilizing the countryside by giving *sobas* real power, deference and the means for a neo-traditional space, the MPLA drastically caps their real role to dimensions it can manipulate. The cheap uniform that *sobas* resent is a sign of subservience, their meagre salaries are often unpaid or pocketed by provincial officials, and at every turn *sobas* are clearly outranked by the party-state.

Discharge of state responsibilities

When referring to the state in the periphery, official rhetoric focuses exclusively on the role of public authorities. In fact, like in the colonial era, the state discharges substantial prerogatives to private organizations and individuals who fulfil tasks that the state can't or won't perform. This includes different modalities, from private companies taking over swathes of territory to the creation of personal feuds and the lawless behaviour of security companies in diamond-rich areas. These modalities share two characteristics. The first is that private bodies enjoy powers that are normally the preserve of the state, including over the means of coercion. The second is that, far from being competitors of the state, they are mandated by it, de jure or de facto, and perform tasks that advance, often counter-intuitively, the power of the party-state in the periphery. The institutional absence of the state does not mean the absence of its regulatory power. The role of unofficial agents is instrumental to the advancement of the state rather than a sign of assertion by non-state social actors.

The most prevalent such strategy is that of having corporations become de facto powers in the context of mineral extraction and (to a lesser extent) agribusiness. A major example is Catoca, the world's fourth largest open air diamond mine, an Israeli-Brazilian-Russian consortium that started operating in Lunda Sul in the mid-1990s in the heat of war. Others include Odebrecht, the Brazilian conglomerate that is the country's largest private sector employer, with a growing role in Malanje, and the Israeli LR Group that is leading agricultural projects in Kwanza Sul, Lunda Norte and elsewhere.

The creation of personal realms through land expropriation and mineral extraction was started in the 1990s by several high profile generals, police officials and provincial governors. This has increased considerably since 2002, partly as a sustained MPLA policy of buying off the men in uniform. General-cum-politician Higino Carneiro's stranglehold over his home region of Calulo in Kwanza Sul is a prominent example. Owning the local football club and having fenced in much of the good land, he runs everything from banking and retail trade to hotels. The municipal administrator happens to be his brother. This sort of domain is happily accepted by the party-state, as Higino delivers the MPLA vote. The analysis of these fiefdoms is beyond this chapter, but according to one estimate, by 2011 the area of arable land distributed to regime cronies exceeded the amount of land controlled by Portuguese settlers in 1975.[112]

At the violent end of the spectrum of discharge one finds the role of private security associated with diamond production, especially in Lunda

Norte. These firms are closely linked with the protection of diamond fields, many of which are owned by FAA generals. The behaviour of outfits such as Teleservice and Alpha 5 is indicative of a brittle, fluid order in areas over which the state has historically had a weak hold. A recent investigation by Rafael Marques showed the extent to which these firms exercise power of life or death over the populations of rural Lunda Norte and the Congolese illegal migrants caught by them.[113] It also unmasked the security firms' sustained collaboration with FAA both in hunting down illegal miners and in establishing protection rackets that enable illegal mining.[114] In a further twist, while the FAA in Lunda Norte is de facto privatized, the provincial government partly subcontracted the armed forces' core function in a border region—border control—to an Israeli defence outfit.[115]

Old-fashioned methods: the Cabinda enclave

If the political economy of Lunda Norte's diamond fields has hindered the postwar normalization of that province, oil has played the same role in the Cabinda enclave. Since oil production started there in 1968, Cabinda has been responsible for most of Angola's output, though production has been steadily moving southwards since the 1990s. Cabinda's status in a discussion of Angola's "periphery" needs to be explained. On the one hand, its coastal and offshore areas have been at the very core of the MPLA regime as the source of the fiscal revenue that afforded the survival of the state during the war. On the other hand, much of its interior, especially the Mayombe mountain range, has long escaped state authority and harboured a long-running insurgency variously supported by neighbouring governments and entities such as the former French NOC Elf Aquitaine. The enclave's physical separation from the main body of Angola, its extraordinary wealth, and a *sui generis* history that includes a separate 1885 treaty with Portugal have jointly fostered a separatist current going back to the 1960s.

Cabinda has always been more complicated than the fleeting references to its remote conflict made it seem. Though FLEC was created in 1963 and claims to have opposed the Portuguese before fighting the postcolonial state, war was never as harsh in Cabinda as it was elsewhere in Angola. Successive Luanda governments, their foreign patrons, and the oil companies all agreed on the imperative of protecting the flow of oil.

Even UNITA's own foreign supporters harshly talked down the rebels' occasional threats against the oil sector and the latter thrived throughout the long decades of the war. For their part, Cabinda's insurgent factions mostly collected payments from the oil firms and the state, and left the oil sector in peace. Yet following the end of the civil war in 2002, Cabinda was flushed by 30,000 troops, a show of FAA power that resulted in a marked increase in killings and human rights violations.[116] Basking in the recent victory against UNITA, the government wanted to show that these minor guerrillas (who actually rarely did much fighting) could be crushed at will, especially now that the regimes in Congo-Brazzaville and the DRC, for long mischievous supporters of Cabindan separatism, were beholden to Luanda.[117]

After this demonstration of MPLA brute force came the co-optation drive: the MPLA signed a 2006 peace agreement with FLEC-Renovada (one of the several splinter groups of the original FLEC) and gave the position of secretary of state for human rights to António Bento Bembe, one of the group's main figures. It showered the province, which, contrary to myth, had never been particularly poor and was now clearly ahead of the Angolan average, with resources and infrastructure, including a stadium and a new airport terminal, and spruced up Cabinda City. At the same time, Cabinda remained under the conspicuous occupation of the FAA and an invisible but ubiquitous stranglehold of SINFO, military intelligence, and various networks of informants.[118] FLEC-FAC, the major faction yet to accept Luanda's writ, occasionally gives a Paris-based press conference and kidnaps foreign workers. During the African Cup of Nations held in Angola in January 2010, it attacked the bus of the Togolese national team (killing three of its staff but no players) instead of a government convoy.[119] But other than giving Luanda a pretext for another crackdown, this and other actions have had no impact on the province, which is under the government's firmest grip ever.[120] Cabinda's unsettled status is a stark reminder, in present-day Angolan politics, of what the party-state is willing to do to affirm its authority.

State agendas in the periphery

The strategies discussed thus far illustrate the broad range of tools deployed by the state to maximize its presence. What these policies do not provide is a knowledge base for quotidian, bureaucratized governance. If the state's approach to knowledge is faulty even at the core, in the periphery it is blinkered to an extreme; in vital dimensions, it does not "see like a state".[121] The state is obsessed with political intelligence and deploys a cast of foot soldiers—FAA, police, SINFO, *sobas*, MPLA structures and associated organizations, private security—for that purpose. Otherwise its ignorance is absolute. As an opposition official complained, "without communications infrastructure and without the census, the provincial government does not know the population [and] has no idea what goes on 100km from here".[122] Key aspects of scientific knowledge—in hydrology, geology, agronomy and public health—remain dependent on outdated colonial-era research. Furthermore, the "state doesn't know that it doesn't know":[123] these matters are either deemed irrelevant or not perceived as a priority. While this limits what the state can achieve in the periphery in terms of developmental governance (particularly in agriculture), it is not a major hindrance in terms of the current priorities.

Other state policies reveal ignorance and arrogance to an equal degree. Take the policy of "village reunification" in the east, which was often championed by Rosa Pacavira, the president's social sector adviser until 2012 and current minister of trade. This entails placing spread-out populations in model villages with "modern amenities". The potentially disruptive impacts are legion. In multi-ethnic provinces such as Moxico, "the bringing together of hunter-agriculturalists with fishermen-agriculturalists and hunter-apiculture peoples is fraught with misunderstanding and potential for conflict".[124] In regions with itinerant agriculture, population clustering results in the reduction of available areas for cultivation and the exhaustion of the land that is cultivated. In addition, a stark fact has been wilfully tossed aside: the history of forceful removals to deny sustenance to insurgents, from late colonial policy to the MPLA's own brutal population uprooting in the last years of the civil war. The government insists that resettlement is voluntary and many people are keen on it on account of service-delivery promises made, but the decision to resettle is on the basis of consultation with the *sobas*, not the population. The developmental failures of villageization (in Ethiopia, Tanzania, Mozambique etc.) known to the MPLA elite further underline this agenda's primarily political, rather than economic or social, goals.

Finally, a key factor in state-rural society relations is the cultural distance between civil servants and the locals. This may not be the case in core regions of MPLA governance but in remote regions many agents of the state do not speak the local languages. On more than one occasion, civil servants privately complained about the "natives" being "different from me and you"; of homesickness and resentment at the long distance from "home", which often means Luanda.[125] The parallels between the colonial administrators marooned in eastern Angola in the great fiction of Castro Soromenho and the complaints of present-day officials are disconcerting,[126] down to the use of the same language and even the perception of what their mission amounts to.

By piecing together the diverse strands of the party-state's actions in the periphery it becomes clear that there is a coherent agenda of occupying abandoned regions and establishing the sort of state grid that briefly obtained in the late colonial years. This agenda resorts to the "available models of state-building",[127] which are overwhelmingly those of the colonial state, for matters ranging from legislation and relations with traditional authorities to private sector engagement. The historical continuities in the relationship between the centre and the hinterland, particularly at the level of elite theories of governance vis-à-vis the periphery, are striking.

The MPLA's peripheral state-building project is driven by two unspoken assumptions. The first is the notion, hiding behind claims of state universality, of the superiority of the Portuguese-speaking, urban and coastal core of the state vis-à-vis the backward periphery. The second is that modernization and "'development' [are] virtually coterminous with control"[128] of rural populations and the expansion of the party-state. The language of systematization and nation building hides an enduringly binary vision of the cities and the countryside, where the latter is to provide the party-state with reliable vote banks and a quiescent population. As mentioned above, this bifurcation scenario may well reflect MPLA goals for the regions under what it calls "peripheral administration" but its static assumptions are belied by Angola's remarkable degree of social transformation. As the Luandan state seeks to master the periphery, Luanda itself is changing under the weight of the rural exodus. The party-state itself unwittingly contributes towards this. The eccentric modernizing projects of the reconstruction era discussed in Chapter 2, for instance, are increasingly present in the hinterland, and larger towns and provincial capitals aspire to become mini-Luandas, absorbing rural populations in the process.

Where is this leading? From the narrow perspective of "state-building" as institutional and administrative creation, the policies outlined above increase the state's capacity to project power yet fall short of producing the bureaucratized apparatus of everyday governance that the population needs. From the point of view of "state formation" as a much broader "unconscious and contradictory" historical process,[129] however, we are witnessing nothing less than the recreation and consolidation of an integrated political space and economy. In view of the dominant MPLA ideas about centre-periphery relations, however, it is unlikely that this will result in broad-based rural development. Optimists might interpret this process as similar to the transformation of "peasants into Frenchmen" described by Eugen Weber: a stern central state, often brutal and always impatient with local particularities, but pushing forward a civic project of nation-building.[130] In Angola, however, there is no civic project or investment in people. The state is dilating not like nineteenth-century France in Auvergne but more in the manner of the colonial state,[131] and in the process creating a society of subjects rather than citizens.

A HAPPY ANGOLAN FAMILY?

By 2008, the MPLA's strategy of nationwide hegemonic consolidation seemed an absolute success. The party had repeatedly postponed the first postwar elections (originally meant for 2004) so that it could tighten its grip across the territory, buy off or tame key constituencies and fully benefit from the oil boom that had started half way through the decade. More important, it sought to buy time to reconstruct the MPLA's grass-roots structure, raised for the 1992 elections but much neglected and underfunded since, into a usable campaigning instrument. This proved a wise move. After a lavish electoral campaign during which the opposition got minimal media exposure and MPLA developmental promises reached fever pitch, the ruling party received an extraordinary 82 per cent of votes (UNITA scored just over 10 per cent).[132] The few international electoral observers in place just about vouched for election-day fairness.[133] Internationally, this was a major upward bump for the regime's reputation; domestically, the MPLA received a mandate on a completely different scale from the qualified majority of 1992. Its complacency knew no limits.

Although the party-state's coercive power underpinned the strategies of consolidation discussed in this chapter, with Cabinda an ongoing example of what it is prepared to do if challenged, it is inaccurate to read MPLA influence on those terms alone. Far from being resented, the MPLA's hegemonic quest was matched by the desires of a geographically and socially diverse set of actors who sought to enter the party-state order and prosper within it. In postwar Angola, opportunities for material improvement and upward mobility became an MPLA monopoly. The power of the MPLA and the prospect of oil money are drivers of social aspirations; "even when perceived negatively, state norms penetrate society".[134] This applies to those within and without the party-state, including the opposition parties, who accepted that political struggle is "itself centralised"[135] and sought to derive benefits from the role they played in the MPLA ecosystem. In any case, this occurs within a national context where, for all their differences, there is an implicit agreement on the character of politics as the distribution of the national cake. This compromised atmosphere is essential for making sense of the MPLA's rapport with Angolan society in the early years of peace.

The pivotal problem in postwar life is the mismatch between this broad "desire for the state" and what the party-state is actually willing to offer Angolans. As we have seen, the MPLA has become a mass party, embraced a nation-building rhetoric and seemingly accepted what Justin Pearce calls the challenge of "making everyone *povo do governo*".[136] In practice, the benefits of the party-state flow through sinuous channels that exclude most people, most of the time, and as private rather than public goods. The opinion-makers, the educated and the would-be middle classes—in short, "the politically relevant"[137]—are pampered. A string of intermediaries with the masses, exemplified by the *sobas* discussed above, is given a stake of sorts. Everyone else is for the most part dispensed with. The urban poor must be surveyed and entertained, and the more astute amongst them billeted into the lower stratum of the party-state, but they do not have to be bought off or included as a whole. The rural poor do not count. Even while the MPLA slowly includes new constituencies, the consolidation of the postwar order is fundamentally premised on exclusion.

Some argue that the party-state is pragmatic in bringing into the fold those it really needs to co-opt. From this perspective, the MPLA excluded large parts of the population because, in the context of social demobilization and many people's de facto acceptance of the iniquitous postwar order, it had no incentive to do so. If this is the case, then one may expect the MPLA to move towards wider inclusiveness in the less placid political atmosphere that is replacing the honeymoon decade.

The alternative explanation emphasizes the values structure of the elite and ascribes it far less flexibility and political foresight. Under its carefully managed exterior as a mass party, it is argued, the real MPLA remains a socially selective outfit controlled by individuals without empathy for the poor and the hinterland. The same individuals and their micro-constituencies, having acquired a rare degree of control over the oil money, understandably have a bias against new entrants. Moreover, for the MPLA elite, the party's legitimacy does not emanate primarily from the people, something that would presuppose a social contract-type relationship. Instead, theirs is a revolutionary legitimacy resulting from the liberation and civil war victories. If this alternative reading is right, the MPLA truly is blinkered and its festering neglect of the population—together with the rapid social change that the party doesn't understand or control—will come back to haunt it.

4

OLIGARCHIC CAPITALISM, ANGOLA-STYLE

"They are stealing absolutely everything and it is impossible to stop them. But let them steal and take their property. They will then become owners and decent administrators of this property."

Anatoly Chubais, Russian economic reformer, 1995[1]

"Either there is morality, or everyone gets to eat."

Kimbundu proverb[2]

Throughout modern history, the accumulation of capital has rarely been a pretty sight, but post-socialist Angola is in a febrile class of its own. What happened over centuries in some societies materialized in Angola as a remarkably compressed process driven by war profiteering, diamond smuggling and the appropriation of oil rents by a small clique. When peace came, reconstruction under the hegemony of the MPLA bore possibilities considerably beyond even the most rewarding wartime business. These possibilities were economic but also related to the consolidation of a socially dominant status, with the beneficiaries of the 1990s hothouse aspiring to establish themselves and their families as Angola's hereditary power elite.

In 2002 dos Santos understood that the old strategies had had their day: for the new potential to be realized, the economy needed to be stabilized, a financial sector created, and the country made safe for an expatriate labour force and some forms of foreign investment. The extraordinary oil-fuelled economic activity that ensued can only be described as the making of a particular type of capitalism, based on rents rather than

productive activity, but one whose depth and sophistication is a departure from wartime resource extraction. This capitalism with Angolan
characteristics is inescapably political in terms of its dependence on state
patronage for access to capital and profit-making opportunities, and the
overarching, if informal, role of the president. His discretionary power
stands in for the formal (and in Angola, inexistent) institutions of capitalism as the new system's chief regulatory force.

Coming to terms with this self-styled capitalism is key for an understanding of contemporary Angola. At heart, this is a story not of an
impersonal process but of the rise of an Angolan affluent group headed
by a minute set of the hyper-rich. Their diversified business groups have
a stranglehold over the domestic economy and increasingly span the
globe. As in other post-socialist contexts, the worldviews, consumer habits and behaviour of the Angolan oligarchs have also proved defining of
societal values in the peace era. In the following pages I examine the
origins and character of Angola's new political economy, the complex
social reactions to it, and its medium-term potential and limits. From
their origins as prototypical robber barons, can Angola's oligarchs
become the more respectable "entrepreneurs" beloved of the regime's
official discourse? And regardless of its messy origins, can this process of
capital accumulation hold positive, if unintended, consequences for
Angola's majority?

POST-COLD WAR PRIMITIVE ACCUMULATION

The future oligarchs stepped into the new capitalist era with a great deal
of hesitation. At its Second Extraordinary Congress in April 1991, the
MPLA formally committed itself to the creation of a market economy.[3]
It did so as a concession to the changing times but not without misgivings; observers even spoke of a "panic" in some quarters of the party.[4]
Understandably, apparatchiks with no experience in private enterprise,[5]
and already beset by the perils of a democratic transition, found it difficult to see how they could recreate domination in an unfamiliar context.
Their inexperience was not simply on account of the socialist period. By
the time of independence Angola had no "commercial and industrial"
black bourgeoisie of any consequence.[6] Its colonial private sector, ranging from multinational extractive industries to the puniest of country
stores, had been almost completely in the hands of Europeans.[7] The

coastal merchant dynasties of the pre-Scramble era had long taken to the civil service,[8] which formed the background and mind-set of the Angolan postcolonial elite. The socialist political system through which they consolidated control of urban Angola further solidified their statist bias. No wonder that the new dispensation initially spooked them.

This handwringing did not last long. The MPLA leadership swiftly broke with the socialist tropes and embraced the idea of creating a "national bourgeoisie" holding not just the state apparatus but also significant private capital; this national bourgeoisie would be constituted by those closest to the party, including the top decision-makers themselves, if only implicitly at the start. There ensued a process of primitive accumulation towards which very few members of the MPLA showed any qualms, if only because the benefits, which disproportionately flowed to a handful of insiders, also flowed to a lesser degree to tens of thousands of urban Angolans with the right connections.[9] Three major strategies were noteworthy: war profiteering after the restart of the conflict in 1992, exchange rate manipulation, and the privatization of state assets.

The manifold opportunities of the war economy were discussed in Chapter 1. Taking advantage of the capital-intensive reorganization of the armed forces, senior FAA and police officers and presidential advisers positioned themselves as key intermediaries between the Angolan state and foreign business operators in logistics, arms deals, private security and militarized extractive sectors such as diamond mining. In possession of a virtual monopoly over air transport to the interior, FAA generals also enriched themselves by using it for personal profit. Much of this activity, which resulted in some of Angola's highest profile fortunes, was corrupt, as it often involved commerce with UNITA and the frequent acquisition of redundant and overpriced matériel that literally came apart in the battlefield.[10]

The second strategy was perhaps the most brazen of all: an unrealistic official exchange rate, utterly out of sync with the real rate in Angolan streets, allowed the well connected simply to enter the central bank and exchange their worthless kwanzas for hard currency, in the words of an Angolan banker, "getting their hands on hundreds of thousands of dollars at a time for next to nothing".[11] This currency exchange arrangement, which would last until 1999, "sometimes permitted enrichment on a factor of 1 to 100" and allowed for the transfer of untold billions into private hands.[12] "This was the way back in the days: one got rich easily, without any work, and the result was [throughout the 1990s] a strong lobby against the normalization and stabilization of the currency".[13] The frenzy of this foundational scam is now remembered in hushed tones, yet is at the heart of many trajectories of accumulation in Angola.[14]

The third strategy was the privatization programme, which sold off 296 of the odd-500 state-owned companies (themselves the consolidated result of thousands of private colonial-era firms) before the National Assembly brought it to a halt in 1994 on account of lack of transparency.[15] Benefiting from this process were the upper reaches of the state and party apparatus and the armed forces. But the highest profile accumulation was by a small group of insiders known as the "empresários de confiança"—literally, "trustworthy businessmen", those whom the MPLA can rely on.[16] The resulting business groups—Grupo Mello Xavier, Grupo Alpega, Grupo César e Filhos, Valentim Amões's Grupo Wapossoka and António Mosquito's Grupo Mbakassi e Filhos—all led by a patriarchal figure, are bywords for the first generation of Angolan capital accumulation. A few became infamous for their brashness and nouveau riche exhibitionism. Yet, with a few exceptions, the performance of the empresários was disappointing: as a prominent Angolan businessman acquainted with most of them put it, "they took to suits and ties and business-speak but were absolutely worthless", and "just kept on losing money and claiming more".[17]

This was unsurprising as there was little entrepreneurial knack about these men or the opportunities (mostly real estate and import monopolies) bestowed upon them; all managed their firms as personal fiefdoms and a few were financially illiterate. Those who benefited did so on account of their insider status and went on benefiting from state largesse and protection even after repeated mistakes. As an Angolan banker put it, "this was all easy money: these people did not need to go to business school".[18] They were creatures of the state, for regardless of its ostensible retreat and privatization, the new dispensation was entirely state-led and articulated by the presidency. As Anne Pitcher put it in the case of Mozambique, the state of the post-socialist era may have been redirected but certainly hadn't withdrawn from the economy.[19] Angola's shift to markets (and elections) cannot be separated from the drastic transformations of "world time"; that is, the liberalizing zeitgeist of the early post-Cold War years. But the specific form of this shift owed greatly to Angola's political economy and the decisions of incumbents able to navigate this complex period.[20]

OLIGARCHIC CAPITALISM, ANGOLA-STYLE

The investment in the *empresários de confiança* shows that the national bourgeoisie agenda was, at least in some ways, not entirely cynical. The exercise of sponsoring a new Angolan business class also revealed that most politicians and members of the security establishment, while busy acquiring chunks of the economy and profiting from the war, were still unwilling to engage in "business" and were more likely to build bank accounts and real estate holdings abroad. This was partly because the context did not lend itself to long time horizons or conventional investments, but also because they did not fully understand the workings of a capitalist economy. Ironically, and in spite of the permissive atmosphere of these years, the open business concerns of politicians and generals were relatively small-scale and often associated with their families rather than themselves. In view of later developments, it is hard to convey the frisson caused in the Luanda society of the early 1990s when it was reported that the president's wife, Ana Paula dos Santos, owned a shoe shop and a hairdressing salon. But the assumption that business and politics were at least nominally autonomous would change quickly.

POSTWAR CAPITALISM: INTRODUCING GROUND RULES

The end of the war was a watershed for the political economy as much as for other dimensions of governance explored in this book. Here too, JES and his people realized that the forms of accumulation of the war years would need to be reconfigured. This was both a matter of adapting to a changed context and of moving beyond the less sophisticated forms of rent appropriation and management of the wild 1990s. As we have seen, the chaos of that decade, with its four-digit inflation, exchange rate madness and sheer lawlessness, was instrumental for the takeover of the economy by those at the top. Once this had been achieved, some of the permissiveness and coarse behaviour of those years needed to be discontinued, for the very state of emergency that had enabled these tactics stood in the way of establishing even the most basic of functioning market economies. This "renewal of the management style",[21] while apparently less disruptive than the initial transition to markets of the early 1990s, was if anything more consequential for the scale and form of elite accumulation.

The stabilization of the economy was a prerequisite for pursuing these ambitions, and in particular for the establishment of a functioning financial sector.[22] As always, the commitment to economic reform was embodied in the sacking of "bad ministers" and the nomination of a reformist team.[23] The star reformers on this occasion, José Pedro de Morais as Finance Minister and Aguinaldo Jaime as Vice-Prime Minister, were actually seasoned political operators implicated in previous rounds of policy. But this time around they had a presidential mandate to curb inflation, prevent the resurgence of forex scams and more generally stabilize the economy. Their nomination was not simply an act of far-sighted reformism on the part of the president. When Morais was nominated in November 2002, the state coffers were so depleted that there wasn't enough money to cover the civil service salary bill for December.[24] In this context, the reformists' international credentials and perfect English were deployed to drag cash-strapped Angola away from the brink. "Without the crisis," argues a Finance Ministry insider of the period, "there would have been no reform momentum, and no reform",[25] but once things started to work well, the president allowed the reformist team a modicum of policy space.

At this stage, reform did not mean acceptance of the IMF diktat, as these were also the years of greatest confrontation on the transparency front.[26] Still, while preventing any degree of foreign oversight and not meddling with Sonangol's space for manoeuvre, the reformist team picked up some suggestions from the IMF laundry list and moved Angola into a more predictable macro-economic setup, imposing "minimal conditions, not for the country's development, but for the functioning of a renewed (even if fundamentally rentier) capitalism."[27] As Vice-President Manuel Vicente put it a decade later, in order to attract investors Angola had "to guarantee people's security [and] contractual stability, which is what we [had] done at the level of the petroleum industry for the last forty years".[28] To a very large extent, this was achieved in the period from 2003 to 2008. Together with the astute management of Angola's international relations discussed in Chapter 5, this is the greatest achievement of the government over the past decade. Positive in its own right, it also enabled a considerable upgrading of opportunities for regime insiders, as I will explain below.

This macro-economic stabilization, when added to the end of the war and the expectation of JES's continued dominance, provided Angola with a degree of predictability absent since independence. The incomplete character of this reformism and the desire to maintain discretionary levers of power are underlined by the fact that legal and formal regulatory reforms were negligible. JES remains the personal arbiter of the system and consequential decisions emanate from the parallel state.[29] Yet the reforms that were introduced amounted to major de facto improvements for foreign firms. Conventional accounts of development make it dependent on a battery of a priori achievements regarding institutional strength and the rule of law, all of which Angola lacks. But Peter Lewis has noted that credible commitments can nonetheless emerge without these conditions, with elites "provisionally crafting" growth-oriented informal arrangements that promote capital formation.[30] This was the sort of implicit understanding prevalent in the oil sector that had allowed investment to pour into Angola despite Marxism-Leninism and war. From 2002 onwards, under the steady hand of JES, the economy was reconfigured in a manner that allowed the opening up of significant non-oil sectors to foreign participation. These foreign players would be accepted, provided their business activity included Angolan co-ownership.[31]

What became possible in this relatively stabilized environment was the state-nurtured expansion of Angolan capital accumulation. As we will see shortly, this was not in order to transcend rentierism. It was about diversifying the sources of rent acquisition and managing rents in more sophisticated ways, a process culminating in the establishment of an Angolan financial capitalism of sorts. The strategy of Angola's state-led capitalism is straightforward. First, to use the financial and regulatory leverage of the state to expand its clout vis-à-vis the foreign private sector, initially in Angola but soon in terms of the "crossed foreign investments" discussed in Chapter 5; second, to act as the facilitator for internal privileged constituencies to become participants in the profit-making opportunities that result from the expansion of the peacetime economy. Some might see this as an evolved form of rentierism rather than a qualitative shift towards capitalism. But it amounts to a major step, in terms of both scale and complexity, away from the amateurish empresários of the 1990s.

The major innovation of this period is the spectacular rise of the Angolan banking sector. With barely US$3 billion in assets in 2003, it had grown into a US$53 billion industry by 2011, when it ranked as Sub-Saharan Africa's third largest after South Africa's and Nigeria's.[32] In the early 2000s, Catherine Boone could accurately describe Angola as an "ideal-type case of a statist regime" when it came to the banking sector.[33] None had been privatized and the state-owned banks were erratically

managed in line with the broader economic policy of the time. (A handful of private banks such as BAI were already in existence though they
remained small and discreet). The government soon promoted the creation of "private" banks, the most prominent of which were partly owned
by the state (often through Sonangol) with ownership shares extended
to elite constituencies. By the end of the decade, the largest amongst
these banks[34] had taken over dominant stakes in leading Portuguese
counterparts such as Millennium BCP.

In Angola itself, this rise was not at all about fostering private sector
development. Though small, bank usage is increasing.[35] For most clients,
it remains a matter of deposits, with the vast majority of individuals and
SMEs unable to access credit: as a senior Central Bank figure admitted
in July 2009, "about 85 per cent of Angolan credit goes to two hundred
or so clients".[36] In essence, this means that bank shareholders are lending
money to themselves and to narrowly defined constituencies around
them. The names of famous oligarchs recur as major shareholders in
Angola's top banks, but the detailed ownership structure (sometimes
with relatively small percentages for family members of politicians—a
sort of trust fund) is highly revealing: those familiar with Angolan society
will recognize it as a veritable *Who's Who*.[37]

In line with their overarching role in Angola's peacetime economy,
external partners played crucial roles in the expansion of the financial
sector: of the 24 Angolan banks in existence in 2012, nine were partnerships with Portuguese banks and one was a joint venture with Standard
Bank of South Africa, which sold 49 per cent of Standard Angola to AAA,
Sonangol's insurance arm.[38] These foreign partners are needed for banking expertise but also on account of their (and their home jurisdictions')
credibility, a major asset for fledgling financial institutions burdened with
Angola's disreputable corruption and money laundering record.[39] At the
same time, these partnerships are formally (through Angolan majority
ownership) or informally (through a bank's dependence on the Angolan
market) calibrated in ways that guarantee Luanda's preeminence. These
partnerships, which are very rewarding for the foreign partners, have
resulted in the acquisition by top Angolan banks such as BFA[40] and BAI
of a highly professional demeanour. They look like generic global banks
and their executives carry themselves in a familiar manner.

As in many sub-Saharan African cases of financial liberalization, this
massive expansion is happening in a context of poor regulation and next

to no prudential measures. The Angolan elite is in no hurry to do otherwise. There are serious limitations of human resources to cope with the burgeoning financial system. But would-be regulators lack the political muscle to patrol the elite shareholders of the banks, who are in many instances current or former officials of the sector regulator (the Angolan Central Bank), Sonangol, and the Presidency. As a result of a major fraud at the Central Bank in 2009, a new team of BNA officials, incidentally headed by two former private bankers from BAI, seems to have received a mandate to rein in some excesses. But to say that regulators have a light footprint in the Angolan financial system would be an understatement. When dealing with Sonangol, the Casa Militar, or elite families, formal regulation plays no role. As in all other systemically vital nodes of the Angolan system, the governance of the banking sector is ultimately at the discretion of the president. If other experiences are to go by, this means that Angolan banks are in for some turbulence.[41]

This remarkable rise has had its hiccups. A 2010 US Senate Report shed light on the opaque ownership structure of BAI, often dubbed "Sonangol's bank" and Angola's largest. BAI had refused to divulge the beneficial owners behind letterbox company shareholders to HSBC, its corresponding bank, despite years of requests (the US Senate chastised HSBC for not rescinding the connection despite BAI's non-compliance). "HSBC," the US Senate report reads, "has allowed BAI to continue to send hundreds of millions of dollars each month through HSBC into the American financial system without providing written assurance of its [anti-money laundering] policies and procedures".[42] Writing about BAI, the activist Rafael Marques even labelled it "the regime's Laundromat".[43] In 2011, Portuguese authorities briefly named Álvaro Sobrinho, the suave CEO of BESA (a partnership with Portugal's Espírito Santo Bank, up to that point at the sophisticated, international end of the spectrum of Angolan banks) a suspect of money laundering, although the investigation was later dropped for lack of evidence.[44] But for now it is the relentless rise of Angolan banking assets and footprint that catches the enthusiasm of market analysts. The culmination of this rise, which also amounts to a qualitative jump in the fortunes of Angola's elite families, is the new law on petroleum payments. Mandating that all oil sector payments be made through the Angolan banking system, this will enlarge the banking sector's capital by an extraordinary US$20 billion.[45]

As always, Sonangol proved to be key for this strategy. To start with, it had the funding to play the role of financier of the new Angolan capitalism, especially in the harnessing of a "private" Angolan banking sector and the internationalization of Angolan investment discussed in Chapter 5. Sonangol also played a vital role in the implementation of an extensive local content policy that, though already in existence, was decisively pursued since the end of the war.[46] On the basis of both the PSAs with international oil companies and increasingly detailed Angolan legal requirements, Sonangol has mandated the use of Angolan companies for procurement and oil services worth billions of dollars a year.[47] Its 1990s restructuring into a holding company with dozens of joint ventures with private foreign firms also make it the ideal vehicle to enforce partnerships with Angolan "entrepreneurs", initially in the field of oil services but soon encompassing non-operating positions in oil blocks for local firms. Especially in oil services, a small number of competent operators emerged who creditably performed increasingly important tasks, but the process of choosing Angolan partners is entirely political. The most frequent outcome is that letterbox Angolan companies, many connected with Sonangol officials, appropriate local content contracts and simply subcontract activities to foreign firms. By 2013, these calls for "Angolanization" of the private sector,[48] reminiscent of Nigeria's indigenization policies of the 1970s, hadn't yet taken Nigerian proportions but significant oil-related business flowed to Angolan-owned private firms.

THE NATIONAL BOURGEOISIE

Even in the official discourse, this "Angolanization" drive was aimed at the vaunted national bourgeoisie rather than the population as a whole. Chapter 2 already alluded to the malleable character of this term, especially the manner in which it can refer in turn, to a sizeable "middle class" minority or a tiny number of privileged Angolans. As applied to the new capitalism, it is highly restrictive and seems to match a few thousand direct beneficiaries surrounding an inner circle of only several hundred insiders. It includes the "professionals of violence" who, in the words of Carlos Severino, the head of Angola's Industrial Association, "had to be fed",[49] such as the leadership of the armed forces, the police and the intelligence services, whether in active duty or in nominal retirement;[50] the upper spheres of the party-state; regional elites, connected with the MPLA but with mostly provincial-level influence; the traditional Luanda elites; and the families and hangers-on of political leaders, with increasing visibility of the President's own family as the decade wore on. Many of these constituencies are of course overlapping and mutually reinforcing. In today's Angola there are no major business trajectories outside the purview of this elite or even in partial autonomy from it. While much academic work on late developers hinges on the complex relationship between the business class and political power, in Angola they are for all purposes inseparable.

Why this narrow social focus? Favouring policies that allow for self-enrichment at the top is certainly part of the story, but there is more to it. The reasoning of a senior MPLA cadre now in the private sector deserves to be quoted at length:

> In the beginning I believed in agriculture but [eventually realized] just how profoundly backward Angolan peasants really are. Think of this: by the time of independence only the peasants in the highlands were using animal traction in agriculture! Almost everywhere else agriculture was still pre-historic! [...] The country needs to develop the cosmopolitan elites it never had [...] which presupposes allowing them access to wealth and power [...] It may not please you to hear it, but Angola needs rich, strong and powerful families that can stand up to international competition. To have a republic of better fed poor people, all with the third grade, is not a viable model for us.[51]

He went on to justify the long-term merits of this process by arguing that "class formation is indispensable historically: one day the poor will emancipate themselves". This spirited defence of what could be called Leninist capitalism is not just the preserve of policy intellectuals or foreign academics seeking to make sense of Angola's political economy. Here is the president's cogent defence of the favouring of the elite in his State of the Nation address in October 2013:

> The primitive accumulation of capital in Western countries took place hundreds of years ago and at that stage the rules of the game were [different]. The primitive accumulation of capital taking place today in Africa should fit our reality. [Why can the West] have large-scale companies, and not the Angolans? Intimidation campaigns [...] are consistently waged against Africans because [Westerners] do not want local competitors and want to continue to take ever more wealth away to their home countries. We need the companies, the entrepreneurs and the strong and efficient national economic groups in the private and public sectors and the elites capable in all domains, so that we can progressively leave behind [our underdeveloped status].[52]

There is no need to elaborate on the self-serving logic[53] or on the fact that many in the elite would be unable to articulate this justification for

Angola's inequities. But at some level this explains the elite's deep-rooted sense of entitlement. Whatever shades of opinion may exist, there is a virtual consensus amongst the powerful that "the Angolan economy is theirs".[54]

The fact that this elite takeover of the Angolan economy has been elevated into national policy is consequential in many ways, the most important being that, contrary to much talk of Angolan grand corruption, much of this process is actually *legal*. Influential people did not just grab money, assets and opportunities; the official policy is that they must be helped in doing so. Some elite ownership of assets and businesses is held by straw men or carefully camouflaged in letterbox offshore companies. But a surprising amount is increasingly available for all to see in the Angolan state gazette, the *Diário da Républica*,[55] in the pages of which one can track the complex web of crossed ownerships that make the top hundred-odd political and military figures partners in some business with just about every other member of that exclusive club. In this context, a selective and self-serving engagement with "the law" amounts to a strategy for consolidating one's business interests and collecting whatever above-board benefits (concessional interest rates, subsidies, preferential treatment for Angolan nationals, etc.) can be had.[56]

Otherwise, the default position of Angolan businessmen is above the law, whether it is a matter of capital flight, money laundering, the unilateral abandonment of partnerships with foreigners, the non-payment of loans and import duties, conflict of interest between public and private roles, the use of coercion to secure extraction, etc.[57] These are not occasional whims, but the very stuff of Angolan private sector life.[58] Such practices are also illegal according to Angolan law, but few Angolan businessmen would describe their behaviour in terms of "breaking the law": they simply assume the latter doesn't apply to them. In what can alternatively be described as the product of arrogance, cynicism or a sheer fit of absence of mind, many progressive laws have been passed in recent years meant to provide some ground rules for Angola's market economy. But they are primarily conceived as tools to regulate foreign entrepreneurs and are not meant to be deployed against the system's masterminds. The activist Rafael Marques' surprising use of these laws to throw lawsuits at some of Angola's most formidable players has therefore been met with anger. Other than the considerable nuisance, this will have no legal consequences. In the words of Inglês Pinto, the former head of Angola's Bar

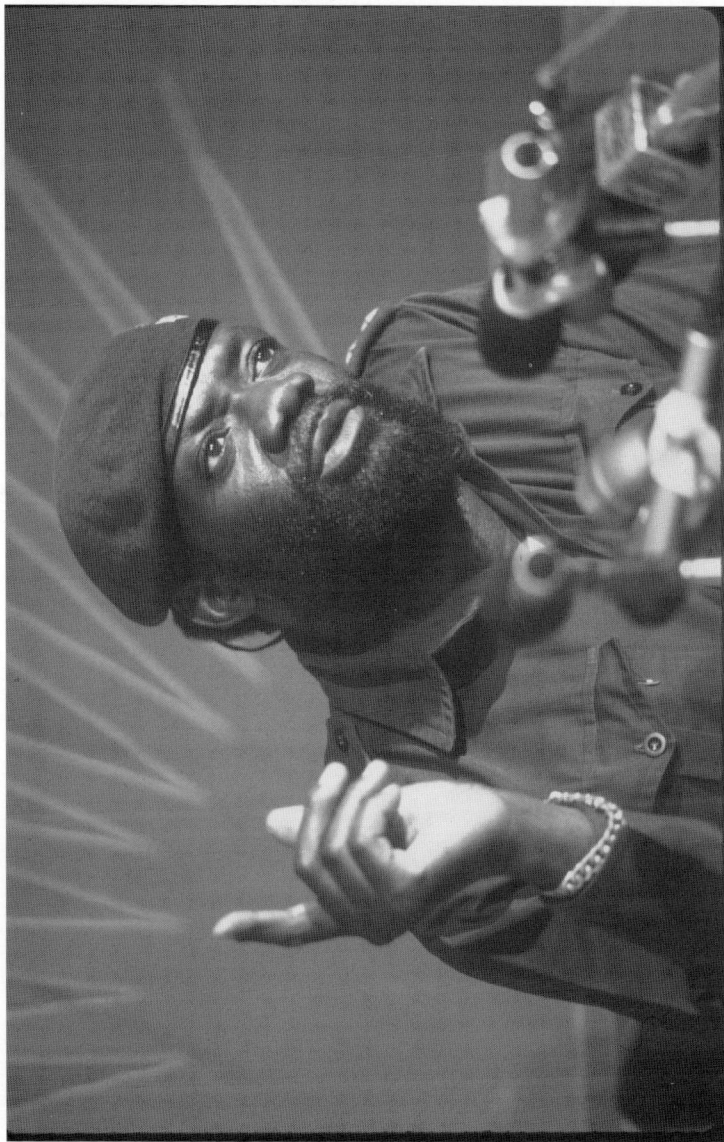

Fig. 1: Jonas Savimbi, the leader of UNITA (Photo: Selwyn Tait / Getty Images)

Fig. 2: A happy José Eduardo dos Santos leaves the US Department of State having met with Secretary of State Colin Powell, days after Jonas Savimbi's death in 2002 (Photo: Alex Wong / Getty Images)

Fig. 3: A Chinese worker rehabilitating Angola's railways (Photo: Per-Anders Pettersson / Getty Images)

Fig. 4: Luanda's construction craze (Photo: Jose De Sousa / Getty Images)

Fig. 5: Luanda bay and the city (Photo: Simon Dawson / Bloomberg)

Fig. 6: Dos Santos as the "Architect of Peace" (Photo: Estelle Maussion / Getty Images)

Fig. 7: Isabel dos Santos at the Monika Bacardi Summer Party, Saint-Tropez, 2014 (Photo: Venturelli / Getty Images)

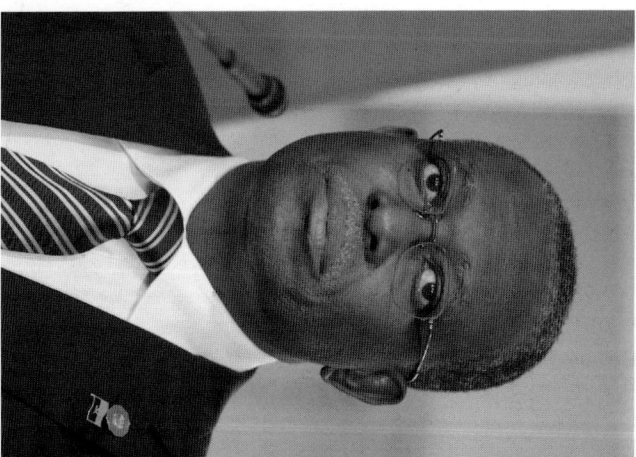

Fig. 8: Manuel Vicente, Vice-President, former head of Sonangol, and sometime dauphin (Photo: Chip Somodevilla / Getty Images)

Fig. 9: Kuduro dancing in Luanda (Photo: Bruno Fonseca)

JUSTIÇA AGARREM QUE É ADVOGADO!
As queixas, os casos mediáticos e os crimes envolvendo profissionais de Direito

VISÃO

www.visao.sapo.pt
Nº 993 • 15 a 21 de março de 2012
Continente e ilhas: € 3,00
Periodicidade semanal

O PODER
DO DINHEIRO
DE ANGOLA

Ordem para comprar em Portugal.
A estratégia angolana para ganhar
influência na banca, energia,
telecomunicações e comunicação social.
A Galp, Zon, BCP e os outros alvos

ENTREVISTA EXCLUSIVA
JONATHAN FRANZEN,
A VOZ DA (NOVA) AMÉRICA

KONY2012
O FENÓMENO
DO YOUTUBE

CAVACO
AS 32 FRASES
MAIS POLÉMICAS

Fig. 10: "The power of Angolan money": Visão, Portugal´s leading news magazine, outlines Angola's strategy and acquisition targets in the former colonial power

Association, "they expose themselves to that extent because they have total impunity."[59] As an Angolan academic noted, "now that we have that information in the public domain, what is going to happen? Nothing!"[60]

For the improvements of the postwar era were not meant to create a genuine rule of law and certainly not to throw open the economy to the unconnected. It is through the power of the state, whether directly or through family, friendship, and other social networks, that the elite access economic opportunities, feed capital requirements, and achieve complete aloofness from regulatory and political pressures. As Renato Aguilar noted, Angola's economy is structured as an "oligopoly of oligopolies" within which competition is kept to a bare minimum.[61] A foreign consultant with fifteen years of experience in Angola even deemed it "ferociously uncompetitive", with whole sectors appropriated by elite networks.[62] My own interviews with Angolan businessmen consistently revealed a strong protectionist culture and reliance on state support, together with a desire to "divide up the market in ways that minimize friction" with other Angolan businessmen.[63]

One of the consequences of this absence of competition is that success is not performance-based. There is no hint of a carrot-and-stick approach by the state, with smart businessmen rewarded with additional opportunities while the slower and incompetent ones are sidelined. A few businessmen of the first generation did show such a lack of business acumen that in the fullness of time their star faded. But the Angolan political economy is best understood as a system of privileged access to spoils, with the identity of the beneficiaries defined through an exclusionary micro-logic, whether political, familial or identity-based. Conventionally defined competence to make money or create value is often irrelevant to the choices made at the top level.

A former worker at the national airline TAAG, for instance, mysteriously materialized as the CEO of Ridge Solutions, an Angolan investment consortium with interests in "Dubai, Abu Dhabi, Hong Kong, Beijing, Luxembourg and Lisbon" and sponsor of the Williams Formula 1 team. His unctuous profile in an Angolan business magazine could not avoid noting that "one knows very little about Ridge Solutions [and] even less about its founder José Ferreira Ramos, who is 46 years old and holds 90 per cent of the capital [in the group]". Ferreira Ramos claimed that Ridge Solutions had assets worth US$15 billion and had seen a 6,000 per cent growth in only three years. According to *Exame* magazine, he is the proud owner "of a collection of luxury watches worth millions of dollars, two yachts, a plane, a personal jet [sic], and a valuable collection of cars where two Rolls Royce have pride of place; [he is also] an avid art collector".[64] A perhaps envious fellow businessman commented: "No one knew him before! He even said in some magazine that he was worth [several] billions! How did he get this money? I think he convinced someone that he was a good investment and so was supported by him."[65]

This is something one would not discern from the relentless official extolling of the Angolan entrepreneur. In important ways, this is an elaborate hoax hiding the realities of rentierism, which instead presents the new business class as "champions of production".[66] This discourse, however disingenuous, needs to be taken seriously if only because it has a degree of traction across Angolan society. For the past decade, almost any public discussion of the Angolan private sector has been steeped in the language of entrepreneurship, and no announcement of government policy is complete without a guarantee that "Angolan firms" are being nurtured. In the self-presentation of Angolan *empresários*, too, demeanour and dress code are increasingly "business-like". Since Angola became the land of the fee-paying, one-week "executive seminar" by "foreign experts", businessmen's talk is peppered with MBA-speak, if often used in inappropriate or superficial manners.

The discourse of entrepreneurship hides the rentier roots of Angolan business and the fact that, in postwar Angola, all business is directly or indirectly with the state. The drumming up of the Angolan entrepreneur also camouflages the absolute dependence on foreign partnerships at almost every level, for Angolan businesses, despite improvements from the days of the *empresários de confiança* in the 1990s, remain inexperienced and inefficient. "There is a genuine lack of capacity amongst Angolan businessmen," a local journalist with deep knowledge of the private sector admits.[67] The most common anecdotes in this regard are those of security-sector toughs who resort to foreign managers to run their interests. But this applies to all levels of Angolan private sector activity. An Angolan notable suddenly given a hotel license will need to go to Portugal and find someone to run it; another with an export license will need a Lebanese wholesaler to conduct the business. Isabel dos Santos will also need Portuguese executives for the heavy lifting at UNITEL, and TV Zimbo must resort to foreign professionals to ensure it is run properly. In a dynamic reminiscent of Nigeria's Mr. 40 per cent-ers in the 1970s, Angolans rarely if ever play an active role in the management of joint ventures with foreign partners. Angolan businessmen prefer to conduct themselves as owners rather than managers and collect their share of dividends without much involvement beyond the cash side of things (in this regard it is not uncommon for Angolan partners to nominate a trustworthy individual, often a family member, to survey revenue generation and keep the foreign partners under control; this measure does not prevent the constant estrangements).

Foreign partners are not unhappy with this arrangement. "The smart Angolans are the ones that don't mess with the business too much; the meddling ones normally ruin things," noted a well-seasoned Portuguese entrepreneur with multiple partnerships with Luanda's finest.[68] Reading the World Bank's *Cost of Doing Business* annual survey, which regularly places Angola near the bottom of world rankings (172th out of 183 in 2012), one would think it an impenetrable, hostile territory for foreign firms.[69] In practice, foreigners have imbibed the Angolan way of business and accept partnerships with the well connected as a prerequisite for operating in the country. Far from being set upon by greedy Angolans, foreign companies engage in active courtship of would-be partners, with access to the presidential palace or JES's family the ultimate prize.

But the World Bank is not entirely wrong. The volatility of the Angolan market often comes back to haunt investors who, having accepted the nature of the game, then go on to rise and fall by its logic. Major non-Angolan investors (such as the oil companies) are protected by arbitrage clauses in foreign courts and partnerships with them are durable and responsibly cultivated by the Angolan side. At the intermediate and lower levels, however, there is a great degree of turbulence, with Angolan partners, especially generals, routinely reneging on payments, going cold on foreign associates, and having them expelled from the country. A number of foreign businessmen have been killed in recent years,[70] and the top legal offices in Luanda are, according to a prominent lawyer, "stuffed with cases of business disputes between Angolans and foreigners".[71]

Volatile their partnerships may be, but Angolan businessmen cannot do away with foreigners. The reasons for this consistent resort to expatriates can be gauged by looking at how Angolan companies are run. Most, including a number of relatively well-known ones, have no bookkeeping, are not audited, and have no board of directors. In all but a few, the owner, his family and associates are likely to use the company's coffers as a personal piggy bank. The Angolan owner and manager of a well-run firm noted: "most companies here are undermined by the owners, who confuse revenue with profit and do not recognize the difference between the business and the businessman".[72] Indeed, the degree of personalization is such that business groups are threatened with implosion when the owner dies.[73] A restricted number amongst the top business groups have made significant strides in corporate governance (in terms of internal organization rather than external transparency) but they are the exception to a near-universal chaotic approach.

Nothing illustrates this better than the fact that the typical Angolan business group is wildly diversified.[74] This is of course true of the multinational business concerns of Isabel dos Santos, General Kopelipa, Manuel Vicente and the other oligarchs, but the very scale of their interests provides some explanation for the extraordinary geographical and sectoral spread. A similar degree of diversification characterizes business groups not quite in the same league, and it is not unusual for media profiles to list countless and shifting areas of involvement. The Veleiro Group started in the ice-cream business, then moved into diamonds, oil services, real estate and restaurant management.[75] The Wapossoka Group is involved in soft drinks, real estate, the selling of motorcycles and ready to wear, hotel management, agriculture, construction, and diamonds.[76] Ridge Solutions claims to have investments in finance, real estate, industry, agriculture and infrastructure.[77] The reason for this spread is that Angolan business groups simply do not specialize. Their opportunities are a product of political access, not sectoral competence. And there is never a hint that some sectors may stretch the group's capacity (which is often dependent on external expertise anyway), for access to new opportunities can always be matched by the hiring of additional expertise. Perhaps the spread of interests is suggestive of a healthy opportunism in taking advantage of whatever comes up, but this is to the detriment of any strategic sense of corporate consolidation.

This is partly because, even a decade after the end of the war, Angolan businessmen are working on a remarkably short time horizon and reveal a preference for import deals, whose turnover is measured in months or, at most, the building of real estate, which is a matter of perhaps two years. Everything else seems to exist on an abstract level. Angolan investors rarely get interested in longer-term undertakings, even if investments requiring a longer timeline also hold the promise of major returns. The examples of this are legion. A foreign consultant told of painstaking months spent putting together a consortium of mostly Middle Eastern investors in a major agribusiness concern, only to have the Angolan partners of the deal pull out at the last minute: the deal was "too complicated, too long-term, and too much upfront investment. This went against their approach of making a quick buck."[78] An Angolan detergent factory owner, when asked about the short time horizons of his counterparts, spoke of an "Angolan philosophy" that consists of businessmen "getting their profit very fast".[79]

This short-termism goes beyond lack of experience or the legacy of the war. As an Angolan banker admitted, "to make things worse, this economy really lends itself to easy, short-term profit."[80] "This is a country that imports absolutely everything, even food: if you just stay on the import economy you will be fine."[81] As interviewees repeated time and again, the whole incentive structure of the Angolan economy rewards arbitrage and wheeler-dealing. Correspondingly, "you really need to be very enlightened to put your money into stuff that will only be realized in a decade,"[82] which includes capital intensive investments in productive sectors such as commercial agriculture and industry.

So, in contravention of the official discourse, these are precisely the sectors no sensible Angolan businessman wants to put his money into. In fact the local business sector is almost defined by its reluctance to engage in productive enterprise, even though every major group's portfolio contains a cursory reference to, say, agribusiness. But with only a few exceptions, the land is either fallow, waiting to be used for "tourism", or part of its owner's weekend estate. Some groups are involved in agricultural concerns, especially in Malange and Kwanza Sul provinces, and have signed up to some form of industrial activity, say, in the industrial park of Lubango or other such state-sponsored efforts. These are often ploys to capture state subsidies or concessional credit for agricultural and industrial development, and they certainly do not constitute the priority for Angolan business groups whose major profits come from import businesses and partnerships with foreign companies. Industry and agriculture remain sideshows to the main business of appropriating the oil rent.

The fact that the Angolan elite neglects large parts of the economy, especially the rural and the small-scale, does not mean that these dimensions are left to a sort of benign neglect. It is virtually impossible for meaningful economic activity to occur outside the charmed circle of the politically protected. Independent businessmen who owe nothing to state patronage are threatening, and those in power labour to undermine them. This is visible in the travails of small and medium enterprises (SMEs).[83] In a series of interviews with owners of SMEs active in the formal economy in Benguela and Huambo provinces, Manuel Ennes Ferreira and I were presented with a consistent picture of harassment, with striving entrepreneurs confronted with protection rackets run by politicians and security forces and often hounded out of business when unwilling or unable to involve the "big guys" in their pursuits.[84] Of course, few of these entrepreneurs are prototypical outsiders. Succeeding in this society means imbibing the rules of the game, and the price for a de facto license to operate is a partnership with, or a share of profits for, a "rainmaker".[85] Business goes on because most entrepreneurs are pragmatic enough to accept the terms. It is noteworthy that those who must be indulged by SME entrepreneurs at the local level are often also regional or national-level notables—often the same people who are non-negotiable partners in joint ventures with foreign entrepreneurs.

There is nothing uniquely Angolan about a commitment towards nurturing a national business class, and most postcolonial governments have rightly pursued these policies, some successfully so. The Angolan specificity, which it shares with other oil-producing states such as Venezuela and Nigeria, lies in the use of this language to favour constituencies that do not fit the description of an enterprising, innovative business class however defined. The actual beneficiaries of the postwar economy consistently shy away from productive sectors and the rural world and reveal little appetite for medium- and long-term strategic investment. These biases match to a large extent the governing mentality of the party-state discussed in the previous chapters, an unsurprising statement in view of the fact that they amount to the same narrow cast of characters.

LIFE OF THE OLIGARCHS

The story of Angola's nascent capitalism has its peculiarities yet shares many traits with other better-studied sub-Saharan African counterparts. Perhaps the most important is the near-total absence of what John Iliffe called an "ascetic tradition" that prizes saving above spending.[86] There are businessmen who "believe in thrift and discretion" but everything around them demands flash and relentless spending. "The diverting of [...] profits to feed social networks, families, women's consumer habits: that's the biggest problem," complained an oil services executive.[87] The most persistent pressure group is the family itself, broadly defined.[88] In interviews with Angolan businessmen, the constant demands of their families were described as a "stressful" and "debilitating" factor. According to a retired politician, "this craving for money, luxury and status" is a big part of "the pressures that my [elite] friends have".[89]

One of the consequences of this is the spawning of a generation of "spoiled children".[90] A relatively high number of Angola's rich have progeny that one of them described as the "kuduro generation" and "good-for-nothings".[91] The children of FAA generals in particular are infamous for an international life of debauchery and consumerism, fast cars and, on one occasion, the acquisition of a personal jet. "They are unacceptable in polite society," noted a foreign diplomat who socializes in elite circles.[92] Like everyone in the elite, the generals spared their children the brutal experience of wartime service in the armed forces, which means that they did not "develop the swagger and violent charisma of their fathers"; but neither were they "educated for business or intellectually".[93] Spoiled children and greedy relatives are genuine concerns yet beside the point. Many Angolan businessmen would like to release themselves from the weight of social networks but also enjoy the "sumptuous lifestyle [of a big man]: parties, cars, the adding of mistresses etc.".[94] Most of all, they share with their dependents the assumption that visible expenditure is key to maintaining their status in society.

For the life of the Angolan oligarch is almost unbelievably excessive in its ostentatious consumption. Pepetela captured this vulgarity in his mordant fictional portrait of a ruthless oligarch, Vladimiro Caposso.[95] A few days in Luanda and the visitor will have seen luxury cars, mansions, fashion shows, private jets, yachts, designer clothes and expensive watches reminiscent of Miami or Rio de Janeiro. Giant billboards advertise the arrival of the new Aston Martin, and invite customers for a test drive.[96] The increasingly raunchy TPA2 lifestyle programmes broadcast the libations of customers at the pricy nightclubs of the Ilha de Luanda. Befitting the elite's internationalized life, the pages of the Angolan press are replete with fawning descriptions of their global exploits and manifold acquisitions. References to Formula 1 sponsorship, the buying up of Portuguese companies and prestige real estate in New York and London and investment in far-off locations are exhibited as proof of Angola's success.

A constant theme is the attempts of oligarchs to outdo each other. This competitive excess is particularly evident when it comes to rites of passage such as betrothals, baptisms, weddings and anniversaries. Events like the 2002 and 2003 weddings of Isabel dos Santos and Tchizé dos Santos, both of which allegedly cost millions of dollars and had guests and food flown in on private jets from all over the world, may be in a class of their own, but they set the tone.[97] No self-respecting member of the elite can afford to host a disappointingly tame event, and price tags of US$500,000 to US$1 million, including the hiring of famous entertainers, are now common. Recent antics have gone as far as include Rolex watches offered to VIP guests.[98] The same applies to elite deportment abroad. Bento Kangamba and his retainers' noisy meals at Pinóquio, a Lisbon seafood restaurant beloved of the Angolan wealthy, always conclude with 500-euro tips; Isabel dos Santos and her husband, while low-key, are also "extremely generous tippers".[99] Reports of the First Lady's largesse towards those rendering her small services in luxury European hotels are often quoted approvingly: "But that is the way it should be—Angola abroad should put money on the table, to show who's the boss!"[100] Often resentful of foreign assumptions that their fortunes are somehow tainted, the Angolan rich want "to make it clear that they are not poor Africans."[101]

An interesting prism through which to consider their mentality is that shameless outlet for elite exhibitionism, *Caras Angola*. The country's *Hello Magazine*, this glossy weekly is modelled on its Portuguese sister publication, mostly produced by Portuguese media professionals since its creation in 2005, and run by the president's socialite daughter Tchizé dos Santos. A handful of more refined oligarchs steer clear from *Caras*, but it is nonetheless representative of the reigning ethos. Angolan socialites seamlessly share its pages with the likes of Albert of Monaco, the Duchess of Cambridge, Cameron Diaz and Justin Timberlake in a hopeful affirmation of their global jet-set status. Its mix of weddings, fashion shows, visible cosmetic surgery, global brands and easy lives in gleaming villas with servants and manicured lawns is tasteless, if in perfect line with its global counterparts. Yet the magazine's sales are healthy, and copies circulate informally to a wide readership;[102] its behavioural codes are influential.

Recognizing the vulgarity of oligarchic behavior, an Angolan intellectual nonetheless argued, "this is on account of the newness of it all; like [people] everywhere, in a few years at least some of them will have sobered up and will be conducting themselves differently."[103] This is an accurate assessment. Even at the time of writing, some amongst Angola's wealthy are endeavouring to camouflage the origins of their money and build internationally acceptable personae that will not be out of place at Davos, Ascot or Miami Basel. José Eduardo Agualusa hilariously explored these status aspirations in a novel whose main character sells a respectable "past" to Angola's elite.[104] As elsewhere, art collecting and patronage is a major avenue in this regard. Sindika Dokolo, Isabel dos Santos' husband and reputedly Africa's leading collector of contemporary art, is the trendsetter but several oligarchs, and increasingly banks and parastatal companies, have become major art buyers. At the time of writing, philanthropy (the time-honoured manner of laundering one's reputation) plays a negligible role in this process of status enhancement.

It is in the oligarchs' aspirational behaviour rather than in actions towards others that the craving for some respectability is apparent. Recurrent, if tentative, traits include providing their children with a global elite upbringing, complete with a British or American education; being "discreet" and especially not showing up in the cover of *Caras Angola*; playing a much more active role in the management of their portfolios than some of the more aloof oligarchs; and diversifying their partnerships away from the usual Lusophone connections. Although much hypocrisy is involved here, criticism is increasingly levelled by successful oligarchs against those who do badly and go on noisily demanding state support as "Angolan entrepreneurs". The story of Riquinho, a music events organizer who by 2011 had accumulated tens of millions of dollars in debt but publicly called on the state to sort him out,[105] was invariably mentioned in pejorative terms. As an Angolan businessman put it, "look at this guy, thinking he is entitled to everything—this is an embarrassment, [it's so] 1990s".[106] This interviewee went on to defend the creation of a truly "normal, open, productive economy". Some observers even argue that the real progressive potential in Angola resides not in the feeble or coopted civil society and opposition, but in the smartest oligarchs who realize that it is time to end the Wild West atmosphere and move on to secure the legitimacy of their fortunes for the long haul.

No trajectory illustrates this yearning to transcend the origins of Angola's great fortunes better than that of Isabel dos Santos, the president's eldest daughter. The poster child of Angola's oligarchic decade, she is also, amongst its richest, the person whose lifestyle and aspirations clearly strive for global respectability. Listed by *Forbes* as one of Africa's richest women, Isabel has accumulated a worldwide business empire of remarkable spread and sophistication.[107] Her upbringing was atypical for her generation (she was born in 1973): the Cold War not yet over, she was sent off to Britain's elite St Paul's School for Girls and graduated in engineering from King's College London. She returned to Angola in the late 1990s to manage a private company tasked with Luanda's waste management as well as Miami Beach, one of the capital's top restaurants and nightclubs. By the early 2000s Isabel, by now sarcastically dubbed "the Princess" by Angolan wits, had emerged as a major player with enormous stakes in diamonds and telecommunications, and her interests have grown exponentially ever since.

Despite her billionaire status, Isabel long kept an extremely low profile. She was so difficult to pin down that, for years, media coverage of her businesses could only resort to a photograph where she looked about eighteen years of age. I phoned her to request an interview in October 2011; she was polite but did not agree to it. Except for her expensive wedding, Isabel has over the years provided few examples of objectionable oligarchic behaviour. Flattering information did transpire: that she was intelligent, respected by her international partners, and well networked in the world of art collecting.[108] But by 2012, sceptical or outright hostile coverage of Isabel, for years a staple of the critical segments of the Portuguese press,[109] started to emerge in the Anglo-American media as well,[110] all the while noting her good looks, poise and business acumen.[111] According to two people close to the president's family, Isabel had "become too big and needed to manage her image", "if you are silent, other people tell your story for you".[112] In the period since, Isabel became less publicity-shy, dining at Scotts in London for a *Lunch with the FT* interview,[113] going to *Hora Quente*, the Angolan equivalent of David Letterman's *Late Show*, to speak about her father, and even attending "Africa Rising"-type events across the continent as an experienced African businesswoman. When asked by the *Financial Times* about her emergence as a paragon of African capitalism, dos Santos replied, "I see what you mean but, like I said, I don't do politics. I do business and I'm not a politician. I've had business sense since I was very young. I sold chicken eggs when I was six."[114]

The search for respectability on the part of Isabel and other super-rich Angolans remains a hit-or-miss affair. Whatever some of the oligarchs' misgivings about the current system—one that, to a man, or woman, spawned them—it is so profitable that all of them remain deeply implicated in it. The rich certainly show no signs of shying away from the methods that characterize the real Angolan economy. Easy credit, foreign partnerships that deliver guaranteed profit at no risk, aloofness from the rule of law: these perks are not voluntarily rescinded. Authoritative knowledge of the Angola economy is difficult to arrive at and excessive speculation has invited lawsuits from the oligarchs.[115] However, a series of international investigations of the country's top bank, BAI, the partnership with Chinese interests, CIF, the dealings of Goldman Sachs-linked oil firm Cobalt, and assorted money laundering in Portugal all point to the deployment of growing sophistication—but in the direction of the usual ends.[116] In an exceedingly frank interview, the Angolan economist Manuel Alves da Rocha pointed out the reason for the strong *esprit de corps* of the Angolan elite regardless of misgivings or a desire to move on:

> Because if ever someone is denounced and brought to trial for being unable to justify how he acquired his wealth, that individual, if he wants to talk, will take everyone [else] to court and to prison. Because the MPLA created a web, bonds between politicians [on account of which] no one will talk about the other[s]. Because if one of them talks, they are all gone. Because the relationships are umbilical.[117]

This "system of general compromising", in Christine Messiant's words, leaves few in a position to dissent from the rules of the game.[118]

Optimistic assessments of this phenomenon tend to hinge on a generational shift towards a "more international" oligarchic offspring. Thousands of elite children were taken out of the country in the 1990s, often to Lisbon, in order to have better schooling and, in the case of males, escape military service. Although Luanda now has a handful of excellent schools such as the Escola Francesa, Escola Portuguesa and Escola Internacional, where fees can reach US$47,000 a year, the trajectories of privileged young Angolans are as worldly as ever (above a certain social standing, for instance, no one would countenance an Angolan university education for their children). But their behaviour is indeterminate, to say the least. Many foreign-trained Angolans from powerful families are seething at the system and venting their anger on Club-K, the leading Angolan Internet news and opinion forum, or Facebook.[119] A small number are even among the organizers of the anti-MPLA demonstrations that started in 2011. But far more are returning home to cash in on their connections. There is certainly no linear relationship between their increasingly cosmopolitan lives, on the one hand, and the pursuit of progressive agendas inside Angola, on the other. Where Angola's "agents of change" will arise is unclear, but the privileged few do not seem to make for obvious candidates.

ANGOLAN SOCIETY AND THE NEW CAPITALISM

At the heart of Angolan public life there is a brute fact: most people in power are perceived as thieves, in the literal sense of the word, having appropriated their fortunes from the siphoning off of oil monies or the use of public office for private gain. Others who have stolen nothing have received, in an utterly legal manner, privatized assets, foreign currency or reward money that they should never have been allowed to access. As in other post-socialist economies, there is no obfuscation here, no pre-existing family inheritance that could partly account for one's wealth. Referring to a series of MPLA barons, a self-described "critical party member" noted succinctly: "twenty years ago no one had anything; now they are all millionaires; it doesn't take much to realize where it all came from".[120] The knowledge that "people at the top are crooks"[121] takes over everything. It gives the rituals and rhetoric of the state—of opportunity, entrepreneurship, innovation, and state support for the hardworking and deserving amongst the citizenry—its publicly affirmed intentions, the media coverage of its initiatives, a markedly surreal character. No one believes anything. Things are exactly the contrary of what they claim to be.

The cynicism on the part of the population vis-à-vis their leaders, however, is more ambivalent than meets the eye. Elite behaviour is lambasted but not simply rejected; a complex reaction mixes criticism with envy, admiration and desire; and there is much emulation. For one cannot begin to understand the societal impact of Angola's oil-fuelled capitalism if one insists on framing it as a morality tale of evil elites and suffering masses. In fact the ethos of easy oil money and its separation of wealth from productive endeavour has come to suffuse Angolan society.[122] This is not a new phenomenon, nor is it particular to Angola. Juan Pablo Pérez Alonso, the founder of OPEC, had early recognized that oil had an impact not just on the state and the economy but also on "the psychology and motivations of the people".[123] In Angola's unsettled, morally uncertain postwar atmosphere, the oligarchs' oil-fuelled behaviour, lifestyle and worldview are highly influential. Angolans may want to do away with the oligarchs, but they also want to become them.

And there is no shortage of elite imagery to go by. Until the end of the war the rich led relatively confined lives and did much of their spending abroad; unless they lived in central Luanda, most Angolans would have known little about the lifestyle of their social betters. In the intervening years, elite visibility increased to such an extent that Luanda became more akin to Caracas and Rio de Janeiro than to other African capitals in its juxtaposition of extremes of poverty and wealth. The familiarity of average Angolans with the lifestyle of the elite increased quickly, not only on the basis of first-hand experience but also because of the display of money relentlessly propagated through the media. A decade ago TV was still reminiscent of the socialist years, but it is now saturated with slick programming. Some of the most popular shows include soap operas and lifestyle shows that unhesitatingly expose the lives of the rich.

The same applies to commercial advertising and its use of alluring imagery of conspicuous consumption. Luanda and the major cities are now covered in billboards peddling anything from soft drinks and banking to mobile phones and cars. Some of this is out of reach for most people but much of it is aimed at the no longer negligible minority of Angolans with disposable incomes and consumer cravings. It is not the product itself but the packaging that is so at odds with the Angolan reality. Mostly produced by Brazilian and Portuguese professionals, these sophisticated advertisements star self-confident, upper class Angolans conversing in flawless Portuguese, either living in luxury surroundings or hanging out (but never actually working) in generic modern offices. Alternatively, they are seen partying in expensive nightspots. *Mestiços* are overrepresented. Advertising always flogs idealized imagery different from actual lives, but the disparity in the Angolan case is quite extreme. And it works: these signifiers of wealth and status are what Angolans have come to crave.

The social and cultural influence of the rich is particularly evident in the outlook of the nascent bourgeoisie of Luanda and the major towns. As discussed in Chapter 2, this state-dependent group is not quite a middle class in terms of education or outlook, but has nonetheless quickly acquired the material culture, lifestyle and status expectations of a global middle class. It includes many individuals who are dissatisfied with the status quo. But as a group, it is not currently an agent of change. Indeed, this middle class, nested as it is in the expanding state apparatus and the state-supported private sector, partakes of the elite's rentier assumptions about the role of the state and the political economy and benefits from the status quo, albeit less than the upper crust. For all the talk of indus-trialization, agribusiness and entrepreneurship, the middle class also has its eyes on accessing its portion of the national wealth to the detriment of any productive conception of the economy. Furthermore, it has a strong sense of entitlement to the national cake, often phrased in nation-alistic terms, and firmly believes in its own intrinsic (that is, on the basis of Angolan citizenship, not merit) access to opportunities for social mobility and capital accumulation. This mindset is present in many areas, but tensions with expatriate workers, relations with the poor, and the middle class's conceptions of the state are particularly revealing.

One of the emerging fault lines of Angolan society alluded to in Chapter 2 is that between locally trained university graduates and expa-triate workers. As late as 2006, Angola had an estimated 28,000 people with university degrees;[124] by 2008, it had 50,000 students in higher education; by 2012, the figure had reached 150,000.[125] As an Angolan journalist tersely stated: "people see university in terms of social ascen-sion and not in terms of knowledge or skills acquisition".[126] Making it to university in a land of illiteracy gives one the sense of having climbed a social Olympus. A higher education certificate brings with it a sense of entitlement to managerial positions, high remuneration (allowing for house and car ownership, travels abroad, etc.) and social deference. These rewards are disconnected from the fact that the Angolan individual in question may be unable to fulfil the technical functions of the position. The individual, while perhaps resenting it, will himself accept that the heavy-lifting be done by a shadow foreign worker, as long as he is deferred to and given the aforementioned markers of status.

The "national" argument used for carving out an economic dividend for the bourgeoisie stops at the latter's boundaries, for it rejects this national rights-based argument when it comes to the poor majority. Middle-class relations with the poor illustrate the accelerated character of Angolan class formation. People who were barely distinguishable from the poor only a generation ago support draconian police measures against the latter and hold to images that emphasize their otherness and latent criminality. But nowhere is the middle class convergence with elite perceptions more obvious than in the widespread discourse about the "capacity" and competence of the Angolan state apparatus, and the avoidance of questions about its lack of service delivery to the poor. The contradiction between the state's claims and capacities discussed in Chapter 2 does not interest the middle class: the state is already delivering for them, and any admission of its incompetence is inherently critical of those who staff it, that is, themselves.

This Angolan middle class also seeks to model itself on the elite in terms of deportment and social conduct. In this regard, the elite's approach to major rituals such as weddings, baptisms, anniversaries and funerals is trendsetting. These moments are important in Angolan society and require the mobilization of extensive resources. The elite's ostentatious and competitive expenditure over the past two decades has increased expectations across society as to what these events amount to, and driven many into debt in order to hold them. In some cases this has resulted in the "dollarization" of traditions such as the *alembamento* (betrothal ceremony), which only a generation ago was a lower profile and more affordable affair.[127] Today, it is a major event in the Angolan social calendar whose details are charted by the media for the benefit of the upwardly mobile. Covering the *alembamento* of the president's niece with Bento Kangamba, the quintessential social climber of the postwar era already encountered in Chapter 3, *Bessangana* magazine noted the groom's handing of a cash-filled envelope to the father of the bride, "in obedience of the rituals of his homeland".[128]

But the social influence of elite behaviour does not stop with the middle classes and ripples down the social ladder; the new capitalism seems to both "magnify class differences [and] undercut class consciousness".[129] It is particularly influential with urban youth, who identify in elite overnight enrichment the trajectory for which they yearn: the sexual success of the rich, especially with *mestiço* women, their material possessions, "their never having to work" and the power "to have anyone arrested" (the ultimate, all-too-real signifier of one's standing in Angolan society). Nowhere is this Angola of the hyper-rich more relentlessly put across than in the programming of TPA 2, a public channel subcontracted to two of JES's children, Tchizé and Coreon Du. Speak to older Angolans on this subject and most will have excoriating views of the vulgarity of shows like Flash or Tchilar, the major outlet for kuduro stars.

The contents of these shows were described by a disapproving journalist as "wild nights, parties, women, showing off of bodies, brands, money spending: this is what young people are taught to aim for".[130]

Some have argued that, at least at the lowest levels of society, mimicry is not a matter of uncomplicated imitation. They underline instead its role as "cultural resistance", "parody" of the rich or even "inventive appropriation".[131] There are of course elements of that but in the Angolan context one must emphasize the non-ironic desire of accessing the material and symbolic markers of modern success that the masses share with the elites, of "being like, of becoming, those they imitate".[132] In this regard, James Ferguson draws attention to the African craving for membership of the "first class world".[133] In Angola, that first class world is to be found not in faraway Europe, but on relentless TV imagery, Talatona condominiums, Ilha de Luanda and Mussulo pleasure enclaves, and the extravagant displays of elite wealth in Luanda itself. Angolans aspire to the modern things that the elite already possesses and consumes in full view: a "Lord's life, soap-opera style", as a popular rap song facetiously put it.[134] However, they are as unobtainable for the majority as Ferguson's remote imagery of developed world success.

By emphasizing the emulative dimension I do not seek to obscure the element of revulsion towards the oligarchs that recurs across Angolan society. There are people who simply reject the moral economy of the new capitalism, often by invoking religious beliefs.[135] Foreign media have paid particular attention to the phenomenon of anti-government rappers, whose lyrics at best encapsulate the system's ills.[136] But for every socially conscious rapper there is a *kuduro* star celebrating booze and ostentatious consumption. Some critics of the MPLA are keen on interpreting every protest as a plea for transformative politics. This is certainly the case of the young demonstrators whose fearless stance since 2011 was discussed in Chapter 3. But other forms of protest are best seen as attempts by specific groups to push for inclusion in the established order, not a root-and-branch attack against it, a point I will return to in the Conclusion. Of course, many political movements start with such concrete grievances only to change their character into a systemic attack. But for the past decade the system of spoils was mainly accepted even as it was contested piecemeal. 2012 examples of such group-focused protest included demonstrations by former veterans left out of the FAA pension fund and strikes by civil servants in Benguela province and Angola's public radio. Keen on preventing disruptions on the eve of elections, the government wisely caved in to their demands.

The broader point here is that elite values may be warped but they are linked to the culture of the masses in more ways than one cares to admit. In turn, the culture of the masses is in many ways compatible with the heightened form of rentierism underlying the new Angolan capitalism. There is a collective inebriation with the notion of an Angolan El Dorado, an oil-fuelled nationalism that takes pride in visible disbursements of money. The culture of the civil service is not merit-based. There is widespread loathing of the rule of law, which is seen as either an alien colonial construct or a tool of elite power, and the resort to illegal means is an everyday occurance across society.[137] Extraordinary stories of individual, unexplained triumph everywhere fascinate even as they appall: success in Angola is generally perceived as a product of luck, the intervention of the occult, or personal connections; it is not seen as based on effort.[138] Patron-client relations of some sort, especially within the extended family, are the rule rather than the exception, and they result in strong, widespread expectations. The rich don't have an imagined community that extends beyond narrowly defined, known members, but neither does the majority of Angolans.[139] There are many Angolans who subscribe to not a single one of these social mores, but they are in a minority.

The danger with this line of argument is that one ends up over-contextualizing elite behaviour. Several Angolan observers relate elite lifestyles at least partly with the pre-existing hedonistic culture of Luanda, of constant partying, sensual women and the good life, and say that this is essential for understanding how the oligarchs played out.[140] In this view, Luandan society already had its permissive structures, its "this-worldly" ethos,[141] and the oligarchs merely behaved according to social expectations. This is an argument that deserves some consideration. Yet the scale of what happened in the last twenty years defies any precedents. Instead of blaming "Angolan culture", we must emphasize the consequential decisions taken in the recent past by a relatively small number of people. These decisions amounted to a "delinquent revolution".[142] There was a time lag between the setting in of the oligarchic free-for-all in the early 1990s and the adoption of similar behaviour by the majority of Angolans. But eventually the logic of the Kimbundu proverb quoted at the beginning of this chapter—"either there is morality or everyone gets to eat"—kicked in.

For the oligarchic mindset of the new capitalism has gone viral.[143] Everything that had once been solid melted into air and now there is only a supercharged sense of flux and moral uncertainty; rules are renegotiated daily; often they are simply abandoned. Corruption has penetrated every recess of public life, to the extent that there is no major aspect of an Angolan's everyday needs—education, health, security, the acquisition of documents, any dealing with officialdom—that is not subjected to steep *gasosa* payments.[144] Nor are these merely symbolic; they constitute a significant percentage of the income of urban Angolans. Top officials orchestrate many of these acts of extortion and actively implicate subordinates in them. The much-resented, thuggish behaviour of Angolan police is exemplary in this regard. According to a Luanda traffic policeman, a significant percentage of the fines that he and fellow officers aggressively collect are passed on to the leadership. But petty corruption cannot be ascribed to senior officials alone: junior officials also "freelance", squeezing the public while lying to their superiors. "The bosses get a bigger share of course, but we do our best to keep more than they would have liked us to keep."[145] A recent survey starkly captured the centrality of the police in the economic life of Luanda: the profits of small entrepreneurs were 26–30 per cent higher when they "knew" (that is, were under the protection of) a local policeman.[146]

The logic of the *gasosa* is ubiquitous in Angolan society. Every day, tens of thousands of Angolans charge bribes for providing other Angolans with access to needed services. In the health sector, for instance, the charging of hidden fees is expected at all levels: to see the doctor or the nurse, to get a prescription, to get the medicine, to get a hospital bed, to get proper anaesthetics.[147] A shocking but by no means isolated case surfaced at Américo Boavida hospital, one of Luanda's busiest. The morgue officials were doing a brisk business by charging bereaved families a fee for refrigerating the corpses of their loved ones: no fee, and the Luanda climate would wreak havoc very quickly.[148] There are people who do not participate in these rackets—to her credit, it was the director of the Boavida Hospital who denounced the morgue affair—but peer pressure is towards compliance. In some hospitals, "other doctors look at you askance if you're known to be 'honest'".[149]

Education is another dimension of Angolan life where venal behaviour is widespread. "Free" textbooks are found on the black market, where students' parents need to buy them at high cost. From primary school to university, grades, exams and diplomas can be had for a price. At all but a handful of universities striving for higher standards, academics will charge for "extra-tutoring" on the subject of their own courses and sell exams and end of degree "theses" to students.[150] The buying of full degrees without ever attending university has also been widely reported. The situation is scandalous to the extent that the government itself, normally keen on putting a positive gloss on public service provision, has taken to running public campaigns to shame professionals into discontinuing widespread practices such as the exchange of grades for sexual favours and the more overt forms of abuse. The situation of the education sector is doubtless reprehensible but it highlights an important aspect of the moral economy of corruption in Angola. Students and their families do not like being squeezed for cash, but they share an understanding of the educational certificate as a lever for social mobility and not a tool for knowledge or skills acquisition.[151] In some circumstances the assumption that exams "are not for real" is so widespread that students themselves approach teachers to buy them off.[152] Similar examples could be provided for virtually every domain of Angolan public life.

In sum, after twenty years of unbridled capitalism, the oligarchs' status at the summit of society—the people others envy but also look up to and imitate—is a fact, as is the Angola they built. Yet the paradox underlying this rentier mentality and political culture is the enduring reality of exclusion of the majority from the benefits of the system. Beyond the confined circles of the elite and the fledgling national bourgeoisie, there is very little distribution going on in Angola. Most Angolans belong to "networks of survival" rather than "networks of accumulation"[153] and are drastically denied access to even oblique benefits from the country's wealth. This results in a gaping credibility deficit for the current oligarchic dispensation, which has changed Angolan society but is failing to secure itself as the rightful order of things. The irony of the oligarchs' success is that this society has learned their lesson only too well. It understands the undeserved and opportunistic roots of their triumph to such an extent that it both wants to become them and confers upon the actual people at the top no legitimacy whatsoever. For years a collective optimism brought about by peace and the oil bonanza seemed to hold the promise of a better life for most. This sense of possibility is now ebbing, and Angolans are realizing that petro-prosperity is only for the few.

WHAT NEXT?

Amidst the darkest moments of Russia's "loans-for-shares" appropriation of the economy by the oligarchs, the leading reformer Anatoly Chubais, in a vacuous attempt at self-justification, expressed hopes that the 1990s robber barons would in time become responsible capitalists.[154] Their subsequent trajectory speaks to the Angolan case. Russia's oligarchs became more sophisticated and expanded their interests worldwide. But the toxic legacy of their takeover is a politicized Russian economy dependent on natural resources, intensely cartelized, and lacking the institutions to deliver broad-based prosperity. Angola's richest, too, are shedding their uncouthness and leaving Angolan shores to explore opportunities in the international economy. After their socialization in the Lusophone world and the Eastern Bloc, which for long gave Angolans little familiarity with the Anglo-Saxon idiom and mannerisms of globalization, the elite has spent the last decade converging with the material life and cultural signifiers of the global jet-setting class. This is a Russian lesson they have learned. But the elite's increased sophistication is having no effect on the predatory basis of its enrichment strategies, which remain tightly connected to the control of the Angolan state and the access it provides to resources and opportunities. They are a "political aristocracy"[155] with an unproductive understanding of their role in the economy that is the exact opposite of their entrepreneurial status in the regime's public discourse.

This assessment does not underplay the degree of change in Angola's political economy, the elite's learning curve or their agility in selectively adopting reforms. Angola's economy, with its growth in trade and services, new roads and airports, (mostly urban) Internet access and mobile phone coverage, consumer-oriented publicity and sleek media, banks and international payment systems, is now in a different league, even if the productive base remains oil-dependent. Many macro-economic reforms over the past decade have been real, if partial. They continued beyond the early reforms mentioned above, even after the 2009 economic slump. The MPLA accepted some IMF prescriptions and implemented those that do not threaten, and even enhance, the status quo.[156] The Central Bank beefed up its reserves to an extent (about US$34 billion in 2013) that provides the country with a significant cushion against price volatility. The president himself, after repeated warnings as to the evils of corruption, pushed for a 2010 Public Probity Law supposed to put a halt to enrichment by state officials.[157] The new Sovereign Wealth Fund discussed in Chapter 5 is, at least on paper, wedded to transparency and the improvement of social conditions. A stock market is in the offing, as is a new round of privatization of parastatals. By 2010, the credit rating agencies were placing Angola above Spain.[158] Under close scrutiny, however, these are revealed as attempts to upgrade the system rather than change it.

Despite these elite-controlled improvements and the rewards that have flowed from them, the current arrangements are "inherently unstable",[159] even if high oil prices and piecemeal reforms continue to pull them along. As we have seen, the reforms are based on implicit commitments by the president but these are not self-enforcing and may be reversed at any time. They cannot provide a viable alternative to the rule of law and the institutions of advanced capitalism, especially in critical sectors such as banking.[160] The elite knows as much—this is why it exports so much capital to foreign outposts of good government and secure property rights, and why it arguably trusts the Angolan economy less than some of its foreign investors. More important, implicit and personalized commitments provide no coverage for major political and economic shocks. Politically, the obvious critical juncture is JES's succession, which I deal with in the Conclusion. But a genuine challenge to the system would come from elsewhere: a durable collapse in the price of oil to shake the foundations of the oligarchs' stranglehold over the economy, and much else discussed in this book.

Angola's achievement of long-term, sustainable growth will demand ambitious political and institutional reforms that the elite currently does not countenance. Ignorance and lack of experience are not the reasons for this. I have interviewed scores of Angolan policy-makers (a number of whom are impressive) who know what good policy is and hold a vision for a rule-bound and diversified economy. Quite the contrary: the elite understands only too well that genuine reform would jeopardize its position by, in Acemoglu and Robinson's words, reallocating "political power from those that dominate today to new individuals and groups".[161] That position being an extremely privileged one, the elite prefers it as it is.

This is not necessarily a matter of their moral makeup. It is tempting to think of the Angolan elite in negative terms and see real reform as incompatible with them. But they are the elite that Angola has been dealt. Their relatively conventional aspirations are sourced from the lifestyle of the global 0.1 per cent and much of their behaviour is widespread amongst elites the world over. Be this at it may, Angola has no alternative, virtuous capitalists waiting in the wings to replace the oligarchs, diversify the economy, and invest in productive sectors. A better option might be to change incentive structures by closing down some avenues of unproductive enrichment, introducing binding constraints on the behaviour of the elite, and channelling its interests into productive enterprise instead. International rules that shut down the elite's discretionary power (such as vigorous anti-money laundering law enforcement, travel bans on the most egregious thieves) are useful but when dealing with an oil-rich state like Angola, they take a back seat to internal reform dynamics.[162] Angola's predicament is that not only is there as yet insufficient pressure for reform, but the people at the top who could enact this internal shift are the same oligarchs and elite families who risk losing from it. As John Githongo, Kenya's foremost anti-corruption activist, noted, "the [big] fish won't fry themselves".[163] In sum, there is movement of sorts, glimpses of an opening, but for now Angola's political economy remains a hostage to the elite's slow, evolving understanding of where their enlightened self-interest resides.

5

ANGOLA RISING

INTERNATIONAL STRATEGIES IN THE PEACE ERA

Angola's international power and influence have soared since 2002. It is now China's main trading partner in sub-Saharan Africa, the USA's second, a major regional power and an expanding international investor. The domestic consolidation of the regime and its oligarchy discussed in previous chapters was a prerequisite for this. But the favourable global realignments of the last ten years, including the emergence of new powers and the advent of expensive oil, have given Angolan elites leeway they had never possessed before.

This chapter focuses on Angola's international strategies in the decade of reconstruction, underlining the steep learning curve and sophistication of decision-makers as they managed the new possibilities. One of the outcomes was the diversification of international relations away from over-dependence on the West. Yet I argue that new partners such as China were perceived not as alternatives to the older rapports with Western states and corporations, but as leverage to recast and consolidate the latter in more favourable terms. The postwar era also saw the emergence of Angola's going-out strategy, the corollary of its foreign policy as well as the major peacetime innovation of the parallel state. In a move reminiscent of Qatar's and other Gulf states' policies, Angola deploys a self-styled state capitalism to simultaneously promote the internationalization of oil rent management and oligarchic interests through acquisitions and investments abroad. This is pursued through the state (mainly Sonangol and, more recently, the Sovereign Wealth Fund) and secretive public-private consortia alike. Unsurprisingly, this strategy contains a strong political component, with investment pouring into locations, such as Portugal, where influence can be had.

Angola has for centuries been firmly, if asymmetrically, integrated in the international system, with powerful local actors using their access to the outside as "a major resource in the process of political centralization and economic accumulation".[1] Furthermore, as Chapter 1 showed, the MPLA state owed its very survival to foreign geopolitical patrons and oil companies. What distinguishes the postwar era is a degree of Angolan traction that goes well beyond the usual patterns of extraversion. Angolan decision-makers not only engage with the outside on their own terms, with the character and preferences of the regime shaping the behaviour of foreign partners. They also re-export the power and wealth of the state to advance an imbrication of official and private agendas, with elite and state interests seen as coterminous and the rewards privatized in favour of the few. From the vantage point of 2014, the Angolan strategy seems effective. The MPLA is no longer fighting for survival or managing scarcity, indebtedness and insecurity; it has greatly limited the once widespread reputational attacks on the regime; and in some exalted corners, there is even talk of Angola as "an emerging power". However, and although oil-addled Angolan politicians seem not to understand it, this relative success is precarious.

AN ENABLING INTERNATIONAL ENVIRONMENT

While the rise of Angola has its own internal momentum, it is inseparable from global dynamics that have, over the past decade, cumulatively resulted in an extremely positive atmosphere for the country. The most symbolic of these has been the renewed geopolitical and commercial interest in Africa. Starting in the late 1970s, Africa suffered a calamitous drop in GDP and significance for the outside world, barely amounting to 1 per cent of global trade by the turn of the century.[2] On account of their indebted status, "weak, poor and subordinate" African states were subjected to often-punitive structural adjustment programmes.[3] Arguing that globalization was passing the "hopeless continent" by, some observers even deemed it a "black hole".[4] Westerners who held a virtual monopoly on what was good for African development spoke of the continent as in need of compassion and, implicitly, incapable of self-redemption.

Yet in the past decade, and without apparent irony, this negative view has been replaced by an often-unrestrained portrait of Africa as the land of boundless opportunity, with consultants and investment bankers penning high-profile publications with titles such as Renaissance Capital's *The Fastest Billion* and McKinsey's *Lions on the Move*.[5] Still, behind this hyperbole there is an undeniable trend whereby countries and parts of countries on the continent long ignored by outsiders have come to look attractive for some types of trade and investment. In the years after the 2008 financial crisis, the diminishing investment returns in stagnant Western economies further stimulated interest in African economies.

A pivotal dimension of this increased interest was the rise in commodity prices. After close to three decades of historically low prices for most of the mineral and agricultural commodities Africa produces, the early 2000s saw, as a consequence of Asian growth and industrialization, a return to higher prices with immediate fiscal benefits for African states. The positive turn in African economies is related to additional factors such as improvements in macro-economic management and debt relief. Resource-poor states also grew steadily. But commodity prices remain the most important continent-wide contributor, and most high-growth countries are also major primary commodity exporters. The price of oil is a particular example of this, having jumped from US$10 in 1999 to US$147 in 2008. This has led to a veritable scramble by investors for acreage, including frontier countries and oil deposits that are technically difficult and costly to access.[6] International interest in Angola's oil endowment is such that it predated the boom years and had been considerable even during the industry's 1998–99 global slump. But the high prices over the past decade unleashed a further degree of external interest, including by new investors from emerging economies.

The increased profile of these new investors was part and parcel of partnerships with rising non-Western states that flocked to the continent bearing none of the baggage or pessimistic assumptions held by Westerners.[7] The interests and investment profile of the emerging powers in Africa are not dissimilar from those of traditional Western investors: all share a strong emphasis on business interests, and the extractive industries in particular. But this pragmatic commercial engagement is nonetheless self-consciously laced in the language of South-South solidarity and a renewed emphasis on sovereignty.[8] After the end of the Cold War, African states felt besieged by an evolving Western approach to sovereignty that is a world away from the formal respect early postcolonial states had received simply by virtue of being states, and is premised instead on the performance of states vis-à-vis their populations. This environment permitted the international campaign against Angolan corruption, something quite unimaginable before the late 1990s. It is increasingly unlikely today, as the emerging players give African states much more deference, "again treating them as states" through elaborate summitry, a show of (often inaccurate) parity in bilateral relations and the eschewing of criticism of their internal affairs. Their presence contributed towards a diversification of African foreign policy options away from over-reliance on the West. A delayed but unequivocal result of this has been the toning down of Western norm activism and conditionality and a quiet return by some Western states to a realpolitik approach towards illiberal African states deemed strategic or commercially important.

The trends just outlined—the perhaps overegged "rise" of Africa, the more tangible increase in commodity prices, and the emergence of new partnerships—jointly gave African elites a reprieve from external criticism, more money, and more space for governance choices and the conduct of their affairs. Today's global economy and its "plethora of opportunities, loopholes, and breaks that the powerful use to their advantage" further expand the leeway of African decision-makers in this positive conjuncture.[9] Its deregulated, permissive character allows capital to pour in and out of countries with no oversight. African elites did not create the international financial infrastructure or the armies of professional facilitators of contemporary capitalism, and have indeed embraced them quite late in the day when compared with their Arab or Russian counterparts. But they have since benefited greatly from their existence.

This is not simply a matter of the more frequently mentioned, labyrinthine banking jurisdictions in places like Bermuda or the Cayman Islands. It includes respectable asset managers, auditors, commodity traders and lawyers in locations such as London, Zurich, New York and Lisbon (and also Dubai, Hong Kong and Singapore) who craftily utilize complex loopholes and offshoring opportunities available in the international economy to deliver value to their clients, as well as regulators in the same locations who interpret their role in a minimalist, lenient manner.[10] This system is seemingly tailored for massive capital flight but many of these strategies are either legal or thread an ambiguous line. This is a world in which elites can pursue extractive agendas at home while taking for granted their "unfettered access to all the advantages of life in the west—from good schools to independent courts".[11] This is an oligarch's ideal world.

In tandem with the increase in commodity prices since 2003, the last decade has also seen the emergence of a new "state capitalism" pursued by resource-rich and often-illiberal states.[12] According to Acemoglu and Robinson, "state capitalism is not about efficient allocation of economic resources, but about maximizing political control over society and the economy".[13] To achieve that, resource-rich states control the revenue-generating "commanding heights" of the economy and deploy instruments such as NOCs and other state-owned corporations, sovereign wealth funds and regime-favoured privately owned "champions" both domestically and abroad. The goal is invariably phrased in terms of the national interest but is in fact a matter of regime consolidation and the advancement of elite interests. The new state capitalism thus brings together "the management of the state as a private business"[14] with formal, conventional state prerogatives.

These two dynamics—the unregulated global capitalism of the neoliberal era and the activist state capitalism of resource-rich states—far from being mutually exclusive, in fact reinforce each other, with the latter using many of the structures and methods created by the former to pursue opaque strategies with global ramifications. Angola has become adept at deploying a shrewd mix of both. The parallel system outlined in Chapter 1 already amounted to an astute exploitation of the manifold subterfuges of the post-Cold War international economy, its deployment of Sonangol a sort of proto-state capitalism. And in the last decade, the stabilization and enhancement of the parallel system happened in tandem with the global dissemination of a state capitalist model that provided Angolans with ideas of how to systematize and amplify the domestic and international influence allowed by the country's resource wealth. In a word, this is a rationalization and upgrading of what, under different names, Angola had been doing for a while.

RECASTING ANGOLAN FOREIGN RELATIONS

We have already seen that, in the years before and after the end of the war, Angola found itself the target of international criticism. Angolan leaders tend to exaggerate this into a narrative of Angolan victimhood, if only to gleefully underline how they have since managed to turn the tables on critical outsiders. The truth is somewhat different. There was sniping at Angolan corruption by Western NGOs and media in the early 2000s. These allegations then became a talking point for diplomats of some Western states that all the while benefited from Angolan oil. But Angola weathered the anti-corruption campaign storms with next to no concessions to critics. Moreover, these pesky criticisms were far less important than the de facto international support the Angolan government received in the final years of the war, especially in terms of the effective campaign for the marginalization of UNITA and toleration for the FAA's repeated incursions into neighouring countries.[15] At their most unbalanced, Angola's international relations were never "donor-recipient" type; oil always gave it extensive leeway. For instance, it was one of the few African states never to undergo a structural adjustment programme during the decades of the Washington consensus, preferring oil-backed loans to the strictures of the IMF. Still, most of the time this was a high-wire act: capable management of dependent relations with geopolitical patrons or creditors did not change the fact that Angola had only a circumscribed space to make decisions. Since the end of the war, however, and particularly since 2004, the favourable context outlined in the previous section has allowed the establishment of international relations that are broadly symmetrical or even characterized by Angolan primacy.

This improvement was assimilated by the existing parallel structures. Nothing demonstrates this better than the continued monopoly of foreign policy by the presidency. In this context, other institutions again play a limited role. Angolan cabinet ministers cannot even go abroad without an authorization from the Palace. The Ministry of External Relations is irrelevant in decision-making. JES could afford a token national reconciliation gesture in nominating Georges Chicoti, a former member of UNITA, as Foreign Minister safely in the knowledge that Chicoti is beholden to him. The MPLA has a prominent if symbolic role in managing relations with liberation-era allies (with emphasis on other movement parties) but anything truly consequential is beyond the party's writ. The president is firmly in control, and informal emissaries responding to the Palace alone conduct much of the business of real diplomacy. In the 1990s, Elísio de Figueiredo, a multilingual, globetrotting Angolan ambassador without portfolio, was an indispensible man for sensitive tasks, and this function has been performed by a small number of (sometimes foreign) intermediaries up to the present day. To a remarkable extent, Angola's remains a foreign policy steered by a handful of individuals.

The role of private emissaries and foreign brokers (and external service providers such as lawyers, bankers etc.) brings out a broader logic of Angolan foreign relations. As the undisputed location of power, the presidency runs the interface between Angola and the outside world in every dimension of geopolitical or economic consequence. The Cidade Alta decision-makers manage traditional bilateral relations with other states and greatly value the formal dimensions of statehood, as would any official of a state whose very international legitimacy was long contested. However, the presidency also acts as the gatekeeper for the full gamut of external connections, including those with the private sector and useful individuals. These multifarious public and private relationships are entertained with a view to advancing equally diverse, if sometimes overlapping, political, economic, military, and image-making objectives. They nonetheless converge on one overarching goal: the management of external relations for the sake of regime consolidation and the enrichment of those in power, elements that, as we have seen throughout this book, are perceived as coterminous.

The upshot of this is that in Angolan foreign relations, there is no hard and fast public-private divide, no separate realm of state-to-state relations or purely non-state interactions.[16] There is instead an imbrication of "public" and "private" interests where grand strategy and elite agendas coalesce under the aegis of the parallel system. This hybridization is systemic[17] and transcends the Angolan side of the equation to shape external behaviour towards Angola. Foreign dealings with Luanda also happen across a wide and porous continuum of public diplomacy, state corporations, private companies, intelligence organizations and political parties reminiscent of the *Françafrique* networks.[18] State credit lines such as China's Exim Bank's are utilized for private profit; apparently private business concerns owe much to the clout of their home governments in Luanda; bottom line-driven firms and brokers nonetheless keep close contact with their governments and intelligence services, which retain the plausible deniability of unofficial dealings. We have seen that this was the case during the war years; the *modus operandi* remains virtually unchanged a decade later.

Lastly, another element of continuity is that Angola's foreign policy remains imbibed in the secretive, illiberal ethos of the party that rules

Land

Luanda. Understandably in view of Angola's recent history of foreign relations, the outside is seen as potentially dangerous and hostile, with sundry enemies trying to take advantage of the country. Angolan decision-makers thus place great emphasis on looking tough and on eliciting "respect" from those weaker than themselves; they often see relations in zero-sum terms, with phrases such as "you either eat or you get eaten" routinely applied to foreign relations,[19] and even minor diplomatic concessions resisted on account of Angola "losing standing publicly".[20] There are a few sentimental exceptions when it comes to relations with old allies like Cuba, though even these tend to be subjected to transactional, cost-benefit analysis by the Angolan side. More generally, Angolan foreign policy is characterized by its realpolitik character and deeply held belief in concrete political and economic power, rather than values or rhetoric. From this perspective, Western criticism on human rights and corruption is exclusively seen as a hypocritical cover for material interests.

These elements of continuity, however, need to be understood in the context of a major shift in Angolan thinking about foreign relations. In a manner that is only apparently contradictory with what was said above, the last decade has seen a massive amount of political and economic learning on the Angolan side. We have already seen this process at play at the domestic level in Chapters 2 to 4. In the international sphere, the purpose of reform has been to diminish external pressures and improve Angola's reputation. Two key strategies analyzed below have been at the centre of Angola's foreign policy in the last decade. The first, and most frequently underlined, is the diversification of partnerships away from over-dependence on traditional relationships. The second is less frequently highlighted but perhaps more important: the recasting of old alignments, especially with Western partners. While Angola has sought to modify them in a way that maximizes Angolan power, it understood the centrality of partnerships with OECD states for the functioning of the oil economy, the needs of reconstruction, and its international standing more generally. Once these partnerships were renegotiated in Angola's favour, the government was more than happy to tone down the Third Worldist rhetoric and profit from them.

Diversification: The new partnerships

Angolan relations with a host of states and private investors, especially from South and East Asia, have multiplied since 2002. As explained

172

above, these partnerships are part of a broad global dynamic of enhanced South-South trade and investment, deepened in the Angolan case by the attractiveness of its postwar economy. In welcoming new investors and furthering previously superficial bilateral relations, Angola sought to create competition amongst external suitors and guarantee that it would never again find itself on the brink of international isolation.

Of these new relationships, that with China is by far and away the most important. In contrast with practically every other aspect of Angola's recent history and politics, which remain significantly under-researched, the China-Angola relationship has received considerable scholarly and media attention.[21] Analysts correctly noted from the onset that this particular relationship did not quite fit the stereotype of clueless Africans outmatched by powerful Chinese minds. On the contrary, a virtual consensus emerged to the effect that the Angolan side had established the tenor of the relationship and channelled it towards the interests of the MPLA regime, if not broad-based national development.[22]

Angolan-Chinese relations in fact go back a long way, with plenty of skeletons in the closet. Despite an earlier rapport with the MPLA, Beijing ended up throwing its weight behind UNITA in the 1960s; bilateral relations with Luanda were finally established in the 1980s but the legacy of suspicion endured for a long time.[23] However, it did not get in the way of the mutually beneficial, strategic post-2004 partnership already discussed in Chapter 2. What happened at that stage amounted to such a change of scale in bilateral relations that it is accurate to see it as fundamentally new. From China's perspective, access to oil and the opportunities of reconstruction were the paramount goals; its Angola policy was part of a broader strategic engagement with the African continent.[24] For Angola, China delivered three interwoven benefits: a prominent attachment to a rising global power that could be used to keep traditional partners in line; the above-mentioned mechanism for infrastructure reconstruction; and the opening of a massive new mechanism for elite appropriation of the country's oil revenue discussed below.

A good deal of South-South friendship rhetoric emerged from the early months of the relationship, and Angolan finger wagging towards the intransigent Westerners abounded. Yet Angola's pushback started soon after the "marriage of convenience" was struck. The Angolans did not want to replace overreliance on Western partners with an excessively dependent relationship with China; the strategic goal was to transcend

Luanda's fragile international status, not shift it around. Therefore, once the Chinese were safely ensconced in the Angolan setting, the authorities signalled to their Western partners that business would not be damaged. The oil sector provides a perfect illustration of this: there was no temptation to either curtail Western interests or give the technically inferior Chinese corporations, in the words of a senior Sonangol official, "more than they can swallow".[25] The resulting limited Chinese access to oil acreage is perhaps the most disappointing aspect of the relationship from Beijing's perspective. Chinese companies obviously fared better in accessing construction opportunities through the credit lines. But Portuguese and Brazilian construction companies, which had been briefly concerned with the Chinese business model, had their stakes protected by the presidency. On the diplomatic front, JES refused to be seen as one of forty-plus African heads of state "kow-towing" to the Chinese and avoided the bi-yearly FOCAC circuit. Angola generally benefits from the rise of the rest and the less Western-centric flavor of the international system. But with ambitions of its own, Angola hasn't become an integral part of the African "followership" sought by China or, for that matter, other rising powers.[26]

For their part, Chinese investors' enthusiasm for the Angolan economy is more hedged than one would think. The oil-for-infrastructure deal mitigates risk and allows Chinese trade with Angola on extremely favourable terms. But China's investment record is puny. While American FDI in Angola totalled US$3.4 billion from 2007 to 2011 (mostly in the oil sector), the Chinese reported figure for the same period was only US$214 million.[27] Despite the conspicuous Angolan commitment to industrialization briefly discussed in Chapter 2, Chinese companies have mostly steered clear from the ZEE and other such Angolan-run schemes, perhaps identifying them as fraudulent or doomed to failure.

Few of Angola's foreign dealings reveal the near-incestuous closeness of relations with Portugal. But ten years on the relationship with China comes across as singularly lacking in intimacy. Elite Chinese and Angolans don't hang out together, let alone strike durable personal friendships; the degree of cultural distance and mutual misunderstanding precludes much by way of Chinese soft power in Luanda. Angolans vibrate with contemporary Western and Brazilian pop culture but are not much interested in China's. The same applies to the low interest and implicitly derogatory view of Angolan (or better put, generic "African") culture in China itself. Attempts at breaking this barrier have had occasionally embarrassing outcomes. During Shanghai's World Expo 2010, for instance, Angola's aspirations to modernity seem to have been lost on the Chinese organizers. The event's website, after describing the "high technical tools" deployed by the Angolan curator, chose instead as the pavilion's "highlight number one" not the sophisticated Bar Luanda but the "aboriginal huts of Angola [...] presented to show original lifestyles and sceneries [...] visitors can have real experiences of African aboriginal lives there."[28] The transactional nature of the relationship was brought into full view during a rare television interview with JES in June 2013: after lauding relations with Israel, Portugal and Brazil in warm tones, he proceeded to describe relations with China as "fair", focused on loans, public works and the importation of Chinese goods but with little "foreign direct investment [on their part]".[29]

So there is little love in this marriage.[30] But this sober reassessment of relations does not obscure their mutually advantageous character. Angola is now China's second largest supplier of oil and its major trading partner in Africa. The same is true for the Angolan side, with the Chinese presence fitting into broader MPLA designs. It continues to deliver on the three regime-enhancing dimensions highlighted above—reconstruction, balancing vis-à-vis Western powers, and elite enrichment opportunities. Most important, the Chinese presence, despite its idiosyncratic aspects, quickly assimilated the pre-existing ways of doing business in Angola; "it sought to join the system rather than change it".[31] It is in continuity with the long pattern of promiscuous international relations where public and private dimensions (on the side of Angola and of its foreign interlocutors alike) are intermeshed and placed at the service of the regime. The result is perhaps the key dynamic of Angola's external relations in the last decade: a sort of mutual convergence between Westerners and Easterners around Angolan-defined terms of engagement.

The same applies to other new entrants, all of whom proved accommodating of Angolan established methods and uncomplicatedly slid into them. South Korea became a player in the construction sector. (North Korea, an older presence in Angola, even got involved in completing the rocket-shaped Agostinho Neto Mausoleum pictured on this book's cover, which the Soviets had started in 1982 but left unfinished at the end of the Cold War). Singapore, Dubai, Hong Kong and other lenient jurisdictions

are increasingly significant in the shifting geography of Angolan investment and capital flight. While Indian investors have not become as
important as expected during Petroleum Minister Mani Shankar Aiyar's
international offensive in 2004 and 2005, they nonetheless now have a
sizeable Angolan presence. And yet one can't help but feel that the centrality of the "new" partnerships has been overstated; the presence and
traction of these players may well soar in future years, but other than
China, none can claim a strategic partnership with Angola. The landscape
has diversified, but some of the most important relationships for Luanda
are unchanged. In that sense, the new partners of Angola may not have
transformed the landscape out of all recognition. But their arrival provided the seasoned Western powers with a warning to recalibrate their
involvement.

Consolidation of older ties

Once empowered by the Chinese connection and an increase in oil prices
and oil production, the Angolan authorities moved to quickly redefine
their relations with traditional partners perceived to be stepping out of
line. On one level at least, that redefinition was uncompromising: international campaigning NGOs and other meddlers, as well as their local
allies, were given short shrift. The Angolan elite dismisses the work of
these bodies as a cynical foreign attempt to keep Angolans down. In dos
Santos's view, "there is a deliberate confusion created by organizations in
Western countries to intimidate Africans who aim to build assets and
access to wealth, because as a general rule [the image has been created]
that a wealthy African Man is corrupt or under suspicion of being corrupt".[32] Therefore it is unsurprising that Angola has become, in the
words of a human rights campaigner for a leading organization based in
the West, "a nearly impossible place to do our sort of work".[33] The fact
that foreign NGOs need the government's permission to operate greatly
limited their scope for action. This diminished space, together with the
receding of Angola as a funder's priority as the decade wore on, meant
that fewer critical NGOs worked in the country.

The reason why the humanitarian-NGO complex could be resolutely
dealt with had to do with Angola's understanding that Western states
would not hold the bilateral relationship hostage to this. Some of the
time, Angolan leaders seem incapable of discerning the pluralist charac-

ter of Western societies. Criminal investigations and critical NGO and media reports are often portrayed as part of a centralized conspiracy, and the home governments blamed for allowing or orchestrating these anti-Angolan activities. But starting in 2004, Western diplomats provided careful signals that they did not share the harshest NGO criticisms and that they too wanted the relationship to proceed on pragmatic grounds. Angola was never an outcast like Sudan and had longstanding supporters in western capitals, especially amongst the powerful oil industry lobby.[34] Now the regime's friends and lobbyists could labour towards the reset-ting of bilateral relations on more productive terms by leaving the politics aside and instead emphasizing the economic reform dynamic in Luanda.

The Angolan authorities welcomed this implicit clarification and, in almost every other way, proved themselves conciliatory. This was itself evidence of the importance Angola gave to its connections with the West. Angola had no intention of downgrading its relationship with Western states and the international institutions where they remained the arbiters of Angolan respectability. Angolan decision-makers saw Western partnerships as crucial for access to technology and service pro-vision in the context of reconstruction. Whatever the fracas with the French government on account of Angolagate, for instance, the status of Total, Thales and other French investors was not tampered with.[35] More generally, the lives of the deeply Westernized Angolan elites, many of whom are Portuguese passport holders, increasingly revolved around access to the West. Children's education, real estate holdings, cutting-edge beauty treatment and healthcare, the management of assets and personal bank accounts are all based in the West, which is also the loca-tion of choice for satisfying the elite's consumption habits and lifestyles.

This process of diminishing criticism was not just a Western retreat from liberal commitments. Many observers concluded that Angola was now a "serious place" that was "open for business", with the regime hav-ing created the conditions for international capitalism to operate.[36] They recalibrated their approach to the country accordingly. This business focus had always been the preference of corporations and chancelleries anyway, and now it became plausible to argue that Angola had improved many policies that had formerly caused friction and embarked on a self-defined reform path (elections, economic stabilization, and the generally more respectable behaviour reviewed throughout the book). It did not take long for formerly critical partners such as Canada and Germany to extend credit lines to Angola, with the United Kingdom declaring it a "High Level Prosperity Partner" in 2013.[37]

The transformed relationship with the IMF is the most consequential instance of this shift. In the early 2000s, the IMF was a harsh critic that fretted about Angolan opaque accounts and the use of oil-backed loans. Its technocratic critique of Angolan finances was never the same as civil society's attack on corruption, but for a time they seemed aligned, especially as the most indicting evidence of malfeasance surfaced through leaks of the IMF's damning Article IV reports. After two decades of dismal relations, Angola called in the Fund during the financial crisis of 2009 and signed up to a stand-by agreement. As Chapter 4 showed, by this stage Angola had already enacted major macro-economic reforms. In addition to the assistance needed on account of the crisis, by 2009 Angolan leaders knew that the IMF's seal of approval was necessary to consolidate the country's reputation and advance their international ambitions. They realized that some of the IMF's technical advice was sensible and adopted a more constructive approach of partial implementation that set aside measures they disliked. For its part the IMF, keen on becoming involved in one of Africa's star economies, had grown tolerant of Angolan particularities and defined its programme in a manner that implicitly recognized that this was no longer a banana republic to be bossed around. As former Finance Minister José Pedro de Morais noted, the IMF wanted "to get in here, [so they] signed up to relatively balanced and generous terms, giving us much more favourable treatment than most African states ever get".[38]

The Angola-IMF relationship deepened considerably after 2009. The US$ 1.4 billion deal, one of Africa's largest ever, proved accommodating to such an extent that critics noted "signs that the Fund is bending the rules to suit Angola".[39] An extraordinary example of the IMF's new-found tolerance was the acknowledgement, in the otherwise upbeat and highly supportive 2011 Staff Report, that US$32 *billion*, or 25 per cent of the country's GDP, could not be accounted for between 2007 and 2010.[40] Stressing that this very estimate could only be made on account of the government's own praiseworthy recent reforms, the report went on to sympathetically survey possible explanations for this gap[41] and ended by allaying fears of a falling out by stating that "discussions with the authorities on this matter are continuing".[42] The contrast with the Fund's ferocious 2001 reaction to a gap of US$4.22 billion it unearthed

ANGOLA RISING

is glaring. As a senior former Finance Ministry official remarked, "now the IMF tolerates off budget accounts, tolerates CIF [the Sino-Angolan consortium discussed later in this chapter]... now that there is a programme, the IMF [wants to stay in] and doesn't criticize too much".[43] There is no doubt that the IMF's Stand-by arrangement from 2009 to 2012 and subsequent monitoring have had a positive impact on Angola's economic management, but these have followed Angola's terms. Once Luanda found ways of implementing the Fund's prescriptions that were compatible with the regime's interests, the IMF went silent on the nature of governance in Angola.

The relationship with the US has also stabilized, if at a more ambivalent level. Despite the long and fruitful relationship with US oil companies like Chevron and Exxon, which are two of the biggest investors in the oil sector, bilateral relations remain, in Alex Vines' words, "prickly and pedestrian".[44] There is a lingering Angolan suspicion on account of US support for UNITA until the 1990s. The nuances of a November 2011 lecture on US democracy promotion delivered in Portuguese by US Ambassador Christopher McMullen, for instance, were lost on a student and academic audience more concerned with oil imperialism and CIA regime change tactics. But at the highest level, Angolan decision-makers are pragmatic towards a relationship they see as crucial. On the US side, too, there is an understanding that Angola is a pivotal African player and a recurrent desire to upgrade the relationship.

The reason for this distrust lies instead in the actions of parts of the US government, including the Senate, the Securities and Exchange Commission and the Treasury Department, which have pursued investigations of Angolan corruption and money laundering.[45] These investigations have typically not gone very far but have been damaging for the improved reputation that the regime wants to cultivate. In 2010, the US complained that Hezbollah used Angolan front companies to finance its activities.[46] Later that year, Bank of America closed the Angolan embassy's Washington bank accounts, believing that the "effort spent making sure government accounts are not being abused for money-laundering purposes" was too great.[47] The Angolan elite experiences these American barbs as a profound humiliation. US State Department correspondence made available through Wikileaks also shows that, official politeness aside, the views of American diplomats on the Angolan elite remain scathing. In a manner reminiscent of relations with China, this too is a marriage of

179

convenience without much love in it. But an excessive focus on imperfections may obscure the areas that are thriving. This is obviously so in commercial terms, if focused primarily on oil. Geopolitically, too, the US now sees Angola as a factor of stability in a turbulent region. Corruption aside, it recognizes that the MPLA has created a durable political order.[48] Angola's neutrality, bordering on tacit acceptance at the UN in regard to the Bush Administration's Iraq invasion plans in 2003 also showed that it isn't an angry, revisionist G77 state, and can be relied upon.

The policies towards the IMF and the US are examples of the broader attempt to either improve, or at least entertain, positive relations with influential international actors with whom Angola has had stormy relations in the past. In addition to these erstwhile critics and the new partnerships, there is another set of relationships that Angola laboured hard to consolidate from 2002: the long standing links with a number of middle-ranking powers. Three crucial bilateral relationships are with Brazil and Portugal, both defined as strategic partners by Angola, and Israel. All three states have long had close ties to the Presidential Palace and a major presence in the non-oil economy. (The many twists of the complex Angola-Portugal relationship, which slumped badly in 2013, are examined in further detail in the next section).

The relationship with Israel has been a crucial one for the Angolan defence and intelligence apparatus for two decades, while Brazilian companies have long held major stakes in the non-oil Angolan economy. The Brazilian construction conglomerate Odebrecht, for instance, is by far Angola's main private sector employer.[49] Both countries have polite bilateral relations with Angola, with relations with Brazil built up by both sides as particularly intimate (though few Brazilian diplomats like the Luanda posting or stay for long). In fact, Brazil and Israel are exemplary in the manner in which private sector interests are at the centre of their presence in Angola. In the Brazilian case, the embassy is less important than the Odebrecht office or Valdomiro Minoru, a Brazilian citizen of Japanese extraction with multiple partnerships with the Angolan elite (allegedly including JES) who has been called "the *éminence grise* of Brazilian-Angolan relations".[50] As to Israel, relations with Angola are dominated by diamond sector and defence interests, complete with their own long-socialized intermediaries with easy access to the presidency. This pattern of relations has evolved in conjunction with Angolan elite interests and serves the goals of all concerned. Most significant, this mix of profit-seeking and/or historical ties meant that matters such as human rights, governance and corruption were never raised. JES was thankful for this, especially in the difficult years of the war, and accordingly showered these partners with extensive business opportunities in the reconstruction era. Whatever their initial stake or niche sector, investors from these friendly states have now built business interests that span the Angolan economy.

The result of these intertwined processes of diversification and consolidation on Angola's foreign partners is ironic: a mutual, realpolitik convergence of methods by old and new players. Formerly critical Western states have mostly abandoned their (always limited) governance concerns and now embrace the business-only attitude of countries such as China, Brazil and Portugal. For their part, the Chinese have, while proclaiming their distance from Western models of engagement with Angola, proceeded to learn from, and emulate, their forerunners. Contrary to the rhetoric of geopolitical rivalry, this has even resulted in occasional partnerships between China and the rest. This is particularly the case in the oil sector where the pattern is collaborative rather than confrontational, with Chinese corporations keen on learning from their technically superior Western counterparts. Angola's foreign partners are not likeminded and do not behave in exactly the same ways—Norway and China, say, still present significant contrasts—but the ironing out of major disparities over the last decade is substantial. In particular, all foreign players accept the privatized character of Angola's external relations. Under Angolan-defined rules, "the Westerners have become more Chinese and the Chinese more Western".[51]

An elusive African role

Some of Angola's desire for a high-profile international role befitting its self-image as an oil-rich power reveals itself on the African stage. As explained earlier, Angola had a defining role in the Congos from the late 1990s, when it helped replace pro-UNITA regimes in Kinshasa and Brazzaville. Though relations with the DRC have gone through difficult moments since, Angola remains influential in these countries. In addition to the regional clout afforded by the FAA, Angola has in recent years become involved in a number of crises around the continent. Its most significant engagements were in Guinea Bissau, a distressed fellow

Lusophone state, and in Côte d'Ivoire, then governed by an old MPLA ally, Laurent Gbagbo. However, both resulted in embarrassing defeats for Angola. A 2012 military intervention aimed at propping up Carlos Gomes, the Prime Minister, and marginalizing Bissau's drug-running junta was foiled by the Guinean military supported by regional interests, including Nigeria, which resented Angola's out-of-area engagement.[52] Angolan attempts at rallying an international response to the muscling out of its mission went nowhere and further exposed its overreach. In Côte d'Ivoire, Angola's last-ditch support of the Gbagbo regime could not prevent its downfall in April 2011.

Angola's blundering in these two West African conflicts, which turned it momentarily away from involvement in high-profile crisis manage-ment, illustrates its uncomfortable status in contemporary Africa. Contrary to expectations, the FAA has not been massively redeployed as a peacekeeping force across Africa. The 2013 crisis in Mali, for instance, saw Angola make pledges of money but not boots on the ground. Angola still sits awkwardly in the African Union and is not a major voice in the continent's major debates. Though a member of SADC that pays lip service to regional integration, Angola has been an obstacle to the removal of trade barriers for fear of South Africa's economic power, pre-ferring instead the continuation of strong import dependence on Brazil, Portugal and China.[53] By early 2014, Angola was reengaging on the Africa front, including as the rotating chair of the International Conference on the Great Lakes Region, but this seemed part of the same pattern of episodic involvement and not a strategic shift towards Africa. In sum, "Africa" is an important rhetorical reference for Luanda, and Angola's sheer financial power does mean that it can be a major player on the continent, but its pursuit of an African sphere of influence has been intermittent at best.

In the decade since the end of the war, Angola's attention has been far more consistently focused on bilateral relationships with "important states" and non-African diplomatic venues that the regime sees as mean-ingful for its international standing. The latter include organizations like OPEC, which Angola joined in 2007 and headed in 2009, the Kimberley Process, where it is vice-Chair, and the Community of Portuguese-Speaking Countries (CPLP), where Luanda has an influen-tial voice. It is symptomatic of Angola's focus on "real power and con-crete material interests"[54] that the only African country that registers as

a "strategic partner" is South Africa (other countries occasionally described as strategic partners are the US, China, Brazil, and Portugal until it
dropped out of the list in 2013). Relations with Pretoria were tepid at
best until 2009.[55] But the accession to the presidency of Jacob Zuma, a
longtime MPLA ally who lived in Angola in the 1980s, led to great
improvements and a flurry of business deals, including with Zuma's family. Other than South Africa, the Angolan elite does not dwell too much
on Africa. Beyond a degree of elite cultural distance from "Africa", captured by a Congolese diplomat's facetious comment that "Angolans are
not African brothers, they are cousins",[56] there is a broader reality:
Angola thinks of itself primarily as a global rather than an African player.

ANGOLA INC.: THE GOING-OUT STRATEGY

Starting circa 2005, scattered reports of Angolan foreign direct investment made their way into the mainstream media. When associated with
Qatar, the United Arab Emirates or China—states that are either
resource-rich or in possession of enormous foreign exchange reserves—
this was unremarkable, but to have a war-torn African state strut the
international stage in this manner was almost unprecedented. In 2010
and 2011 alone, Angola invested an estimated US$6.1 billion abroad,
substantially more than the FDI it was receiving.[57] These investments
were but the most visible elements in a worldwide, relatively well-crafted
(if never explicitly outlined) external strategy that goes beyond traditional patterns of extraversion. This strategy is an instance of state capitalism whereby the Angolan state uses its control of oil revenue to pursue
internationalization through vehicles such as Sonangol, the SWF and a
number of public-private partnerships.

This "state capitalist" internationalization is the pivotal dynamic in the
deepening of the parallel state since 2002. Defenders often highlight
legitimate reasons for it, including the risks for the economy if Angola's
cash surplus is not invested outside. However, the rationale for the
deployment of this state capitalist strategy abroad is intensely political.
On closer inspection, we find a public-private enmeshment with state
interests advancing oligarchic interests, the pattern we have come to
associate with Angola's political economy and the workings of the parallel system. In this context, the main goals are the internationalization of
rent management and the redeployment of state resources in the inter-

national sphere for regime and personal advancement. Each of the stories discussed below—the role of Sonangol as a de facto sovereign wealth fund (SWF), the creation of a discrete SWF in 2012, the CIF-linked Angolan-Chinese partnerships, and the politico-commercial offensive in Portugal—reveals this dual logic.

Sonangol

It will come as no surprise that the weapon of choice for this internationalization agenda was again Sonangol. This was unavoidable. Whether Sonangol should have been tasked with the postwar missions reviewed in earlier chapters such as industrialization, housing construction, and the fostering of a national bourgeoisie is a moot point; for the purpose of Angola's going-out strategy, Sonangol was ideally suited. Following restructuring in the early 1990s, the NOC had been transformed into a mighty group with more than thirty subsidiaries and scores of joint ventures with foreign firms. Before internationalization became official policy, Sonangol already spanned the globe, with offices in Singapore, London, Houston and Hong Kong. As well as holding a virtual monopoly on technically capable Angolan personnel able to function in the international economy, Sonangol had always been the centrepiece of the parallel state, long mastering the public-private arts required for the new internationalization policy. Remarkably, despite this centrality for the parallel state, the company's international reputation had emerged unscathed from the corruption scandals discussed in Chapter 1.[58] Sonangol—ranking as Africa's second largest corporation by 2013—was ready for redeployment.

The internationalization of Sonangol has proceeded breathlessly since the end of the war, and especially since Angolan coffers started to fill up with oil revenue from 2004. Directly or through its subsidiaries, Sonangol investment locations as of 2013 included Brazil, Iraq, Cuba, Venezuela, South Sudan and Algeria, in addition to Portugal. There are also a series of joint venture investments, some of them attracting critical scrutiny, such as the partnership with Cobalt in the Gulf of Mexico and China Sonangol, which is reviewed in detail below. The Sonangol strategy is simple: the company leverages its resources and role as gatekeeper to Angola's domestic economy (both oil and non-oil) to build partnerships abroad. Most of Sonangol's partners abroad are already actual partners in Angola itself[59] while others see a foreign deal with Sonangol as a precondition for entering the Angolan market on privileged terms. This policy of "crossed investments" is an explicit Angolan goal: "if companies in Portugal or elsewhere want to invest in Angola, then Sonangol will seek to invest back into that country".[60] This brings out a characteristic that distinguishes Sonangol's internationalization policy from many other sovereign investment vehicles. Most go out of their way to deny that their decisions are in any way political, especially if they clearly are. For instance, the overt concern of the Angolan SWF created in 2012, which is supposed to take over from Sonangol as the country's leading foreign investment player, is profitability and politics are never mentioned. Sonangol officials, however, have spoken openly of political goals being at the centre of their decisions.[61]

Sonangol's buying spree is also political in terms of the structural pattern of association between its "state" investments and the cortege of Angolan oligarchs that ride on its coat-tails. On some occasions you find "private" Angolan companies moving in with or shortly after Sonangol becomes a major investor. On others, Sonangol acts through companies (such as Angola's largest bank, BAI) where Sonangol is the major shareholder but where the oligarchs have important holdings. A constant partner in Sonangol's internationalization drive brings this political character fully into view: Isabel dos Santos, the president's daughter. Through a number of different investment vehicles, Isabel is the major Angolan investor abroad after Sonangol. Though ostensibly private, Isabel's investments come with the strongest political backing. "For me [Sonangol and Isabel] are the same: both come with the President's seal of approval. When you deal with her, you know you are dealing with the Palace," said a top Portuguese investor.[62] This is part of a wider pattern of oligarchic business interests advancing with state interests: where Sonangol is, you often find Isabel dos Santos, Manuel Vicente, Kopelipa and others. Sonangol is the spearhead of the oligarchs' internationalization.

By 2007, CEO Manuel Vicente was adding a goal to the lengthy list of ambitions he liked to boast of in interviews: Sonangol's public listing in a major international stock exchange by 2010 (references were made to New York and also London and Johannesburg).[63] A few years earlier, this would have been impossible in view of the company's opaqueness, but two major changes had occurred: the first was the partial transparency reforms and improved accounting standards which brought the company closer to the (arguably undemanding) standards for listing.[64] The second was a process of "downstreaming of corruption",[65] that is, the reorganization of rentier opportunities within the Sonangol Group, whereby the summit of the group was increasingly "clean" and fit for listing while the more dubious activities shifted to the labyrinth of subsidiaries and joint ventures. Over the years, current and former Sonangol officials have mentioned examples of successful flotation against the odds. These included Petrochina, an international subsidiary of China's CNPC that was listed abroad as a "better version of CNPC, but with none of the toxic stuff [such as the Sudan investments] in it".[66] The favorable outcome of Russia's Rosneft 2006 IPO, which many had expected to be marred by the company's inheritance of Yukos' confiscated assets, was also highlighted.[67] The lesson from these cases was that moderate cleanup and corporate reorganization could provide Sonangol with enhanced international respectability without the need for systemic transformation.

Since the 2009 crisis, Sonangol's public listing is referred to far less often. Although it remains an official "long-term goal",[68] the contradictions between listing and having Sonangol continue to play its political role became less easily avoidable. "SONIP, SIIND [the real estate and industrial subsidiaries discussed in Chapter 2], all of these new roles: if anything the firm looks even less conventional now that it did five years ago," complained a former official.[69] Francisco de Lemos, the economist who replaced Vicente as CEO in 2012, is said to be critical of Sonangol's large footprint and to want to bring it "back to its primary focus on the petroleum sector",[70] but two years later, the scope of the company's involvement remains huge. There was, however, one major exception to the long-term accruing of ever-larger responsibilities to Sonangol: the creation of a dedicated sovereign wealth fund meant to perform the foreign investment role played by Sonangol over the past decade.

The Sovereign Wealth Fund

Sonangol was and remains, in all but name, Angola's sovereign wealth fund. Yet in tandem with the global expansion of such instruments on account of high commodity prices and accumulating foreign exchange reserves, from 2007 the Angolan government expressed a desire formally to establish a separate SWF. For this purpose the president created a commission of technocratic insiders to study different SWF models and advise on the creation of an Angolan fund. This commission was a typical JES parallel state outfit, run out of the presidency without consulting the Finance Ministry or the Finance Minister himself.[71] Its members included Archer Mangueira, the President's then economic adviser and now charged with establishing the Angolan Stock Exchange, Francisco de Lemos, then a Sonangol official who has since become its head, and Ricardo Viegas de Abreu, a former private banker and later BNA vice-governor. This commission went to the United Arab Emirates, Brazil, China, and Norway to study different SWF models and their functioning.[72]

Although talk of a SWF abated amidst the 2008–09 economic crisis and the near-depletion of Angola's foreign exchange reserves,[73] it continued to be referred to as a long-term policy goal. Finally, a high profile SWF, the Fundo Soberano de Angola (FSDEA), was established in October 2012 as Africa's second largest after Botswana's. The actual launch of the SWF took place amidst an impressive media offensive by hired image-makers from Dubai, the United Kingdom and Portugal. Foreign journalists, including those with a record of critical reporting on Angola, were flown in for this inaugural event. For Angolan standards, the Fundo was certainly unusual in emphasizing the centrality of good governance and transparency for its operations, pledging allegiance to the Santiago principles of SWF best practice. "The FSDEA has been founded in accordance with established international governance benchmarks and best practices. The activities of the FSDEA will be guided by the core principles of accountability and transparency," read its founding press release.[74]

Despite these commitments, the FSDEA was immediately the subject of negative publicity. The most polemical aspect was the choice of José Filomeno "Zenu" dos Santos, JES's eldest son and would-be heir apparent, as a member of the three-person board. As part of the well-oiled PR machinery that staged the launch of the SWF, the articulate Zenu showed up in international media outlets like CNN and, in perfect English, argued that his appointment was based on his personal qualities and experience: "I am here as myself," he said,[75] while the FSDEA website states that the nomination is based "absolutely on merit".[76] Zenu's business experience and British degrees notwithstanding, reactions were sceptical.[77] A further point of contention is the SWF's relationship with Quantum Global Investment Management, a Swiss-based asset manager with deep connections to the dos Santos family and run by a Swiss-Angolan close friend of Zenu's, Jean-Claude Bastos de Morais. Ever since discussion of an Angolan SWF started in 2008, the only constant feature has been the association of this consultancy with it.[78] Without a public tender, Quantum Global was given the task of managing a significant chunk of the fund (according to some reports, up to US$3 billion of the initial US$5 billion placed in the SWF; further amounts are meant to accrue to the FSDEA from the yearly surplus of Angola's Strategic Financial Oil Reserves Account, although details of this remain confusing at the time of writing). Finally, the strenuous promises of transparency were actually non-committal, as they refer to adherence to voluntary, unenforceable codes.

The initial scepticism continued into 2013. While government officials kept on repeating that Sonangol would now stop performing SWF-like functions and return to its core business, it remained in control of the portfolio of foreign investments described above. This means that Angola will in practice have two SWFs for years to come. This did not create friction with the FSDEA since the fund barely moved in the intervening period, apart from the rumoured acquisition of expensive real estate in London's Mayfair;[79] the publication of the SWF's investment strategy was repeatedly postponed. After a government reshuffle that led to the nomination of Armando Manuel, the SWF's first chairman, as Finance Minister, Zenu took up the top position.[80] In his first public statement in this role, Zenu finally divulged the long awaited investment strategy, which contained the usual commitments to a mix of medium and long-term investments, both in Angola and abroad. However, the investment he chose to highlight—the building of a chain of hotels—is of questionable profitability and hardly fits the commitment to social development that the SWF had claimed for itself. In brief, it is unclear whether the SWF will play a developmental role, however defined. But merely on the basis of the resources that will accrue to it, the FSDEA will be a key player in the Angolan political economy.

With somewhat of a cookie cutter approach to these matters, the IMF has been a keen promoter of the SWF. A properly run fund can of course be used to manage the impact of revenue volatility or put aside resources for future generations. With an estimated US$34 billion in foreign exchange reserves parked in the Central Bank, this is the sort of instrument Angola is expected to develop. But as all observers of actually exist-

ANGOLA RISING

ing SWFs know, these are in fact neither a good nor a bad idea. They are what decision-makers do with them. Worryingly, the management of SWFs is almost always a function of a government's overall economic management. In the case of the FSDEA, while the modern, transparent self-presentation is reassuring, the bald facts point to yet another—perhaps the most sophisticated yet—strategy of the parallel state, and any claims to innovation need to be set against the obvious parallels with other Futungo-engineered black boxes of the "Bermuda Triangle" world described in Chapter 1. Through his son, JES has absolute control over the SWF, most of whose money will be managed by an asset management consultancy he is close to.

The president's ambitions for the FSDEA are the subject of some discussion in Luanda: reacting to early speculation about the setting up of a SWF, a top economist even wagered that "this is the [ultimate] parallel system" and "part of a retirement strategy for dos Santos".[81] Most likely the president is seeking to realize a mix of state and private goals in full continuity with Sonangol's foreign investment strategy described above. JES wants a moderately respectable SWF to be able to claim plausible success, both in terms of a return on investment and the advancement of his son's reputation. He also wants to extend and deepen his grip over Angola's political economy and its global ramifications.[82]

CIF-China Sonangol

Since its operations started to fall under scrutiny, many epithets have been levelled at the so-called Queensway syndicate: "corporate vultures" and "buccaneers" are perhaps not the unkindest. The syndicate was established in 2003 by three Chinese individuals who brought with them complementary skills verging from contacts in the highest reaches of the Communist Party of China, SOEs and military intelligence to African networks established over decades of trading and arms dealing. Plainly stated, the aim of this conglomerate of companies (sometimes known as the Queensway group after the Hong Kong address where scores of them are legally located, and often referred to as CIF after one of the most important brands in the group) was to intermediate "between African governments, international banks, and Chinese commodity buyers and construction firms".[83] Its strategy—to first gain access to natural resources that could be used for getting commodity-backed loans from international banks, subsequently redeployed for financing infrastructure work—was simplicity itself; its functioning over the last decade, however, is a labyrinthine lesson in the world economy's opaque possibilities. The Queensway Group has been the subject of a number of in-depth investigations.[84] Though the claims made about it are serious, their impact has not gone beyond spurious PR attempts at image cleanup (a series of websites and cursory commitments to CSR, mostly) and glaring questions remain. My purpose here is not to advance knowledge of the Queensway Group, a protracted task fit for a team of investigative journalists,[85] but to look at it from the prism of the Angolan side of the partnership.

This partnership started shortly after CIF's creation: an Angolan official privy to the Beijing bilateral negotiations between Angola and the Chinese authorities in late 2003 and early 2004 even claims that some Angolan officials "slipped away in the evening" to discuss parallel deals "with private groups, including the [CIF] people."[86] Key in these early contacts were longstanding Futungo insiders such as Pierre Falcone, by then resident in Beijing, and Helder Battaglia, the discreet co-owner of the politically connected Escom group.[87] By late 2004, a major deal had been struck with Sonangol: the creation of a joint venture, China Sonangol, that is 30 per cent owned by Sonangol, with the remainder owned by CIF. China Sonangol served three interlinked purposes: the first was to be the official borrower for a new string of oil-backed loans;[88] the second was as a vehicle for CIF's involvement in the Angolan oil sector, including as a broker for Angolan oil sales to China;[89] thirdly, and more important for our purposes here, it was to be the instrument for a going-out strategy rivalling in scale the above-described ambitions of Sonangol itself.

Within a few years China Sonangol had become involved in more than a dozen countries. 2004 ventures into Venezuela and Argentina had garnered access to Presidents Chávez and Kirchner, but the setting proved inimical to the particular brand of CIF business. The group also made high-profile real estate acquisitions in the West, including the Morgan Building on Wall Street.[90] But it was in Africa that CIF proved successful. In Zimbabwe, Guinea, Tanzania, Mozambique, Madagascar and other African countries, variants of the infrastructure-for-oil model were deployed, with cumulative promises of a total US$18 billion by 2011.[91] Manuel Vicente, as one of the directors of China Sonangol, co-fronted many of these involvements. While successful as a mechanism for the enrichment of insiders, the Queensway mechanism doesn't deliver on commitments. Early analysts of CIF's shortcomings emphasized its incompetence and lack of experience, especially in building infrastructure. However, these shortcomings seem linked to its very business model. Critics argue that CIF has overpriced infrastructure while underpricing the commodities that back it.[92]

In view of this opaqueness and (from a conventional perspective) disappointing performance, it is unsurprising that CIF would collect enemies all over the place. From the very start, sections of the Chinese state rallied against it, even while others, including prestigious SOEs such as Sinopec and CITIC, happily worked with the group.[93] According to an Angolan Finance Ministry official, MOFCOM and Eximbank "warned us many times [against CIF]", saying that this "wasn't a serious company, that Angola should not be dealing with them".[94] This hostility was echoed on the Angolan side, with the CIF connection perceived by many in Luanda as "another swindle by the Palace".[95] It only got worse when, after 2006, CIF started to default on payments to Chinese SOEs and most of its construction sites were deserted. International criticism abounded, especially after the publication of an investigation by the US-China Economic and Security Review Commission in 2009.[96] This scrutiny extended to China itself.[97] According to J.R. Mailey, by 2010, a number of investigations by different Chinese government agencies were being conducted into CIF's global network of interests. At this stage, Chinese authorities would repeatedly distance themselves from CIF, with the Chinese embassy in Luanda making a public statement to that effect. But, in the end, no punitive action was taken. The four jurisdictions where CIF could have been brought to task—Hong Kong, Mainland China, Singapore and Angola—never moved against the group. Two interviewees with knowledge of the Angolan side alleged that the Presidency pressured the "Chinese not to be publicly critical of CIF, as so many regime interests were invested in it".[98] In China itself, the undisclosed friends of CIF ultimately proved more powerful than the critics and, by 2011, the Chinese government was referring to CIF's African investments as "strategic".[99]

The Queensway Group's activities elicit a number of comments. The first is its innovative character. Chapter 1 surveyed the schemes made possible by Angola's unique wartime conditions. China Sonangol builds on that legacy but contains new elements. According to the *Economist*, "the syndicate's corporate structure is fiendishly complex [...] Individual companies are not vertically integrated—it is not a group in the usual sense" as there is no holding company.[100] While we have an inkling of who ultimately profits, the use of offshore structures is so intricate that there is no way of ascertaining final beneficial ownership. J.R. Mailey, perhaps the person who has spent more time following the Queensway Group, calls its Angolan operations "a state within the state within the state".[101] The syndicate is also original in its internationalized character and extreme diversification. This goes much beyond the wartime focus on arms and commodities, even if the latter are the lynchpin of the Queensway model: this mechanism now allows insiders to profit from everything going on in a given economy.

The second noteworthy characteristic is the manner in which China Sonangol is presented as a private group although it is a state-backed instrument with the power of the government of Angola and, more ambiguously, sections of the PRC behind it. One is again confronted with a public-private divide that is manipulated by power-holders for their own benefit. On the Chinese side, recurrent denials of high-level protection are belied by CIF's close links to SOEs and the fact that the Chinese state never moved against it. Thirdly, this partnership shows Angolan power at work, its very existence a precondition for Chinese market access to Angola.[102] Finally, the Sino-Angolan identity of the Queensway Group partners may be historically original and innovative in method, but its core activity—profiting from natural resources in weak African states—is entirely familiar. When provided with the opportunity for easy profit, new actors in the African scene, including both outsiders and internationalized African actors, are as liable to exploit asymmetrical rapports as the old plunderers of the continent were. Indeed, if one is to believe some estimates on the scope and scale of this process, few Western involvements in Angola compare to the scale of misappropriation that CIF allows.[103] As co-stewards of this effort, one finds our usual cast of elite Angolan characters.

Portugal: Angola's new colony?

Chapter 2 noted the critical role played by Portuguese expatriates in Angola's postwar economy. I will now outline the much less common role that Angola has come to play in Portugal's economy and society.

Portugal is hardly the most shocking case of a Western state's dubious dealings with resource-rich partners in the developing world: BAE Systems' business with Saudi Arabia, the UK's exceedingly close relations with Gaddafi's Libya and assorted Russian oligarchs, or *Françafrique*'s long-standing shenanigans come to mind. And as mentioned above, northern European states with usually pristine foreign policies have not hesitated to bend to local mores in their relations with Luanda. That said, the expansion of Angolan interests in Portugal is unusual for two reasons. The first is its considerable weight in Portugal's trade and investment. This is not just one amongst many other relations but a vital bond for the former colonial power, especially in view of the depth of Portuguese involvement in Angola itself. The second is the fact of Portugal's fragile status as a cash-strapped and stagnant economy. FDI is welcomed and increasingly fewer questions are asked about its provenance and the compromises it entails. Together these factors mean that Angolan interests have, in a brief amount of time, reached the heart of Portugal's economic and political life.

Despite the expected opaqueness as to real ownership, especially in the media sector, many of the largest Angolan investments in Portugal are public knowledge.[104] Starting around 2005, these interests have quickly reached into the major private banks (BIC, BPI, BPN and the leading private sector bank, Millennium BCP, where Sonangol is now the major shareholder), telecommunications (ZON), the media (the weekly newspaper *Sol* and the media group that includes *Correio da Manhã*, Portugal's highest circulation daily newspaper),[105] and energy (Galp Energia). Although estimates vary, somewhere between 4 and 7 per cent of shares in Portugal's stock exchange were Angolan-owned by 2013, and Angolans are the largest foreign presence in it.[106] There are two major, apparently distinct sources of Angolan FDI: Sonangol in its role as a de facto sovereign wealth fund, and a few investors closely connected with the presidential family (with pride of place for Isabel dos Santos) and the Palace. In fact, here too private and public are fully intertwined.

This increased Angolan presence has played out very much under the Portuguese public's attention. The Portuguese media are replete with salivating portraits of the "new Angolan settlers", their ostentatious habits in the capital's five-star hotels and posh restaurants, and the crazy Lisbon nights of Angola's *jeunesse dorée*. According to staff of luxury boutiques in Lisbon's Avenida da Liberdade, it is primarily Angolan clients on binge shopping trips that have kept them going throughout the crisis, in some cases accounting for 30 per cent of sales.[107] Angolan clients spending more than US$100,000 at Lisbon's Loja das Meias even have a privileged "Luanda Card".[108] From cars to jewellery and designer clothing not a week goes by without a preposterous, sometimes apocryphal tale of Angolan excess. Angolans are also leading in acquisitions of luxury real estate, accounting for an estimated 15–20 per cent of this segment of the market with emphasis on high-profile wealthy enclaves such as the Algarve's Quinta do Lago, Cascais' Quinta da Marinha and the best Lisbon neighborhoods. Among the many Angolan investments, the media zoomed in on General Kopelipa's acquisition of two old-money port wine estates in the Douro valley *without even having visited them first*: surely a sign that the world is upside down.[109]

Angolan interests are now an inescapable aspect of the Portuguese economy. Furthermore, the buying up of important stakes has happened in tandem with what amounts to the Angolan cooptation (or outright hiring) of segments of the Portuguese elite. In some ways, this is a process of mutual assimilation, with the Angolan elite densely networked within Portuguese masonic lodges and Opus Dei.[110] But the Angolan element holds the upper hand. Whether in the banking system, construction companies, the media or the legal profession, Angolan employers are now significant voices defining professional behaviour and worldview. This is deepened by the revolving door between private sector and public office amongst Portugal's small political and economic elite. Both in Angola and in Portugal itself, numerous interviewees argued that this Angolan influence went to the very centre of the political system through large-scale financing of Portuguese political parties. I have not found any evidence for this, but the widespread belief that this is the case is itself revealing.[111]

Nowhere else do Angolan interests have as much traction and respectability as in Portugal. With exceptions such as Portugal's daily and weekly newspapers of record, *Público* and *Expresso*, press coverage has been superficial and, in the case of media partly owned by Angolans, sycophantic. There is extensive sniping at Angolan "corruption" but the extent of Portuguese participation in Angola's political economy has curbed outbreaks of civic-mindedness. A March 2009 exchange on the TV show *Prós e Contras*, a sort of Portuguese *Question Time* whose subject was Portuguese-Angolan relations, provided an example. Confronted by a question on corruption, the wily Aguinaldo Jaime, at the time head of

Angola's foreign investment agency, claimed that this "cancer" was not unique to the country nor was it "[the Angolan state's] policy to institutionalize corruption", before turning to the front rows studded with the crème de la crème of Portuguese investors in Angola and executives working for Angolan companies. "If you ask the Portuguese businessmen who are present here today, and who have been present in the Angolan market for a long time, if they ever needed to resort to less transparent [or] illicit schemes, I am convinced that they will tell you [that their answer is no]."[112] The embarrassment was palpable but the high-powered members of the audience remained silent.

From an Angolan perspective, there are complex reasons for massively investing in a country going through a rough decade even before the 2008 financial crisis. The economic reasons are actually strong. Portugal provides Angolan investors with a familiar setting, in both linguistic and cultural terms, for venturing outside of Angola. It has armies of essential banking, legal, accounting and managerial experts, particularly as most Angolans, in contradiction with the recurrent desire to pull rank on their employees, do not want to manage their holdings on a daily basis. Portugal is a major investment site even for the savviest oligarchs who have gone global; for everyone else in the lower rank of Angola's oligarchy, it is almost the only foreign location not a tax haven where they are comfortable taking their money to. Angolan investors have understood the benefits of a respectable OECD/EU jurisdiction, especially as many have had bruising experiences with US regulators or have had to dwell in the obscurity of tax havens. This is not to say that other jurisdictions are strict on Angolan capital flight, but the benefits of owning reputable banking institutions with a façade of European professionals while being politically influential are obvious. In addition, there is the fact that Portugal's anaemic growth allowed easy pickings amongst leading corporations that Angolans would not have been able to afford elsewhere or even in Portugal under less straitened circumstances.

A mainly economic explanation for Angolan investment in Portugal could therefore be advanced. However, the fact that Angolan FDI has continued despite serious underperformance and asset depreciation in the past five years points to additional reasons for this presence. At some level, there is *Schadenfreude* about the former colonial power's shambolic economic performance and loss of status. One cannot overstate the extent to which actually owning chunks of the Portuguese economy a generation after the end of colonialism is itself a mobilizing factor for wealthy Angolans: far from wearing their newfound authority lightly, Angolan bosses have made their presence felt in Portuguese boardrooms. Manuel Vicente provided a high-profile example with his blunt statement that "We are the bosses [now], we will dictate the rules of the game" at Galp Energia, Portugal's leading oil and gas firm.[113] And in ways that are only apparently contradictory with what has just been said, Angolan oligarchs also like Portugal. All have a house in Lisbon, and their children will have been educated there; most will also have a (secret) Portuguese passport. While the rhetoric of Lusophone brotherhood is often deployed in Angolan-Brazilian relations, it is in Lisbon not Rio or São Paulo that the Angolan wealthy hobnob with the upper classes, regardless of the strong influence of Brazilian popular culture and the status of Brazil as an ideal society for many urban Angolans. Postcolonial score settling and enjoyment of the Portuguese *dolce vita* go hand in hand here.

Some observers, perhaps naïvely or self-interestedly, see this process of increased Angolan involvement in the Portuguese economy as a contribution towards "Europeanizing" and "professionalizing" Angolan businesses. But others fear that it is the Portuguese economy that is being made to serve the agendas of the Angolan elite. In a biting 2013 report on Portuguese implementation of anti-money laundering measures, the OECD notes that despite the fact that a full third of all foreign bribery allegations in Portugal concern Angola, "not a single investigation into the activities of a PEP [Politically Exposed Person] has led to prosecution for money laundering".[114] The lead examiners expressed "concerns over Portugal's capacity to effectively detect, prevent and prosecute laundering of the proceeds of foreign bribery by PEPs, especially those from jurisdictions with pervasive corruption and close economic ties to Portugal".[115]

The upshot of this complicated turn in bilateral relations is that Portuguese institutions proved more unruly than expected. To the utmost embarrassment of Portuguese politicians keen on a smooth relationship, the Attorney General's Office went on to pursue numerous investigations into alleged Angolan money laundering in Portugal. The first conflagration came with the naming of Álvaro Sobrinho, then the highly regarded CEO of a top Luso-Angolan bank, BESA, as suspect of fraud and money laundering in late 2011.[116] For the subsequent year and a half, Angolan frustration at myriad investigations rose steadily as leaks showed that Manuel Vicente, by then the Vice-President of

Angola, General Kopelipa and other members of the elite were all under scrutiny. A Portuguese journalist mentioned that these cases were "the tip of the iceberg" and that more than thirty oligarchs were under investigation.[117] A bitter conflict was raging, with the MPLA mouthpiece *Jornal de Angola* routinely pouring vitriol on Portugal.[118]

Yet as late as June 2013, dos Santos was describing Portugal as a strategic partner.[119] So his uttering of two brief sentences in the State of the Nation address in October 2013 could not but unleash a storm: "Only with Portugal, sadly, things are not fine. There have been misunderstandings at the level of the summit [of power] and the current political climate presiding over this relationship does not advise the construction of the strategic partnership announced earlier."[120] The Portuguese political world went into a tailspin, with blame ascribed to the Portuguese foreign minister Rui Machete, who had bizarrely apologized on Angola's national radio for the nuisance caused by the investigations.[121] This instance of brazen Angolan blackmail partly worked, for within weeks, a number of prominent investigations had been shut down. But others rumbled on, and open resentment about Angola's role became widespread.

THE LIMITS OF "EMERGING POWER" ANGOLA

This chapter surveyed what is perhaps Angola's greatest achievement of the last ten years. After only three decades of self-government, much of it under foreign invasion, civil war, and successive asymmetrical foreign relations, the country holds a much more balanced and self-confident position in the international sphere. This was made possible by a positive international environment, oil revenue, and shrewd decision-making at the top. As a result, Angola set up new partnerships and renegotiated the terms of preexisting ones in a manner favourable to the MPLA regime; external actors have fitted into Angolan designs as a condition for access. Angola has even forged a foreign investment strategy that is fast turning it into a political-economic player far beyond its shores. Throughout, Angolan decision-makers have shown a steep learning curve in marrying the prerogatives of sovereign statehood with the ample profit opportunities of a deregulated world economy. These possibilities are taken straight out of the rulebook of today's global capitalism. Even when pushing legal boundaries (and occasionally going beyond them), Angolans do not subvert the rules and seek instead to carve out a profitable space for themselves within the world as it is.

Punch-drunk on this meteoric rise, elite Angolans and more than a few foreign commentators speak of the country as a force to be reckoned with, even an "emerging power" in the making. Although references to the mighty FAA's regional clout recur, it is Angola's economic power that is at the centre of the country's newfound stature.[122] Can Angola be an emerging power? It would not be the first energy exporter to gain international influence while run by a regime focused on self-perpetuation and oligarchic advancement: this in fact describes most oil-rich states in the developing world. Nor is the reputation for corruption the defining factor of yesteryear. There is certainly a lingering whiff of disrepute about Angola, daily fed by money laundering scandals and schemes such as CIF. But beyond wounding the pride of elite Angolans and feeding PR contracts in London and Washington it is not clear that concrete negative consequences flow from this.

Still, these emerging power aspirations are unrealistic and reveal much about the megalomania of Angolan decision-makers and their hangers-on. In addition to the long-term threats posed by the inequitable internal order examined in the other chapters, three factors prevent Angola's international status from going much beyond the gains of the last decade and may even imperil those gains. The first has been succinctly labelled as the "arrogance" of Angolan decision-makers flush with cash and self-confidence.[123] It takes the form of foreign policy blunders, as when Angola is emboldened to act alone in unfamiliar settings such as Côte d'Ivoire and Guinea Bissau. It also takes the form of a pervasive assumption that every interlocutor is driven by the profit motive and, therefore, that solutions, and people, can be bought. This leads Angola to throw money around in a manner that is highly visible, clumsy and sub-optimal. (In the case of Portugal, for instance, the Angolan elite's imperious behaviour has made life difficult for apologists for its investment in the country.)

The second disabling factor is Angola's all-too-frequent unilateralism and unwillingness to compromise. This is the result of a "Manichean worldview",[124] where the world is divided between friends and foes and negotiation means weakness. As a foreign diplomat put it, "the Angolan foreign policy culture is inflexible: for them, partnership means you do what they want, 100 per cent, otherwise they leave you hanging".[125] An IO official commented that, "ironically, the fact that so many former critics have been enticed into a business-only [approach to] Luanda has actually emboldened the elite into thinking that they don't have to make real concessions".[126]

Lastly, there is nothing definitive about this renegotiation of Angola's international status. It is based not on a durable transformation of Angola's insertion in the world economy, but on an enabling international conjuncture that may deteriorate very fast. As one of the world's most oil-dependent states, Angola's swagger literally hangs from the price of oil. A durable oil price shock would unravel many of the gains outlined above, and throw Angola back into a pattern of unequal, shifting engagements with the outside world.[127]

6

CONCLUSION

POST-POSTWAR ANGOLA

"Produzir mais para distribuir melhor [To produce more in order to distribute better]"

MPLA 2012 electoral slogan

"[In the years after the war] we didn't give enough attention to people; but now we will"

Vice-President Manuel Vicente, June 2013

On 31 August 2012, Angola held its second legislative elections since the end of the war and, contrary to the much-delayed 2008 elections, on this occasion everything happened on schedule. Elections in postwar Angola, while useful for gauging the party-state's evolving approach to power and to relations with society, are strictly non-competitive. No surprises were expected. But the elections provided a vantage point to reflect on Angola's decade of peace. The MPLA presented 2012 as the "end of reconstruction and the beginning of national development",[1] while the opposition campaigned against the MPLA's governance record. Normal life stopped in expectation of the voting day; the country's state schools were closed for the month of August to allow for "the full mobilization of the state at this important time",[2] much aggravating Angolan parents.

Mindful of appearances, and safe in its electoral domination, the MPLA cultivated a show of pluralism.[3] The head of the national electoral commission, an MPLA official, was replaced following protests as a sop to the opposition. The other parties were allowed free rein during their (extremely brief) televised airtime. While the smaller parties, many MPLA creations, scarcely made sense, CASA-CE did not mince its words. CASA-CE's leader, the former UNITA cadre Abel Chivukuvuku, had partnered with Admiral "Miau" Mendes de Carvalho, a charismatic dissident from a leading MPLA family with a reputation for honesty. Denouncing a degree of corruption that he saw as worse than Nigeria's or the DRC's, Miau portrayed Angola as "walking toward the abyss, [something that] cannot be hidden by cement or asphalt". He also questioned the sources of the President's daughter's money before making unprecedented attacks on JES himself. According to Miau, the President was "hiding under the skirt of the MPLA [by avoiding direct presidential elections]": "What is the legitimacy of a President who has never been elected"?[4] A transient onlooker might have construed this as a sign of real democracy. At any rate, no one wanted to prod too deeply. After realizing that its presence would not be welcomed, the EU boldly concluded that electoral observers were unnecessary on this occasion, and the only missions came from the AU and SADC.[5]

The ruling party left nothing to chance. Outside their airtime, the opposition parties barely featured in the long procession of MPLA propaganda that passed as TV news coverage. While the public channels were predictably sycophantic, TV Zimbo also fell in line. Brazilian "political marketing" consultants were again hired to run the MPLA media strategy. This time, it was President Lula's "A team", fresh from working with President Hugo Chávez of Venezuela.[6] Towns and cities were covered in billboards trumpeting the achievements of the regime, including images of the vacant Kilamba. UNITA was again labelled the party of destabilization, the enemy of order, while the PRS, already reeling from MPLA-sponsored desertions of senior cadres, was deemed homophobic and backward on account of its president's anti-gay comments (incidentally, this allowed the MPLA to further burnish its modern credentials, though it is hardly pro-gay).[7] Senior figures engaged in a hectic circuit of inauguration of public works (JES ran through several such ribbon cuttings on 29 August alone). Some of these works had already been inaugurated months before, while others were closed again immediately after the ceremony, as they were not yet finished; all were deemed good TV material on the eve of the elections. Alert to agitation among potentially disruptive constituencies throughout the year—a civil service strike in Benguela, demonstrations by former soldiers excluded from the FAA's pension system—the government announced just before the elections a 10 per cent salary increase for civil servants, war veterans, and traditional authorities.[8]

The MPLA's electoral victory duly followed. Results started to emerge on 2 September, the day of the president's televised 70th birthday party. JES, surrounded by his family, advisers and MPLA barons, seemed happy; one flatterer even labelled him "father of the nation". But the results proved equivocal. The MPLA got 71.85 per cent of votes, down from almost 82 per cent in 2008. UNITA nearly doubled to 18.67 per-cent, while the neophyte CASA got a respectable 6 per cent. National abstention (only 11 per cent in 2008) leapfrogged to 38 per cent of the electorate. Worryingly, the MPLA obtained its second worst national score, 56 per cent, in its Luandan heartland, losing the ethnic Ovimbundu neighbourhood of Cacuaco to UNITA and not doing as well as expected in upper-middle class neighbourhoods like Maianga. The MPLA retained an impressive majority but cracks opened in its carapace. Amidst half-hearted opposition protests of fraud, the electoral commission declared the winner and the whole matter was officially wrapped up, yet intense speculation ensued.

What inferences can one draw from these results? Anti-MPLA read-ings often amounted to wishful thinking; after all, 72 per cent is a land-slide and the MPLA remained in firm control of the country. But a degree of exasperation had nonetheless crept into the world that the MPLA had effortlessly mastered since 2002. For some inside the party, the fact that it got fewer votes than the number of registered MPLA members showed a "dangerous lack of commitment" by the rank and file.[9] Others worried that too many members of the "MPLA urban middle class were turning against it".[10] Influential cadres spoke of the "cooling of enthusiasm for the government's promises".[11] Fernando Pacheco, a public intellectual and historic (if estranged) MPLA figure, called it a "yellow card, for now".[12]

Accomplishments and limits

From the perspective of 2012, one overarching fact about Angola's decade of reconstruction emerged: Angolan elites did it their way. As argued throughout this book, the MPLA regime was able to turn a unique convergence of factors—its war victory and resulting hegemonic position, the oil bonanza and the emergence of new international partners—into an unprecedented degree of autonomy from both domestic forces and international pressures. Angola shares much in this regard with states such as Ethiopia and Rwanda, to name but a few instances of locally generated "illiberal peacebuilding"[13] where elites are also pursuing robust state-building projects, although development economists seem less enamoured of the Angolan approach than they are of Paul Kagame or the late Meles Zenawi.[14] Africa's illiberal state-builders are articulating cogent ideas about the future they desire for their states and societies. As in Angola, these ideas bear little similarity to Western donors' prescriptions on political rights and poverty reduction[15] and are not premised on convergence with Western models.

Yet those same Western donors, after initial scepticism about Angola's sovereign assertiveness, soon welcomed the regime's simultaneous focus on market expansion. "Whatever you say about [the MPLA], they have hugely broadened the space for foreign investors in Angola," a construction sector executive mused, "objectively speaking, their role has been extremely progressive [in this regard]".[16] In its own way, the regime has turned a dangerous enclave economy only fit for oilmen and mercenaries into a relatively accessible, if still unpredictable, one where business opportunities can be found subject to the indulging of local appetites. This massive enlargement of foreign material interests in Angola—and the increased rationality of capitalist activity in the country—endeared the MPLA to outsiders and improved its reputation in influential international circles. Oil companies, management consultancies and global banks explicitly embraced the regime, as did the governments and private sectors of myriad emerging economies. Western chancelleries implicitly did the same. Never a contributor to peace, security and prosperity in Angola, the international system over the last decade has fostered the empowerment of the status quo. Angola's globalized "looting machine"[17] would certainly not have been possible without the elite's foreign associates and the extensive opportunities afforded by today's deregulated world economy.

The Angolan trajectory examined in *Magnificent and Beggar Land* is both exceptional and part of wider dynamics playing out in contemporary Africa and the international system. The decade of reconstruction took place in the midst of Africa's best economic conjuncture since the early

1970s. These circumstances favoured most countries on the continent but disproportionately benefited commodity producers and oil producers in particular. Rising from the doldrums of the early 2000s, when the barrel of oil was very cheap, oil-rich states saw an exponential increase in revenue. The widespread outcome has been the strengthening of the state and of elite interests, as resources empowered the latter and diminished the influence of internal and external forces on their actions. This process of state strengthening was taken much further in Angola than in the other African petro-states. Contrary to chronically turbulent Nigeria, Angola enjoyed political stability and elite cohesion as well as a state that is capable in some key areas, which allowed it to generate a strong degree of purposive power.

What are the accomplishments of Angola's first postwar decade? The most important is the end of large-scale violence and the building of peace. This may be a victors' peace, but it has proved non-vindictive and even accommodating of the losers. A civil war in Angola is now almost inconceivable. This is a fact that is cherished in its own right by the population regardless of misgivings about the character of the political order established by the MPLA. Second, Angola is no longer a colonial fiction. There now is, fifty years and one million dead later, an Angola where everyone is pulled into a single political society and unitary state apparatus. Although the Cabinda issue remains unresolved, all major political forces accept the national space as the legitimate political framework.[18] Third, there were two major policy successes, the rebuilding of the communications infrastructure and macro-economic stabilization. The latter points more broadly towards a much improved approach to economic management and to the continuing development of enclaves of competence, such as Sonangol, which have the potential to serve national development under the right circumstances. Lastly, postwar Angola's aloofness from external pressures allowed the country to open itself to the world largely on its own terms, a notable accomplishment in view of a long history of foreign intrusion.

While recognizing these successes, I have underlined the limitations of Angola's postwar reconstruction. The victory guaranteed that there would be no return to violence but also afforded the MPLA a rare concentration of political, coercive and ideational power. As mentioned at the start, this book is about what the victors did with this power: the Angola they imagined and tried to bring into existence. The result was both eccentric (even utopian) in its high modernist ambitions and pragmatic in terms of the economic and status goals of the elite. It materialized in the form of a continued MPLA stranglehold over the political economy, and a rhetoric of universal inclusion contradicted by a practice of mass exclusion.[19] Public expenditure flowed to cities over the rural world (and within cities, to the urban core over the peripheral shantytowns); to a loosely defined "bourgeois" constituency of regime supporters to the detriment of the poor; and to consumption and physical infrastructure instead of diversification of the oil-dependent economy or investment in human capital. The state distributed private goods, not public goods, through party channels rather than through administrative channels. The overarching objective was to consolidate the MPLA's grip over Angola in perpetuity. Though the rituals of democracy were performed, this amounted to a particularly constraining species of electoral authoritarianism in which the party-state went unchallenged. The building of popular legitimacy was for much of the time a secondary concern for the regime, which saw its legitimacy as emanating from the war victory as well as the inherent superiority of the MPLA vis-à-vis the other nationalist projects.

The Angolan lesson for wider debates about contemporary development in Africa is therefore dispiriting. Touted as one of the continent's biggest successes of the last decade on account of the tenfold expansion of its GDP, the Angolan achievement is in fact largely built on sand. Worse, far from being an exception, it is a magnified version of a dynamic occurring across many resource-rich states around the continent. Elites in these states have used the dramatic increase in revenue allowed by the upturn in commodity prices—a pivotal trend of the "Africa Rising" conjuncture of the last decade—to pursue their own, allegedly developmental, agendas. But more often than not, these elites have failed, the enrichment of insiders notwithstanding, to use the rewards of the boom to transform resource wealth into development, support genuine African entrepreneurs and transcend the perennial handicaps of African economies.[20]

Challenges

Back in 2008, it seemed that the MPLA had firmly secured its grip over Angola and that the country was going into one-party lock-down for a generation. But things are not turning out that way. A decade after the end of the war the status quo as described in this book has started to be tested across the board. JES's autocratic rule, assumptions about a politically quietist population, and the certainties of oil-based development are all in different ways under stress. The MPLA "peace dividend" has ended and Angolan society is noisily kicking back into life.

Of all the open questions regarding Angola's future, none has garnered more attention than dos Santos's succession. As mentioned above, this has been a recurrent concern since the late 1990s. But since 2011 the matter has emerged fully into public view and JES's prolonged absences throughout 2013 (allegedly for treatment at a Barcelona clinic) have resulted in frenzied speculation about what comes next. JES himself has admitted to being in power "for far too long", but remains reticent about the timing of succession.[21] This is not simply a case of wanting to hold on to the throne, for the process of succession poses serious challenges. In the words of a longtime observer of Angolan politics, JES "is a hostage to the need for protection of his family and allies".[22] Their collective stake in the economy is so large that there is nothing left on a similar scale for newcomers to appropriate. Merely in order to consolidate his own patronage structure, a new head of state would have to redistribute privileges away from JES's core supporters. His successor would also be tempted to blame dos Santos's long tenure for myriad policy failures. In addition to the internal politics, JES fears the prospect of foreign legal prosecution should he retire. He knows that, once he relinquishes power, he will be able to count on few foreign friends;[23] a cozy Riviera exile can no longer be taken for granted. JES's perception of how the succession will play out is vital because if he is not confident that a transition can be operated that protects the status quo, he will simply stay on until he dies.

Like many other autocrats in this difficult position, JES's preferred solution is to keep the presidency within the family. But his earlier attempts at pushing through his eldest son, José Filomeno "Zenu", were met with hostility by the party (Zenu's current high-profile role as head of Angola's sovereign wealth fund leads many to think that JES has not yet discarded this ambition).[24] Short of a family member, someone from the inner sanctum of the president is the next best option, even bearing in mind that trustworthy dauphins historically have a knack for betrayal further down the line. In many ways, Manuel Vicente, the current vice-president and former long-time head of Sonangol, seems a judicious

choice. In view of dos Santos's penchant for discarding would-be successors, much scepticism remains as to whether he really is serious about
Vicente. This remains, for the time being, the most likely outcome.
Vicente has a close relationship with JES and owes his career-long ascent
to him alone; he obviously has intimate knowledge of Angola's political
economy and the functioning of the parallel state. Moreover, Vicente
does not carry with him an alternative clique that might replace dos
Santos's. He would need to accept the existing JES network rather than
do away with it. JES might even remain involved in governing Angola by,
for instance, leaving the presidency but remaining head of the party, and
having Vicente do his bidding. However, what makes Vicente palatable
to JES also makes his bid a fragile one. Though a member of the
Politburo since 2008, Vicente is seen by MPLA barons as someone
without a party history, "not really a comrade"; in a case of the pot calling
the kettle black, powerful voices also criticize his extensive business interests accumulated during the years as head of Sonangol.[25]

Angola's concern with presidential succession is amply justified. JES,
together with President Obiang of Equatorial Guinea Africa's longest-
serving head of state, is the very heart of the country's functioning. As he
has allowed little by way of autonomous decision-making or institutionalization, his demise is likely to be as traumatic as one would expect.
There are strong incentives for the transition, in whatever shape or form,
ultimately to go smoothly: everyone, from foreign investors to elite rent-
iers, would have so much to lose if it didn't. But this moment is beset
with dangers. Even if the immediate succession works courtesy of hugely
expensive buy-offs and assurances of continuity, decision-making under
a new executive (say, by a weak Vicente beholden to multiple constituencies) will be much more fragmented and faction-ridden. From party
barons and army generals to senior civil servants and the leading Luanda
families, the Angolan elite will not allow the parallel state to survive in its
current form.[26] A seamless shift from personalized rule to transparent,
institutionalized politics is unlikely. Released from JES's tight grip, the
elite will want not just the fruits of Angola's political economy, which
they have long accessed, but the discretionary power that the president
has jealously hoarded away from them.

The role of two key organizations, the MPLA and the armed forces,
deserves particular scrutiny. This book has emphasized the power of JES
and his coterie for understanding Angolan politics, arguing that the peace

era represents the apogee of the parallel system the president concocted from 1979. Dos Santos' longevity is partly related to the capacity to keep in mind, and deliver on, the interests of different elite constituencies, but there is no doubt about who's in control. Nevertheless the MPLA exists externally to dos Santos and will be around when he is no longer in power. The legitimacy of the succession process is partly cloaked in its approval; without it, no one can replace JES. And though Angola has little experience in presidential transitions other than Neto's death in 1979, the party at least provides a quasi-institutional context in which the elite can regulate conflict. The MPLA's dealing with the succession issue is a function of the broader elite incentives for continued cooperation as opposed to fragmentation. Dos Santos has kept everyone at the top happy and rich, and they have obliged by suspending old disputes and agreeing on the merits of party cohesion. But the MPLA is inherently fissiparous and its rifts may reopen, especially when the stakes are inordinately high and there is fear of losing out. At the end of the day, much depends on the complex calculations of a handful of powerful Angolan players who, with their unique trajectories, passions, and personal limitations, may not behave according to external expectations of cool-headed maximization of self-interest.

The same unpredictability applies to the armed forces, which remain among Africa's largest and best equipped (15.4 per cent of the state budget went into the security sector in 2012 and 16.4 per cent in 2014).[27] Throughout the period covered in this book, the FAA stayed in the political background, their immensely wealthy leadership quiescent and loyal to the president. Though riven with corruption, especially through their opaque, cash-rich procurement system and their pension fund, the FAA have emerged as perhaps the most legitimate public institution in Angola, one where the divisions of the war seem to have been transcended.[28] In truth, however, the world of the FAA is virtually unknown to outsiders, and there is next to no understanding of how it sees the near future. The armed forces and the ruling party will be defining for the succession process, but for now their calculations remain shrouded in mystery.

The second major challenge is economic diversification. Only a genuine transformation of Angola's economy can provide its population with the opportunity to transcend mass poverty. We have seen that the commitment towards diversification away from oil, and particularly towards industrialization, is central to the regime's rhetoric. But Angola remains as dependent as ever on oil rents and exposed to external shocks, with virtually all the important investments (the development of Angola's LNG sector, the opening up of the pre-salt oil frontier) taking place in the hydrocarbons enclave and resulting in jobless growth. Stripped to its essentials—by 2012, oil still represented more than 95 percent of total exports[29]—the last decade seems little more than a new configuration of Angola's perennial role as a commodity producer on the periphery of the world economy. This economic model still has some mileage to it, provided the global conjuncture remains positive. But the 15 percent annual growth rates of the golden years that made Angola, as Ernst & Young breathlessly put it, "the world's fastest growing economy for the first ten years of the new millennium",[30] are probably gone forever.[31] And the flashy gains of the boom—the conspicuous consumption, Angola's apparent high standing in the world—can all be reversed overnight. There is no sign of structural transformation and the economy's full possibilities remain untapped. With little emphasis on the development of domestic social capabilities or improvement in state capacity, the same applies to the talents of its population.

It is not too late for a complete rethink. This would entail the wholesale discarding of what passes as industrial and agricultural policy; the replacement of informal guarantees by the president to investors by formal, contractually binding commitments by Angolan public authorities; the development of Angolan capacities, including a genuine qualitative investment in education and health; and the overall redeployment of fiscal resources for productive purposes. But there is little chance of this happening at the present time. This outcome will not surprise experts on oil booms, who know that a long-running fiscal windfall is the least conducive context for policy-makers to enact bold and potentially difficult reforms, especially when these hurt their own interests.

This failure elicits a larger question: whether the Angolan state can even conceivably be tasked with a developmental role.[32] Costly attempts at industrial development are occurring through the building of factories and the recent adoption of protectionist policies, but both seem designed primarily to favour special interests close to power rather than increase Angola's productive capacity. There are factors other than good or bad public policy at play here. An extensive development literature explains the genuine difficulties faced by primary commodity producers in turning resource wealth into broad-based development. There is no doubt that Angola presents serious challenges in this regard. In addition to the crushing legacy of the war, the country lacks the human resources, the technologies of administration and the regulatory framework necessary for sustained diversification; its land system is a shambles and scares away most investors; Dutch disease effects seriously hamper would-be productive sectors in the face of competitively priced imports.[33]

However, these structural explanations are not enough. As Atul Kohli put it, states can undertake "sustained actions that alter [...] contextual conditions"[34] when they deem such alterations an overriding priority. An exclusive focus on the very real shortcomings of the Angolan state apparatus does not take into account the manner in which Sonangol—a competent entity that few if any African states possess—has been built up, or the extent to which the post-socialist system of spoils is the product of state intervention throughout. As acknowledged in JES' 2013 State of the Nation Address (quoted in Chapter 4), the state has promoted an agenda that fosters elite accumulation, professionalizes the commanding heights of the economy and mixes state intervention with a judicious resort to politically controlled market tools. In short, the regime has shown a degree of strategic vision and capacity to implement it, but economic diversification and poverty alleviation have not been at the forefront of its concerns.

The third challenge facing Angola is the increase in popular mobilization. In the immediate aftermath of the war, average Angolans were exhausted and demobilized. For a long decade, this afforded elites a free hand. Oil-rich states are known to hold asymmetrical relations with their populations but in the case of Angola this autonomy from social pressures reached an extreme form in these years. Now this apathy on the part of the masses is withering away and their reawakening will be a major test for the ruling party. Perhaps inevitably, the nascent demands revolve around the distribution of oil revenue. As I have shown, the population took the promises of oil wealth and the MPLA's developmental language at least partly seriously and showed a "desire for the state" and for service provision; many sought to improve their condition by seeking inclusion in the established order.

By 2012, however, there was a general understanding that the national cake was not being shared, and might never be. Despite a GDP per capita of US$5,700 in 2012, most Angolans are very poor, suffer and die of preventable diseases, and have a life expectancy that barely reaches 50 years; access to potable water, sanitation and electricity remains scarce. People are not finding their way into jobs in the modern economy, but rather scraping by in the big cities, seething at the prosperity that excludes them. If left unheeded, these social claims have the potential to fester into anti-MPLA mobilization. This may not materialize as a revolt threatening the party's hold but will increase the costs of domination and eat away at its legitimacy claims.

Can the regime change?

To stave off these threats, out of self-preservation if not altruism, can the regime change and take Angola down a developmental path? Many Angolans, including active members of the opposition, incessantly ask themselves this question. This is because they share a tacit understanding that the ruling party is going nowhere and that the vagaries of its internal politics will be defining for the country. After years of trying to answer it, I have come to a sceptical view: the regime cannot revolutionize itself, certainly not in the sense implied by the small number of older idealists who, against the grain of decades of misrule, still believe in the party's ultimate goodness. The regime has no inclusive project of national development.

There are several reasons why this is so. The regime's elite is remarkably like-minded. Regardless of disagreements about the political management of the state or the dishing out of spoils, there is a virtual consensus amongst them about the political economy and their lordly role in it. There are no meaningful MPLA constituencies articulating a productive understanding of capitalism, a social democratic project, or a particular focus on the poor. Individuals holding to such beliefs are few and powerless. The Angolan elite benefits immensely from the country's extractive institutions and its stranglehold over them, and opposes "development" if this means a loosening of that grip. Even more important for the character of state-society relations is what I defined in the Introduction as the MPLA's "idea of Angola". This cluster of beliefs, which are core to the MPLA's identity, remains intact and is unquestioned by the regime's upper castes. It includes deep-seated assumptions about relations between the cities and the "uncivilized" countryside, the MPLA's project of building the nation in its own image, and the agenda of coercive state expansion in the interior that, in important ways, resembles the completion of colonial modernization.

Of course, my scepticism is towards the prospect of the MPLA abandoning an oil-based, rentier extractive system in favour of a productive post-oil political economy. Yet the MPLA is not static. There is no doubt that, within the confines of a patrimonial system, the regime has shown a capacity for steep learning and overcome disparate domestic and international trials over the past two decades. If one accepts that Angola is not for the foreseeable future, going to possess a developmental state, there is still ample ground for establishing a rentier system that is much more inclusive than the current oligarchy. This option—the establishment of a broad-based clientelism that includes a plurality of Angolans— would go a long way towards coopting the most pressing challenges to MPLA rule.

There are, in this regard, people inside the MPLA who defend a wider distribution of rents. This is not a liberal faction arguing for transformation but a pragmatic persuasion seeking to buy off potentially influential segments of the population for a generation or more and thus perpetuate social tolerance for the elite's position.[35] Regardless of their involvement in the regime, middle-aged, highly educated men such as Manuel Vicente, Bornito de Sousa, Manuel Nunes Júnior, Aguinaldo Jaime, Archer Mangueira, Job Graça, António Pitra and many òthers know that some expansion of the constituency of beneficiaries is both necessary and (if carefully conceived) compatible with their interests and of those closest to them. In comparative terms, this does not seem a very ambitious upgrade, but in the Angolan context it is almost a progressive programme. As we have seen, the MPLA has over the last decade shown some dexterity in including new constituencies when they are important enough or loud enough. But this extension of regime benefits to the so-called national bourgeoisie, an improvement in regard to the war years, still only targeted a tiny proportion of the population.

Starting in 2012, the MPLA drummed up the promise of social expenditure, with references to distribution deployed throughout the National Development Plan for 2013–17.[36] Vice-President Vicente even acknowledged that social investment had not been a priority up to 2012 and promised that this would change.[37] Priorities for the coming years are said to include electrification, water supply, job creation in agriculture and manufacturing, and a specific focus on women, the elderly, war veterans and youth. The new priorities are praiseworthy, but while the rhetoric is relentless, the party has not shifted towards mass distribution. Critics point to the fact that social expenditure is still interpreted in terms of "infrastructure" and other capital-intensive scams that benefit the usual handful. Bizarrely, the otherwise expansionary 2014 budget even saw a major decline in the share of government expenditure in social sectors.[38] Education experienced a massive 23.6 percent cut, all of it in the lower-level state schools that poor Angolans are likely to attend (primary schools, secondary schools and technical schools suffered cuts of 33 percent, 2.3 percent and 19.3 percent respectively). But funds for university education—the social mobility ticket for the national bourgeoisie—increased by 20.9 percent. Health sector expenditure was slashed by 14.5 percent. Angolans remain some of the world's worst educated and unhealthiest people. Yet twelve years after the end of the war, the defence, security and public order budget is three times larger than the education budget and four times larger than the health budget. In this context, "to produce more in order to distribute better" seems like the latest iteration of the MPLA's piecemeal, defensive inclusion of rising constituencies rather than a change of scale in distribution, let alone a game changer.

Any major expansion of distribution towards new constituencies will therefore come about through social pressure rather than a public-spirited shift by the regime. However, it is unclear at the time of writing to what extent those exercising this pressure will have a very different understanding of what Angola should be. Quite apart from the matter of whether there are political alternatives to the MPLA, most influential actors in present-day Angola do not articulate markedly different approaches to the political economy. There are impressive rights activists and remarkably lucid public intellectuals but their support base is still very small. The MPLA's particular culture has determined important aspects of Angolan life, but it exists within a political world where many ideas and practices are shared. This includes the major opposition party, UNITA, which has not decisively broken with its authoritarian legacy. It also extends to large segments of the population, which yearn for a better life in the context of a functioning distributive system. Ideas of hierarchy, dependency, private disposal of public goods and particularistic attachments overriding abstract ones are all widespread. These values have entered the mainstream of Angolan life and are no longer simply those of the elite. In short, popular perceptions of exclusion, rather than

CONCLUSION: POST-POSTWAR ANGOLA

visions of a radically different society, are what is likely to result in mass mobilization.

In this regard, the opposition parties are slowly navigating the constraints outlined in Chapter 3. The demonstrations that started in 2011, though failing to galvanize wider segments of society, have been decisive in that they have pushed the opposition towards far more assertive postures. CASA-CE, though powerless, is an articulate critic of the government's policies. At least in the urban setting, and partly as a response to the rise of CASA-CE, UNITA is increasingly deploying the language of the social contract and is no longer cowed by the MPLA's constant associating of it with disorder. Still, there are unresolved tensions between the "modern" urban politics UNITA is trying to master and the way it relates with its heartland constituencies in the Highlands.[39]

But formal parliamentary activity is proving less important than the mobilization of popular constituencies ranging from the urban young to disgruntled interest groups that can more easily pull together (lower civil servants, war veterans, etc.). Their claims are growing louder, increasingly take the form of street protests, and exhibit a degree of hostility towards the elite, and JES in particular, that was unknown as recently as four years ago. In turn, the MPLA, which likes to cultivate an image of tolerance when the going is good, is reacting to perceived challenges as existential threats and resorting to bellicose language and the deployment of harsh policing to deal with the emerging contestation.

In our lifetime, Angolans may not get a welfare state or anything resembling a just society. But if they are lucky (in other words, if sustained popular mobilization unleashes a degree of enlightened self-interest at the elite level), they may get some of the distributional clientelism of petro-states like Saudi Arabia, Venezuela or Iran, which provide large, but not overly large, segments of their populations with some disbursements. Such a "pacted" arrangement has, over the last five decades, already proved dysfunctional in many resource-rich states.[40] It is bound to leave rural dwellers and the poorest in the lurch: they will not benefit from the expansion of patronage, and will likely remain second-class citizens in their own society. In the Angolan context, however (and this testifies to the exclusionary, barely distributive character of the current system), an increase in rent distribution will amount to a major expansion of benefits to a wider segment of Angolans than ever before and is likely to deflate the most articulate challenges to the regime.

According to this distributive scenario, the elite is able to continue to learn and adapt to their fast-changing society by using the state's resources to solidify the MPLA's rule and their own social preeminence for the long haul. In a society with historically deep asymmetries of power, some argue, the structures of inequality are very dynamic and can conceivably withstand rising demands, even major upheavals. The result would be a long-lasting oligarchy that locks in state power and assets and uses its sovereignty over them to strut the world stage.

But don't count on it—greed and lack of vision are as likely to carry the day. This situation may seem untenable to outsiders but, as a former ministerial figure put it, "most people [in the summit of the party] have no sense of urgency; Angola has so much money, they think they can make mistakes and start all over again [and still] come out on top."[41] Throughout 2013, examples of the regime's ham-fisted approach were legion, from the mishandling of a severe drought in the south and the killing by intelligence agents of two campaigners to the brutal repression of street demonstrations. Moreover, the regime's long-term stamina depends not just on deft political management but on the fluctuations of its major revenue-generating sector. In Manuel Ennes Ferreira's words, "the only opposition party capable of unseating the MPLA is the oil barrel".[42] The price crash of late 2008 already showed the Angolan economy's high degree of exposure. A major and long-lasting fall of production or price collapse would snatch this lever from the hands of the MPLA, undermine every choice the party-state has made, and introduce a remarkable degree of unpredictability into Angolan life.

Post-postwar Angola

The medium-term implications of a turbulent political transition, increased social mobilization and a resource-dependent, volatile economy are clear: Angola will face a stormy decade as it awakens from its postwar political hibernation. Angola's historical fault-lines have not been decisively bridged; they will reopen in new, unexpected forms. It is safe to assume that many of the old fractures remain fertile ground for social conflict.

The regime's ongoing dynamic of exclusion will interact with the massive social change occurring throughout Angola in unpredictable ways. The mass migratory movement towards the cities shows no signs of abating, in the process emptying the countryside and creating new social and ethno-regional constituencies in the urban environment. As elsewhere in Sub-Saharan Africa, the postwar demographic expansion is resulting in a remarkably young population[43] (by 2012, an estimated 63.7 percent of Angolans were below twenty-five years of age, with 54.2 percent below eighteen)[44] for whom the war is a distant memory, if remembered at all, that no longer works as a deterrent to action. While their parents compare the current dispensation with the terrible plight of the conflict (and are therefore likely to still view it in positive terms), the reference point for the young is the global culture of consumerism that they are bombarded with but cannot access. Their frustrated yearnings are coming to a head. Angola is changing at an extraordinary speed. The party-state does not fully understand or control this process, even when it is the unintended consequence of its policies. The MPLA's legitimacy tropes—the liberation struggle, the civil war victory, even the early postwar threat of *confusão*—are quickly becoming redundant in Angolan political discourse.

In this cauldron, disruptive political phenomena are bound to emerge. The elite will be able to reproduce itself, its privileges and access to power. But it will do so in a fractious and contested Angola. A civic-minded alternative to the MPLA that brings to power patriotic techno-crats committed to "getting to Denmark" is implausible.[45] Far more probable are populist reactions that marshal ethnic, regional and racial resentments, laced with xenophobic sentiment against expatriates, into a rousing critique of the postwar order. Dormant under the current national reconciliation rhetoric are a host of derogatory elite views about "backward" Ovimbundu (the "*sulanos*" or "*bailundos*" of Luandan street slang) and the popular perception of *mestiço* and white overrepresentation in the elite.[46] The elite's dependence on foreigners, already a lightning rod for criticism of the regime, will prove as unsustainable as it has been in other African contexts, ranging from Uganda to Côte d'Ivoire, where the locals played only a peripheral role in the running of economies.[47] Shrewd political entrepreneurs in the Hugo Chávez cast may come to mobilize these frustrations into a more structured discourse of class grievance. Luanda's vast shantytowns in particular seem prone to this sort of mobilization, with 1970s *Nitismo* providing a powerful portent.[48] Alternatively, the increasingly criminalized slums may explode into the sort of gangland violence typical of Latin American cities. Either way, the urban poor will not stay at the margins of Angolan political life.

MAGNIFICENT AND BEGGAR LAND

Angola's potential remains unrealized. The "magnificent" promise of this book's title continues to be elusive, the abject poverty of most Angolans far too real. Yet Angola's long-term prospects are more optimistic than those of so many African countries that are landlocked, internally divided and stuck with non-viable economies. We don't know what the political future of, say, the Congo holds, but in a hundred years there will be an Angola. Angolans will not build their future from scratch; Angola is growing within its battered confines as well as accumulating new contradictions that result from the MPLA's choices. But Angolans have more space for self-fashioning now than ever in their tortuous history. With the trail of blood of the last decades, only someone irresponsible would wish further radical transformation upon Angola. A better life for the masses, however, can only be the outcome of the relentless press of political mobilization, the rallying of Angolans around aspirations for a more dignified life. Nothing will be given to them for free.

Whatever comes to pass, Angola will not stand still. There is electricity in the air. *Angola começa agora*. Angola starts now.

NOTES

INTRODUCTION: "ANGOLA STARTS NOW"

1. Theroux (2013); see Soares de Oliveira (2013b) for a review of Theroux's book.
2. See Soares de Oliveira (2011) on Angola and Jones, Soares de Oliveira and Verhoeven (2013) for a comparative perspective.
3. Movimento Popular de Libertação de Angola, Angola's ruling party since 1975.
4. União Nacional para a Independência Total de Angola.
5. Ferguson (2006).
6. There were some variations to this phrase such as "the future starts now" and "the country starts now", but the meaning was the same.
7. I am following Cramer (2006: 143–165) that provides a judicious assessment of each of these competing explanations.
8. Cramer (2006: 20).
9. Pélissier (1986).
10. For the early settlement of Angola see Birmingham (1966).
11. For the Angolan slave trade, see, e.g., Miller (1983) and especially Miller (1988).
12. The Angolan poet Mário Antonio (1968) popularized the term in his influential essay *Luanda, "ilha" Crioula*. Pepetela, one of Angola's leading novelists, dislikes the term "Creole" and refers to extensive debates with another prominent Angolan writer, José Eduardo Agualusa, who frequently resorts to it. Pepetela also admits that he doesn't have an alternative term that fully encapsulates Luanda's and Benguela's peculiar histories. Interview with Pepetela, Luanda, September 2012.
13. Cahen (2012: 12).
14. "*Filhos da terra*" (literally, "sons of the land") was the self-identification most commonly deployed by Creoles in the nineteenth and early twentieth centuries; it referred to their broadly defined community and not to the totality of those born in "Angola".

219

15. Dias (1984). *"Angolanidade"* can be translated as "Angola-ness".
16. Newitt (1981: 144).
17. Bayart (1989: 50).
18. See, e.g., Bender (1978).
19. Messiant (2006: 322).
20. Some of Angola's peripheral regions were de facto run by other entities, as was the case of Lunda district (presently the provinces of Lunda Norte and Lunda Sul), where a diamond company, Diamang, was all-powerful from 1917 onwards, or parts of Malanje district, where a cotton farming corporation, Cotonang, presided over the destinies of the population.
21. Contrary to myth, the movements that eventually coalesced were less about ethno-regional similarities and more about the networks of sociability of different individuals. However, in a society as fractured as Angola's, the result was relatively homogeneous nonetheless. The MPLA, which more than any other movement appealed across ethnic and racial boundaries and had senior cadres from all backgrounds, was still an overwhelmingly Creole/Mbundu movement, while UNITA had very few Luandans in its ranks.
22. Frente de Libertação do Enclave de Cabinda.
23. I thank Michel Cahen for emphasizing this point.
24. See Christine Messiant's seminal work as well as Marcum (1969 and 1978) and Pélissier (1979), amongst others.
25. Messiant (2008: 50).
26. União dos Povos de Angola.
27. Frente Nacional de Libertação de Angola.
28. The political ownership of the 4 February 1961 attack remains a highly contentious issue in Angola. An Angolan clergyman, Manuel das Neves, who acted without coordinating with the nascent MPLA, is now seen as the key organizer of the Luanda uprising. Another major revolt by cotton workers in the Baixa do Cassange (Malange district) in January 1961 seems to have been similarly unrelated to the liberation movements. Research on these events is still scarce but see, e.g., Keese (2004).
29. Cann (1997).
30. On the Cuban presence in Angola see George (2005). Between 1975 and 1991, more than 430,000 Cubans (an estimated 5 percent of the Cuban population) served in Angola in military and civilian roles.
31. Pacheco (2002b: 2) refers to "UNITA's exercising of a certain state power, less formal and structured, but much more authoritarian".
32. Messiant (1994) and Messiant (1995).
33. Brigada de Informação e Defesa do Estado.
34. Matloff (1997: 231) contains a great description of Jamba as "a guerrilla theme park".

35. Bridgland (1988).
36. Muekalia (2010: 173).
37. I thank Didier Péclard (2014a) for this point; see also his forthcoming monograph (2014b).
38. Heywood (1998).
39. Muekalia (2010: 86).
40. Messiant (2008a: 40).
41. In his memoirs, Samuel Chiwale, UNITA's then military commander and one of the movement's top officials, tells of his sudden removal from the inner circle and torture on spying accusations in the early 1980s. Several months later, Chiwale was taken to a wedding celebration and sat in the front row: this was his wife's wedding, Savimbi having decided to give her to someone else (Chiwale, 2008: 268). Memoirs by Alcides Sakala (2006), the current head of UNITA's parliamentary caucus, and by Jardo Muekalia (2010), a former party representative in Washington, DC, dwell less on internal repression but also make disturbing revelations about the reality of life under Savimbi's rule. *Patriots*, by Sousa Jamba (1992), a lightly fictionalized treatment of the author's experience in the ranks of UNITA, is an accurate portrait of the inner life of the movement in the 1980s as well as an admirable work in its own right.
42. See Crocker (1993) for an account by the then Assistant Secretary of State for African Affairs of the US involvement in Angola from 1981 until the signing of the New York Accords in 1988.
43. Anstee (1994) is a memoir by the United Nations SRSG given the thankless task, but not the means, of running UNAVEM II.
44. Again, contrary to MPLA propaganda, UNITA always had senior personnel from other regions of the country; it was not an ethnic Ovimbundu vehicle in the manner of the FNLA for its Bakongo constituency. This said, the salient fact of UNITA is the personal rulership of Savimbi; the ethnic composition of its leadership is of lesser import.
45. See Maier (1996) for an account of the 1992–94 war and Vines (1995) for the siege of Cuito.
46. Matos (2002).
47. Karl Maier, "Divide that fuels the world's 'worst war': Country-city struggles divide Angola", *The Independent*, 21 November 1993.
48. For a very useful account of the years 1994–98 see Human Rights Watch (1999).
49. Forças Armadas de Angola, the post-1991 national armed forces that replaced the MPLA's pre-1991 FAPLA army.
50. Matos (2002: 91).
51. The analysis by Charles Tilly (1985), whose insights on European early modern state-building are perceived by some as having limited relevance for postcolonial Africa, fits the Angola experience to a considerable extent.

52. Nascimento (2002: 115).
53. Linz (2000: 34).
54. Birmingham (2012).
55. Arguably, many Angolans who are not supporters of the MPLA have imbibed this dichotomy. Even UNITA politicians, routinely dubbed country bumpkins or even savages by the MPLA, argue against their internal adversaries by dismissing them as "rabble from the bush" (*"malta da mata"*; interview with senior UNITA official, Luanda, February 2012). For a succinct, pitiless illustration of these assumptions, see José Eduardo Agualusa's short story, "Os pretos não sabem comer lagosta" (1999).
56. Vines, Shaxson and Rimli (2005: 21).
57. Messiant (2008a: 50).
58. This is the ironic expression often used to decry the capital's overbearing domination of the country. Luanda's towering influence sometimes elicits a degree of ambivalence and even hostility from non-Luandans, but apparent rejection often hides an enduring fascination.
59. A study of the following decade will very likely give more prominence to non-MPLA political forces, but that is not the story of the first decade of peace.
60. This said, the incumbents strenuously entertain the formalistic fiction that these are different entities. In this view Angola is a democratic state with a constitutional order; the MPLA is simply the party that won the elections and formed the current government; the public administration and the armed forces are above politics, etc.

1. IN THE SHADOW OF WAR: OIL AND THE MAKING OF THE PARALLEL SYSTEM

1. I am following Benjamin Smith's emphasis on "macro-origins and political trajectory" (Smith, 2005). According to Smith, "the initial conditions surrounding regime consolidation set in motion coherent institutional trajectories" (p. 422) and "the circumstances under which single-party regimes come to power have important effects on their makeup" (p. 427).
2. Interview, Luanda, May 2012.
3. See, e.g., MacQueen (1997).
4. Rela (1992: 47–8).
5. Interviews, Luanda, January 2010, July 2011, February 2012.
6. Interview with former senior civil servant, Luanda, February 2012. The interviewee gives an example from the Finance Ministry. In late 1975, a dispatch was sent out asking the most senior personnel still available in the finance department of each province to travel to Luanda. For three provinces, the lowest possible grade (*"aspirante"*) was the highest available, and they were nominated as heads of their departments.

7. Laban (1997), Messiant (2006).
8. Pimenta (2006: 126).
9. In the propaganda battles of the late colonial era the liberation movements and their foreign supporters strenuously denied any amount of transformation. But scholars from all perspectives accept that late colonial Angola saw an accelerated degree of social and economic change. See, e.g., Clarence-Smith (1979), (1985) and (1981), Heimer (1973) and (1979), Roque *et al.* (1991), Castelo (2007), Newitt (1981), Wheeler and Pélissier (2010), etc.
10. On developmental colonialism, see e.g., Lonsdale (1981), Cooper (2002) and Pomeranz (2005). In the context of Mozambique, Pitcher (2002: 31) notes that, despite "Frelimo negative propaganda and lack of research", there is no doubt that the Portuguese government "had become much more aggressively developmentalist, earmarking funds for large projects in the colonies and soliciting foreign investment".
11. See, e.g., Clarence-Smith (1985).
12. JMJ Angola (2011:16).
13. Ferreira (1999: 44).
14. Ferreira (1999: 484).
15. See Ferreira (1999) for numerous examples. "The MPLA administrators", a journalist noted, "embodied the worst of Portuguese bureaucracy, African lack of training and Marxist-Leninist inefficiency" (Matloff, 1997: 66).
16. Vidal (2011: 15).
17. Interview with senior civil servant, Luanda, June 2012.
18. This sub-section is a modified version of parts of Soares de Oliveira (2007b).
19. Soares de Oliveira (2007b).
20. Author interview with Percy Freudenthal, Lisbon, August 2005.
21. The Portuguese cautiously waited till late February 1976, by which time the other armed parties had been driven back.
22. According to this agreement, they would staff the new company and their years there would be counted as service to Petrogal for the purposes of promotion and retirement benefits when and if they decided to return to Lisbon.
23. Interview with Sonangol official, Luanda, January 2004.
24. Soares de Oliveira (2007b: 600).
25. Ibid.
26. Although I have found no hard evidence, two interviewees mentioned that the Algerian President wrote to Agostinho Neto personally assuring him that ADL "was independent and objective and a good consultant for Angola". Interview with former Sonangol official, Lisbon, September 2006, and phone interview with oil consultant, March 2012.
27. Phone interview with oil consultant, March 2012.
28. The fact that the same individual, a US consultant named Philip Hawley, man-

aged A. D. Little's dealings with Angola from 1974 to 1991 lent a strong element of personal trust and even intimacy to the rapport.

29. Marc Rich quoted in Ammann (2009: 183–85).

30. Rich was the "most important oil supplier to South Africa", providing it with at least 15 percent of its oil from 1979 until 1994 (Ammann 2009: 193). Much of this came from countries such as Angola, the USSR and Iran, sworn enemies of the apartheid regime. This was hardly untypical for Rich, who busted sanctions the world over and specialized in deals between mortal enemies (Ammann 2009: 84, 99). It is noteworthy that the MPLA regime had also established a diamond sector relationship with De Beers, reportedly on the initiative of President Neto. This relationship, though extensive, proved less successful. Interview with diamond sector executive, Luanda, October 2011.

31. Ferreira (2005: 5).

32. Interview with Finance Ministry official, Luanda, June 2012.

33. World Bank (1989: viii–x, 16).

34. Le Billon (2001).

35. Soares de Oliveira (2007b).

36. Karl (1997: 44).

37. Amundsen (2014).

38. The largest company in Africa is Algeria's SONATRACH.

39. This process, which happened across West and Central Africa, is studied in Soares de Oliveira (2007a).

40. Interview with oil company executive, Cascais (Portugal), September 2005.

41. Interview, London, October 2010.

42. Alvesson *et al.* (2003: 80).

43. Shaxson (2008: 73–4).

44. This may well have been the foundational scam in Angola's oil sector, and reportedly contributed to the firing of the company's second CEO; author interviews with former Sonangol officials and foreign oil executives, various locations, 2004–2012. Extrapolating from this oil trading fraud, a retired Sonangol executive noted: "even in the 1980s, Sonangol was already the main tool for doing all sorts of things beyond the core mission, if you know what I mean". Interview, Luanda, August 2012.

45. Vallée (2008: 22).

46. "Oil-fired warfare", *Africa Confidential*, 14 May 1999.

47. Of course, as we have seen with Marc Rich, the presence of such individuals predated the 1990s.

48. See Melman and Godoy (2002) for an account of this.

49. Oil equity stakes were also given to companies linked to arms suppliers. However, in a decision typical of Sonangol's careful approach to the oil sector, the operator role was always left in the hands of a reliable Western multinational corporation.

50. Interview, Luanda, July 2010.

51. Cramer (2006: 147) correctly notes that war in Angola "was always associated with international linkages, political and economic". This section's brief discussion of the specificity of the 1992–2002 political economy of war assumes its insertion within that longer set of trends. See "Pre-humanitarian surveillance", *Africa Confidential*, 21 January 2000, for information on private intelligence companies active in Angola.

52. Reno (2000b).

53. Global Witness (2002).

54. Soares de Oliveira (2007a: 253–61).

55. A recent report by Corruption Watch UK (2013) contains additional information in this regard.

56. See the seminal contribution by Hodges (2004), which remains essential for understanding this period.

57. IMF (2002: 47).

58. Hodges (2004: 142).

59. Global Witness (2004: 50).

60. Conversation, London, January 2007; he was referring to Global Witness.

61. Shaxson (2008: 78).

62. Interview, New York, February 2013.

63. Neto's death is still deemed mysterious when not squarely blamed on the Soviets who, according to the prevalent version, had him killed during surgery in Moscow. As a former MPLA member remarked, "in Africa no one dies of natural causes: even if Neto was known to be seriously ill, the conspiratorial interpretation is much more popular!" Interview, Luanda, March 2012.

64. Interviews, Luanda, February 2012, June 2012 and September 2012.

65. Interview, Angolan academic with access to Neto's circle, Luanda, September 2012. *Mais-velho* is a common Angolan expression of deference towards older individuals.

66. A further rationale for JES's strengthening of his power structure vis-à-vis the MPLA was his relatively poor performance in the 1992 elections, which created the widespread belief that he is less popular than the party (he got 49 percent of votes, while the MPLA got 53 percent).

67. Sciascia (2002: 30).

68. Interview with Angolan academic, Luanda, September 2012.

69. Interview with Marcolino Moco, former Prime Minister, Luanda, May 2012.

70. "These individuals owe everything to him—who were they before he pulled them up there?". Interview with senior MPLA official, Luanda, June 2012.

71. Two senior MPLA officials referred to the presidency in such terms. Interviews, Luanda, May and June 2012.

72. Interview with senior MPLA official, Luanda, May 2012.
73. Numerous interviewees referred to this exchange though the details were much embellished by the Luandan rumour mill.
74. Interview, Luanda, March 2012.
75. Interview, Luanda, May 2012.
76. Hansen-Shino and Soares de Oliveira (2010).
77. Interview with Finance Ministry official, Luanda, June 2012.
78. Interview with MPLA official, Luanda, June 2010.
79. Interview with Angolan journalist, Luanda, June 2012.
80. Interview with Angolan journalist, Luanda, June 2012.
81. Shaxson (2008: 9).
82. Interview with defence sector specialist with FAA experience, Lisbon, March 2012.
83. Interview with defence sector specialist with FAA experience, Lisbon, March 2012. These units fought the war and were well fed and resourced, but even in 2002 many army recruits were underfed, shoeless and under punitive command.
84. In the 1980s and 1990s, and ironically in view of subsequent developments, Mugabe preferred to favour white commercial agriculture to the detriment of its African counterpart, as he saw whites as lonely individuals who could not possibly mobilize against him. Likewise the MPLA (and to a lesser extent UNITA) has always used white Angolans as performers of key tasks without the downside of political ambitions. Theirs is now a "small, isolated tribe", over-represented in technical positions but politically marginal.
85. JES, who has since styled himself the "president of peace", did not want Matos to overshadow his "war hero" credentials (interview with Angolan journalist, Luanda, January 2010). In a typical JES move, João de Matos wasn't exactly sent off to Siberia: married to a former Miss Angola, he is one of the country's wealthiest businessmen. This is certainly a better fate than that meted out to Savimbi's potential rivals.
86. Another example is the fact that the military chief of UNITA in 2002, General Kamorteiro, is now deputy head of the FAA for logistics.
87. As a longtime MPLA cadre notes, JES "dominates all the meanders of intelligence [...] what he has is more information about everything and everyone than anyone else in Angola—this is crucial for his control". Interview, Luanda, June 2012.
88. Slater (2010).
89. Hodges (2004: 56).
90. Interview, Luanda, September 2012.
91. Vu (2010: 150) underlines the importance of state genesis both for "durable institutional complexes within state structures [...] and particular patterns of relations with society".

92. Vandewalle (1998: 29).
93. See, e.g., Reno (1995).
94. For months, JES allowed rumours to spread regarding his preference for João Lourenço, the then Secretary-General of the MPLA, as the successor. When Lourenço finally expressed his ambitions, he was swiftly marginalized.
95. ICG (2003b: i-3).
96. Celia W. Dugger, "Angola moves to make President stronger", *New York Times*, 22 January 2010.

2. THE SPECTACLE OF RECONSTRUCTION

1. Abrantes (2009: 99).
2. Hobsbawn (1995:199).
3. Angola Country Report, *Economist Intelligence Unit*, May 2002.
4. Justin Pearce, "Angolan Ceasefire Signed", *BBC News*, 4 April 2002.
5. Cramer (2006: 245).
6. Of a number of reports and contributions on DDR in Angola, by far the most comprehensive is Porto, Parsons and Alden (2007).
7. This included a sustained policy by MINARS of claiming responsibility through ambiguous language such as "the government called upon/authorized the UN and the NGOs" ("*o governo autorizou*"; "*o governo chamou*") for activities that were in fact wholly funded and conducted by UN system agencies and NGOs. I thank Justin Pearce for insights into this process. Conversation, London, April 2012.
8. General Hélder Vieira Dias "Kopelipa", a presidential insider and one of Angola's most powerful men of the last two decades, was one of the beneficiaries of this process, with his company Entreposto Comercial receiving a US$50 million contract to supply the UNITA cantonments. See "Whose peace bonanza?", *Africa Confidential*, 14 June 2002.
9. Porto, Parsons and Alden (2007: xix).
10. Craig Timberg, "Between old allies, A profound divide", *Washington Post*, 16 September 2004. See also ICG (2003a: 7).
11. Vines and Oruitemeka (2011: 260).
12. This was compounded by hostile creditors threatening to seize Angolan assets abroad; see *Angola Country Report*, Economist Intelligence Unit, February 2003.
13. Benner and Soares de Oliveira (2010).
14. See especially IMF (2002).
15. See "Banking on the donors", *Africa Confidential*, 14 June 2002 and "Clinging to the cash box", *Africa Confidential*, 11 October 2002.
16. Soares de Oliveira (2007a); Benner and Soares de Oliveira (2010).
17. Carola Hoyos and John Reed, "Angola forced to come clean", *Financial Times*, 2 October 2003.

18. Interviews with Angolan diplomat, Washington, DC, May 2010 and two MPLA politicians, Luanda, July 2010 and July 2011.

19. James Traub, "China's Africa Adventure", *New York Times*, 19 November 2006.

20. "Angola: Interview with Aryeh Neier, President of the Open Society Institute", *IRIN*, 10 December 2003. These negotiations with the Finance Ministry and Sonangol allegedly involved George Soros himself. Angolan officials always described this brief engagement with OSI (frequently placed by them at the centre of an all-encompassing anti-Angolan conspiracy said to include the CIA) as insincere on their part and the product of the straitened circumstances of 2003.

21. In the words of a former Finance Ministry official (*"diálogo da treta"*); interview, Luanda, June 2009.

22. See Vines, Wong, Weimer and Campos (2009: 5).

23. *Angola Country Profile*, Economist Intelligence Unit, 2009.

24. Interview, New York, February 2013.

25. See, among others, the various contributions in Alves and Power (2012), Corkin (2013), Ferreira (2008), Campos and Vines (2008) and Power (2011). For the broader context of China-Africa relations, see Alden (2007), Alden, Large and Soares de Oliveira (2008), Brautigam (2009), and Taylor (2009).

26. Brautigam (2009: 274). The arrangement in short order of more than US$4 billion in oil-backed loans through syndicates headed by Standard Chartered and Calyon places the Chinese loans in this wider framework.

27. Downs (2007).

28. Interview with senior Angolan official involved in negotiations with China, Luanda, May 2012.

29. Interview, Luanda, August 2012.

30. See Corkin (2013) for a study of Exim Bank's credit lines and state-to-state China-Angola relations more generally.

31. Vallée (2008: 37).

32. Levkowitz, Ross and Warner (2009).

33. UNSA (2002).

34. *Angola Country Profile*, Economist Intelligence Unit, 2008.

35. World Bank (2005: 2–3).

36. *Angola Country Profile*, Economist Intelligence Unit, 2008.

37. Pushal and Foster (2011: 11). The same authors note that, of this amount, a full US$1.3bn is lost to "inefficiencies" (5 percent of GDP).

38. Pushal and Foster (2011: 21).

39. This was mentioned by many interviewees during my research, and is easily observable on the main roads.

40. I thank Ana Duarte, one of the leading experts on the Angolan railway system and the Lobito Corridor in particular, for very useful insights into this subject.

41. Interview with railway official, Luena, September 2012.
42. Duarte (2013: 1).
43. Fernando Pacheco, "Mandela, manifestações e OGE", *Novo Jornal*, 20 December 2013.
44. In October 2011, I travelled along the Saurimo to Dundo segment of the Luena to Dundo national road, the main North-South artery in the east. It was in a state of utmost dereliction and, according to locals, in a worse condition than in 2002. The Saurimo to Luena segment, which I drove through in September 2012, had some repaired stretches but most of it was also in terrible condition.
45. Interview with José Oliveira, an Angolan energy sector expert, Luanda, July 2010 and CEIC (2011b).
46. Interview, Luanda, August 2012.
47. CMI and CEIC (2011).
48. Wells (2011: 17).
49. Interview, Luanda, February 2012.
50. The five officials with knowledge of the ZEE whom I interviewed in February 2012 and November 2013 made it clear that there was virtually no contact between ZEE and the GRN officials who set up the ZEE. The current senior personnel have no clue as to the costs of the ZEE until 2010. At least one government official admitted that he had got most of his information through Google.
51. "Ministério da Indústria realiza primeira conferência nacional", *Angop*, 15 November 2013.
52. Conversations with the author, Talatona, November 2013.
53. Interview with government official, Luanda, March 2012.
54. Interview with Angolan journalist, Luanda, June 2012.
55. Domingos Bento, "CEAST 'abençoa' Kilamba e ZEE", *Novo Jornal*, 23 March 2012.
56. Interview, Luanda, May 2012.
57. Interview with government official, Luanda, November 2013.
58. According to the government, the "initial" goal is import substitution industrialization, with export-oriented production a "future goal". Interview with government official, Luanda, March 2012.
59. Interview, Luanda, November 2013.
60. Interview with Angolan academic, Luanda, March 2012.
61. Interview, Luanda, November 2013.
62. Interview with Angolan journalist, Luanda, September 2012.
63. Conversation with senior MPLA official, Luanda, June 2012.
64. Interview with foreign management consultant, Luanda, May 2012.
65. Interview, Luanda, February 2012.
66. Conversation with the author, September 2012.

67. See Louise Redvers, "Angola's Chinese Built Ghost Town", *BBC News*, 2 July 2012 and other coverage by Redvers, who has closely followed the Kilamba story.

68. President José Eduardo dos Santos, "Que todo este esforço do Estado seja correspondido pela nossa população", inaugural speech, Cidade do Kilamba, 11 July 2011, my italics.

69. Interview with Angolan urban expert, Luanda, January 2010.

70. Santos Vilola, "Imobiliária da Sonangol gere novas centralidades", *Jornal de Angola*, 28 September 2010.

71. When asked whether Delta Imobiliária had received the Kilamba contract from Sonangol without a public tender, and why it was fit for the task, the company's administrator Paulo Cascão answered that "these are concepts that I do not want to broach". See Faustino Diogo, "Entrevista: Delta Imobiliária: Kilamba é um modelo?", *Novo Jornal* 27 January 2012.

72. Louise Redvers, "Angola's Chinese Built Ghost Town", *BBC News*, 2 July 2012.

73. Interview, Dundo, November 2012.

74. Sources in the provincial government of Lunda Norte went as far as declaring that the long term goal is to house about 300,000 people in the new city: "all the inhabitants of the province could, if they so wished, move into the buildings under construction". Miguel Gomes, "Dundo ganha a sua Kilamba", *Novo Jornal*, 19 August 2011.

75. Yossi Melman, "Angling in on Angola", *Haaretz*, 4 January 2002.

76. Interview, Luanda, July 2009; similar points were made by managerial staff during my visit to Aldeia Nova in January 2010.

77. I thank Fernando Pacheco, Angola's leading agronomist and an early critic of the Aldeia Nova project, for a number of valuable conversations on this subject.

78. An Aldeia Nova worker lamented that, in the beginning, things had worked smoothly, but "afterwards, when the Israelis started to leave, everything went on getting worse. We are in a bad situation here". Miguel Gomes, "A Aldeia que era nova está a ficar velha", *Novo Jornal*, 8 June 2012. See also UCAN (2013: 73–5).

79. JMJ Angola (2010: 54).

80. Interview with José Cerqueira, Luanda, July 2009.

81. Interviews, Cacanda and Dundo, November 2011.

82. Interview, Luanda, June 2012.

83. "Angola: Governo angolano investiu 600 milhões de dólares no Presild", *Macauhub*, 18 March 2009.

84. Aylton Neto, "Rede Nosso Super reabre com gestão privada por uma década", *Expansão*, 1 June 2012.

85. Interview with NGO official, Malanje, September 2012.

86. I thank António Tomás, whose excellent study of Luanda (Tomás, 2012) is a reference in this regard, and also Sylvia Croese, Chloé Buire, Claudia Gastrow and Ricardo Cardoso for interesting conversations on the transformation of

Luanda since 2002. This theme, which for reasons of space is dealt with only briefly here, is resulting in some of the best research on contemporary Angola.

87. Conversation with Angolan economist, Luanda, November 2013.
88. Luís Ferreira Lopes, "Baía de Luanda: Os Megainvestimentos na Nova Cara de Angola", *Rumo*, December 2011.
89. Luís Ferreira Lopes, "Baía de Luanda".
90. "Sai daí que é feio".
91. See Amaral (1968), which remains the best geographical study of Luanda.
92. Angola's SOS Habitat has played a leading role in this. In addition, Human Rights Watch (2007) and Amnesty International (2007) have published reports about the demolitions.
93. In fact, by 2012 two thirds of companies active in Angola still depended on generators according to Jover, Pintos and Marchand (2012: 2).
94. World Bank (2005: 4).
95. UCAN (2009).
96. In a rare interview with Portuguese TV channel SIC in June 2013, JES mentioned the inflated figure of 200,000 Portuguese expatriates, perhaps to emphasize the importance of Angola for the Portuguese economy.
97. UCAN (2009); Vines, Wong, Weimer and Campos (2009: 420).
98. David White, "Benguela railway transformed by loans from Beijing", *Financial Times*, 18 July 2012.
99. After attending the 2011 Luanda Fashion Show, a Portuguese businessman with extensive experience of pre-independence Angola quipped: "It felt like 1973 all over again... 70 percent whites, 20 percent *mestiços* and 10 percent blacks; and the blacks and *mestiços* almost the same people as in the old days!" (conversation with the author, Lisbon, December 2011).
100. "New KPMG in Angola", KPMG press release, Luanda, 4 May 2010.
101. The quotes in this paragraph are from an interview with an executive of a leading international consultancy, Luanda, March 2012.
102. The government's 2025 Development Plan tersely labels the DRC "an out-of-control migratory threat, very serious for the Angolan territory" (Ministério do Planeamento 2007b: 12).
103. Benoit Faucon and Sherry Su, "Hostility towards workers cools Angola-China relationship", *Wall Street Journal*, 8 September 2010.
104. Interview, Luanda, August 2012.
105. Interviews, Luanda, October 2011.
106. Jorge Fernandes, "Controvérsias nas noites de Luanda", *Novo Jornal*, 27 January 2012. In reality, the discrimination is class-based, with nightclub managers exclusively concerned with revenues: inside these nightclubs one finds a multiracial elite clientele spending recklessly until dawn.
107. Interview with European businessman, Luanda, July 2010.

108. Interview, Luanda, October 2011. He further noted: "It is extraordinary that there are people who come here thinking that they are getting into a normal place of emigration like Switzerland and Germany [where they will be able to build normal lives for the long haul]."

109. Interview with Portuguese management consultant, Luanda, July 2011. Many of these consultants are an integral part of Angola's clientelistic structure. They have an attachment to particular Angolan politicians and are brought along every time their patrons get nominated to a new post, the health and education sectors being egregious examples of this.

110. Interview with international official, Luanda, February 2012.

111. Interview, Luanda, July 2010.

112. Interview, Luanda, June 2009.

113. UNSA (2002: vii).

114. Interview with international official, Luanda, February 2012.

115. MAT (2004: 7). Some of the high-flown character of the president's speeches (which are available in expensive, illustrated hardback editions with titles such as *José Eduardo dos Santos and the Challenges of His Time: Words of a Statesman*) owe to José Mena Abrantes, his main speechwriter and communications adviser who doubles as Angola's leading playwright.

116. Interview, Luanda, May 2012.

117. Amsden, DiCaprio and Robinson (2012: 356).

118. Hibou (2005: 260).

119. Hibou (2005: 262).

120. Ministério do Planeamento (2007).

121. Interviewees from diverse backgrounds made this point on almost every occasion the 2025 strategy was mentioned. Conversely, ministerial speeches are peppered with invariably vague references to the 2025 agenda every time individual policies need to be fitted into a grand narrative.

122. James Scott (1998) defines high modernism as the belief in science and technology to reorder the natural and social world, an especially dangerous mindset when associated with the modern state and its statebuilding, systematized aspirations.

123. See Karl (1997); Soares de Oliveira (2007a).

124. See Vines, Shaxson and Rimli (2005) for one of the earliest studies seeking to understand the reconstruction mindset of the MPLA.

125. Interview, Luanda, July 2009; see also Power (2011).

126. Vines, Shaxson and Rimli (2005: 6).

127. World Bank (2006: 9).

128. Ferguson (2006: 39).

129. Interview with Angolan academic, Luanda, October 2011.

130. Costa Oliveira (2005).

131. In a prescient article written immediately after the end of the war, Fernando Pacheco, one of Angola's foremost intellectuals, had already alerted to the danger that the Angolan elite might adopt a reconstruction model focused "on the restoration of an order identical to that of the last colonial years". See Pacheco (2002b: 47).
132. Interview, Luanda, 20 July 2012.
133. Messiant (2008a: 40).
134. Birmingham (2012) is a brief, powerful statement of the Angolan elite's Brazilian fascination.
135. "Expensive Angola: Hot on Dubai's heels", *Economist*, 9 February 2011.
136. Interview with Rui Santos, CEO of Sistec, Luanda, February 2012.
137. Conversation with Angolan human rights activist, Luanda, January 2012.
138. Seeking to make sense of Angola's Brazilian and Chinese mélange of influences, Manuel Ennes Ferreira termed it the "Chindubra model". See M. E. Ferreira, "Angola: hora de mudar o modelo Chindubra", *Expresso*, 8 September 2012.
139. CEIC (2009).
140. MPLA (2008).
141. CEIC (2010: 16).
142. António Nogueira, "Dívida do Estado ascende a 9 mil milhões de USD", *Expansão*, 23 July 2010.
143. "Professores reclamam atrasos salariais em Luanda", *Angop*, 18 February 2009.
144. Interview with international official, Luanda, July 2010.
145. Africa Economic Outlook (2012: 12).
146. Apter (2005: 14).

3. THE CONSOLIDATION OF THE MPLA PARTY-STATE

1. Interview with party official, Luanda, January 2004.
2. The party-state dilutes boundaries but likes to reaffirm them on occasion, especially when the president or the MPLA want to put space between themselves and policy failure.
3. Although the trajectory of the MPLA after 1977 is poorly researched, the earlier history of Angolan nationalism is well covered in Messiant (2006), Heimer (1979), Marcum (1969) and Marcum (1978). For the MPLA the key work is Mabeko Tali (2001a).
4. Mabeko Tali (2001a, volume 1: 25).
5. Newitt (2007: 83); see also Brinkman (2003).
6. This cultural distance was mutual: "I became an ethnologist in my own country", reminisced Mário Pinto de Andrade on the subject of his complete lack of familiarity with the Angolan east, where much of the MPLA's activity was concentrated after 1966 (Laban, 1997: 187).

7. Mabeko Tali (2001a, volume 2: 65).

8. For the 1974–77 period, see Cahen (1989).

9. There are a number of memoirs and journalistic accounts of the Nito Alves coup and its aftermath, but no thorough academic treatment. See Pawson (2014) for a searing investigation into the repression and its consequences. Agualusa (1997) is a fascinating novel partly inspired by the events.

10. Messiant (2006: 3). Amongst well-born Angolans, there is no shame in (let alone *Harki*-style retaliation against) having worked in the Portuguese civil service or served in the colonial army. In fact, those with meaningful professional experience who were deft enough to embrace the MPLA in 1974–75 soon found themselves in very senior policy positions after independence, even if the high-profile political leadership positions went for more conventional exile, guerrilla or prison leadership. In this regard, family connections and the "*necessidade de quadros*" (need for educated personnel) invariably eased their integration in the regime. The MPLA's pragmatism was also evident in the recycling of secessionist Katangese militias (exiled into Angola in the 1960s and formerly at the service of the Portuguese colonial army), which became a crucial part of its coercive machinery in the late 1970s and 1980s.

11. Cahen (2012).

12. As Heywood (2000: 204) notes, "like the *assimilados* under the New State, Ovimbundu who became involved in the ruling party conformed to MPLA (Afro-Portuguese) cultural norms".

13. The MPLA's Security Department had been created by Iko Carreira in 1962 but the post-colonial secret police, DISA, was built with Soviet and East German assistance.

14. Pacheco (2002: 3).

15. Pitcher (2002: 6).

16. Heydemann (2007).

17. The *Grande Família* strategy remains under-researched but see Messiant (2008a: 116) for a brief discussion. This strategy for creating an anti-UNITA electoral front seduced few of the many intellectuals who had suffered in the 1977 repression but was successful among professionals, *mestiços* and whites, who perceived the rebels as an existential threat. Discussing the success of this strategy, an MPLA official boasted, "we even managed to pull Chipenda [the leader of a 1970s splintering MPLA faction] back in!" Interview, Luanda, June 2012.

18. Even in the 1980s, JES had already shown a willingness to accommodate stray former *Nitistas* and FNLA members, but co-optation since the early 1990s, and particularly since 2002, is on a different scale altogether.

19. See Marques (2010) for an excellent exposé of GEFI and its business empire.

20. Interview, Luanda, February 2012.

21. More recently, attempts at improving Angola's image abroad have included adver-

tisements on CNN International, courtesy of a contract with a media company belonging to two of JES's children.

22. Soares de Oliveira (2007a).
23. Brownlee (2007: 33).
24. Crystal (1995).
25. See "Inteligência externa espremida por dentro", *Voice of America*, 3 March 2006 and Luís Costa, "Como Angola transformou a sua inteligência externa", *Voice of America*, 23 February 2007. By 2012, Miala, who was imprisoned for two years, was making a comeback as the president's personal emissary.
26. Péclard (2008: 9–13).
27. The following quotes are taken from interviews with many MPLA party members (most of whom were primarily interviewed on the basis of their professional capacity), various locations in Angola, 2009 to 2012.
28. Vidal (2007).
29. Interview with Abel Chivukuvuku, Luanda, February 2012.
30. Many Angolans distinguish between a Cuban presence, towards which they have a range of opinions, and that of other Eastern Bloc advisers, who tend to be remembered in resentful tones. Despite years of geopolitical intimacy, the Angolan-Socialist Bloc relationship was mired in mutual ignorance and rampant prejudice. Amongst the thousands of Angolans who studied in Eastern Europe, I have rarely met anyone who did not highlight racism and even brutality as their most memorable student experience. East Germany in particular seems to have garnered little soft power from this historical encounter.
31. An additional way in which this impact is still felt is the manner in which Soviet networks were "reinvested" and proved amazingly useful in the subsequent years of crony capitalism.
32. McGregor (2010: 12).
33. The classic example was the nomination of Marcolino Moco, a rare and then relatively young Ovimbundu cadre, to the prime-ministership in 1992 as the country went back to war. This was to underline the non-sectarian character of the MPLA, but did not prevent thousands of Ovimbundu from being massacred in Luanda; Moco held no real power until his belated discharge in 1996.
34. "Criado grupo para a investigação da História Geral de Angola", ANGOP, 19 August 2008 and "UNITA e FNLA protestam exclusão de comissão de história de Angola", *Voice of America*, 6 May 2013.
35. Messiant was subsequently barred from Angola for four years on account of her landmark article on FESA (Messiant 1999).
36. "Primeiro Colóquio Internacional sobre a História do MPLA", Final Communiqué, Centro de Conferências de Belas, Luanda, 6–8 December 2011.
37. For a good discussion of Angolan civil society see the contributions in Vidal and Andrade (2008).

38. During this period, the anti-corruption agenda found a charismatic spokesman in Rafael Marques. But the import of corruption issues for wider civil society networks was limited in view of their politically explosive character and the fact that the war was clearly more important at that stage.

39. Interview, Luanda, 12 March 2012.

40. For instance, *Diamantes de Sangue*, the book on violence in the diamond-rich Lunda Norte province by the irrepressible Rafael Marques, is available and in full view in at least two bookstores only metres away from the main entrance of the Sonangol building. This would have been inconceivable a decade ago. At the same time, Marques has been repeatedly sued by some of the Angolan targets of his accusations both in Lisbon and in Luanda.

41. A major example is the annual Prémio Nacional de Cultura e Artes. Incidentally, as fiction and poetry writing are status enhancers in the Lusophone world, many senior MPLA officials dabble in them, with uneven results.

42. Every professional field has one such organization, and new ones are constantly created to keep up with the increasing number and diversity of Angolan graduates. In 2013, the Ordem de Psicólogos, with 68 members, held its first Congress.

43. Some information on the special cadre committees made briefly available on www.mpla.org (accessed 18 April 2012) was removed when the MPLA website was refurbished for the August 2012 elections.

44. Interviewed on TPA after voting on 31 August 2012, Minister Carolina Cerqueira thanked, with remarkable precision, the "1905 accredited Angolan journalists" as well as the "64 foreign journalists" for their coverage of the elections.

45. "Maboque maior para Gustavo", *Semanário Angolense*, 13 October 2012. For the 2012 round, and in addition to the main prize, there were another seven prizes and the total amount of money disbursed was US$330,000.

46. At any rate, getting foreign funding became progressively more difficult in the years after the war as donors moved to other trouble spots. In some cases, donors also became wary of being seen to fund activities critical of the government. Interviews with two NGO officials, Luanda, July 2010 and July 2011.

47. Many interviewees mentioned JES's disappointing electoral performance in the 1992 elections as the stimulus behind these presidential outfits: while the MPLA won against UNITA in the first round, JES had fewer votes than his party and was scheduled to face Savimbi in a second round, which was never held.

48. Messiant (1999).

49. Literally, "the entrepreneur of youth", a daft moniker meant to convey Kangamba's extensive expenditure on youth-related activities such as those described in this paragraph.

50. Kangamba retired as a general for pension purposes.

51. João Marcos, "Convulsões sociais abrem a porta a Bento Kangamba", *Angolense*, 18 May 2012.

52. Interview, Luanda, May 2012.
53. Interview, Luanda, November 2011.
54. Interview with senior MPLA member, Luanda, October 2011.
55. Conversation with the author, Luanda, June 2012.
56. "Tribunal Constitucional extingue 67 partidos políticos", *ANGOP*, 2 May 2013.
57. In Michel Cahen's felicitous expression used in the context of Mozambique, this even leads opposition parties to take "the enemy as model" and to mimic the mannerisms and internal organization of the MPLA; see Cahen (2011).
58. "Cabinda is not poor, the Lundas are: this shows that dialogue has no rewards; the Cabindans [make] *'confusão'*, and the regime is afraid", which results in attempts to buy them off. Interview with Eduardo Kangwana, PRS president, Luanda, October 2011.
59. For the gleeful pro-MPLA coverage see, e.g., "Chibatadas de regresso na UNITA", *Angonotícias*, 15 July 2011.
60. Many interviewees, including three senior members of UNITA, referred to Gato's 2002 request.
61. Senior UNITA leaders have had low profile but rewarding partnerships with MPLA heavies such as former Vice-President Nandó, former Minister of State Carlos Feijó, General Kundi Paihama, etc.
62. Nelson Sul d'Angola, "General 'Black Power' poderá reforçar campanha do MPLA", *Semanário Angolense*, 28 July 2012.
63. Interview with Abel Chivukuvuku, Luanda, February 2012.
64. Interview with UNITA official, Luanda, May 2012.
65. This reputation is often presented as Chivukuvuku having "stood up to Savimbi". It is true that he kept his distance from Savimbi's bellicose post-1994 stance and had no contact with him after 1997. A complicated intrigue led to the end of the rapport. In Chivukuvuku's telling, President Omar Bongo of Gabon, "the victim of MPLA disinformation", complained to Savimbi that "his people" in Luanda were going astray, which raised Savimbi's suspicions. But this break was accomplished not by a dramatic confrontation, but by Chivukuvuku's never returning to Savimbi's court (a wise decision). Strictly speaking, no one ever stood up to Savimbi. In his years with UNITA, Chivukuvuku was as awed by Savimbi, and as silent about the movement's internal life, as other officials. He would have been killed otherwise. Interview with Abel Chivukuvuku, Luanda, February 2012.
66. Interview, Luanda, February 2012.
67. Matumona Félix, "Entrevista com Pepetela", *Novo Jornal*, 23 March 2012.
68. Conversations, Luanda, March 2012.
69. Former Prime Minister Marcolino Moco's reaction explicitly referred to the need for the *"grande família"* to come together. See http://marcolinomoco.com/?p=558 (accessed 14 April 2012).
70. Literally "big daddy", a paternal Big Man who generously takes care of his dependents.

71. In turn these derive a measure of local legitimacy from an association with the party-state. See Croese (2012) for a case study of the Zango neighbourhood with lessons for an understanding of Luanda.

72. Every major football club is intimately tied to the regime and receives lavish funding on account of this: Petro (Sonangol), Inter (police), Libolo (General Higino Carneiro), Primeiro de Agosto (FAA), Kabuscorp (Bento Kangamba), Asa (TAAG, the national airline), Recreativo da Caala (António Mosquito), Benfica de Luanda (Tchizé dos Santos), etc.

73. See Moorman (2013) for an insightful analysis of *kuduro* and its wider political and social context.

74. Despite the sympathetic foreign media attention that rappers like MataFrakos, MCK and Brigadeiro 10 Pacotes have received, the content of Angolan rap can be problematic. The rappers' railing against poverty and inequality, packed in the vernacular, has considerable social reach. But mixed in with the lyrics about the elite's hidden billions you will also find abuse against foreigners—the Portuguese, the Congolese—as well as hints at the suspected São-tomean origins of the President, a xenophobic trope frequently used to delegitimize him.

75. "Sétima Sessão do Comité Central: Discurso do Presidente José Eduardo dos Santos", MPLA, Luanda, 7 February 2014 (http://www.mpla.ao accessed on 27 February 2014).

76. Schubert (2013: 2).

77. Hibou (2006: 17).

78. MacGregor (2010: xx).

79. Author interview, Luanda, July 2011.

80. Soares de Oliveira (2013a: 167–172).

81. The fact of state absence until 2002 makes the Angolan experience similar to that of other post-conflict states, but different from most of the case studies in the African literature on decentralization that tends to focus on "reform" to a long-standing central state-rural state rapport.

82. On UNITA's governance structures, see Pearce (2011) and ongoing doctoral research by Paula Roque.

83. Quoted in Guedes (2003: 79).

84. MAT and PNUD (2007: 53–54).

85. In Lunda Norte, three out of a total of nine municipalities were unoccupied, as were between ten and thirteen out of a total of twenty-six communes. In Lunda Sul, only one municipality out of four was unoccupied, but nine out of fourteen communes had no state presence; see Guedes (2003: 79).

86. These are studied in Herbst (2000).

87. He added that the goal here was to show that in case of dissent, "the destruction of all those who go against the state is guaranteed" [...] the message is clear: the state has authority over you, but it is not responsible for you [i.e., for your welfare]". Interview, Luanda, July 2011.

88. There were instances of banditry by former UNITA soldiers in Huambo province and elsewhere, but this fell short of the fears of early observers of demobilization.

89. Communities below the level of municipalities still have no official police presence, but networks of SINFO (Angola's main intelligence agency) informants are strong and have a close relationship with local party structures. Interview with senior MPLA member, Luanda, March 2012.

90. These are numbers provided by the Angolan Bar Association. See David Filipe, "96% dos advogados concentrados na capital", *Novo Jornal*, 23 August 2013.

91. In this regard, the provincial governor is most often the provincial party head. During interviews with two top officials in Lunda Sul (both high-ranking MPLA members), phone calls and personal requests were met with a "Ring me/Look me up at the party headquarters this afternoon and we will go over it". Interviews, Saurimo, July 2011.

92. Interview, Luanda, March 2012.

93. Interview, Luanda, February 2012.

94. The situation of senior technical staff was even worse: 97.5 percent worked at the provincial level, 2.5 percent at the level of municipalities, and 0 percent at the level of communes; see MAT and PNUD (2007: 74).

95. Bowerbank (2010: 32).

96. Interviews with two MAT officials, Luanda, February and June 2012.

97. Carvalho (2003: 258).

98. On the CACs see Orre (2010: 191–214).

99. The MPLA reasoning is circular: municipal elections cannot be held until capable local government exists, and the requisite degree of local governance "is likely to take a very long time to become operational". Conversation with Carlos Feijó, Talatona, November 2013.

100. Bowerbank (2010). The role of decentralization in advancing state power has been identified by analysts in other contexts; see, e.g. Otayek (2009).

101. Interview with MAT official, Luanda, June 2012. This includes more than 7,500 in the fractious province of Uige alone. "Because there is money involved, traditional authorities are mushrooming all over the place, many of them with competing claims! The situation in Uige is a real mess," this official noted.

102. There are different designations for traditional authorities according to region and ranking; *sobas* is the most prevalent one and usually used for generic discussions of traditional leaders.

103. Orre (2008). Even in the socialist years, Presidents Neto and dos Santos held meetings with traditional authorities.

104. While UNITA's wartime approach to traditional authorities is beyond this chapter, I thank Fernando Florêncio for pointing out that the rebels also made extensive use of them for the purposes of "indirect rule of populations and territory".

105. Interviews with UNITA and PRS provincial secretaries, Dundo, Lunda Norte, November 2011.
106. Pacheco (2002a) is an excellent analysis of traditional authorities.
107. Pacheco (2002a: 10).
108. *"Acham que o estado é pai"*. Interview with João Fukungo, Secretary of the Lunda Sul Provincial Government, Saurimo, July 2011.
109. Alexander (1997) also perceives local elites as motivated by the desire for inclusion in the state instead of seeking to "oppose or reform it".
110. Angolan critics argue that the policy on traditional authorities empowers male, older rulers in aspects of local governance to the detriment of the young and females. These are recurrent concerns in the literature on traditional authorities in contemporary Africa.
111. Feijó (2012).
112. JMJ Angola (2011: 22).
113. Marques (2011).
114. Marques (2011: 75).
115. Cândido Mendes, "Angola boosts security at border with Congo to help secure diamond fields", Bloomberg News, 2 August 2011.
116. Human Rights Watch (2004).
117. See Mabeko-Tali (2001b: 60–62) for a discussion of Congo-Brazzaville's support for Cabindan separatists.
118. See Human Rights Watch (2009) for a detailed report on the widespread human rights violations by state security forces.
119. Adding to the confusion, FLEC-Posição Militar, a dissident offshoot, also claimed responsibility for this attack.
120. Henrique Almeida, "Angola arrests a third rights activist in Cabinda", Reuters, 17 January 2010.
121. Scott (1998).
122. António Tchikanawe, PRS official, Saurimo, July 2011.
123. Interview, NGO official, Luanda, July 2010.
124. Interview, local official, Luena, September 2012.
125. Interviews and conversations with municipal- and provincial-level officials, various locations, 2011 and 2012.
126. Soromenho (2010: 57).
127. Tilly (1975: 82).
128. Clapham (2002: 17).
129. Berman and Lonsdale (1992: 5).
130. Weber (1976).
131. Tilly notes that expansion "from a highly organized centre into a weakly organized periphery" is a rare historical pattern that only became the "dominant experience [...] in European colonial expansion" (Tilly, 1975: 24).

132. See Roque (2009) for an analysis of the 2008 Angolan elections.
133. European Union (2008); the full electoral observer reports nonetheless hinted at a host of electoral authoritarian practices.
134. Hibou (1998: 55).
135. Mann (1984: 206).
136. Conversation with the author, London, April 2012.
137. Interview with Angolan academic, Luanda, June 2009. An old-fashioned Portuguese expression, "*as forças vivas*" (literally, society's "live forces") is also used by some interviewees.

4. OLIGARCHIC CAPITALISM, ANGOLA-STYLE

1. Quoted in Freeland (2005: 67).
2. Quoted in Rocha (2011: 254).
3. The MPLA had already abandoned Marxist-Leninism in its Third Ordinary Congress in 1990.
4. Ferreira (1995: 17).
5. Of course, the elite had benefited extensively from the parallel market, especially since the early 1980s: see e.g., Morice (1985).
6. Messiant (2006: 322).
7. See e.g., Guerra (1979) and Clarence Smith (1985).
8. The sophisticated trading networks of the era of slavery and "legitimate commerce" which spanned the coast and the hinterland were eliminated at the time of the Scramble for Africa in the late nineteenth century. While a counterfactual approach may posit that in time they would have developed into "capitalist" enterprises, their character was decidedly pre-capitalist.
9. See Hodges (2004) and Ferreira (1995).
10. See among others Cilliers and Dietrich (2000), Human Rights Watch (1999), Le Billon (2001) and Cramer (2006: 145).
11. Interview with Angolan banker, Luanda, February 2012.
12. A further exchange rate scam was tightly connected to the rampant inflation: a considerable profit could be made by simply delaying payments by a few days or weeks during which the real value of the amount would decrease considerably.
13. Interview with Angolan banker, Luanda, February 2012.
14. Shaxson (2007: 51–52) and Hodges (2004: 115–18) provide good descriptions of the functioning of this currency scam.
15. See Ferreira (1994/1995) for an analysis of the first round of privatizations.
16. It is symptomatic of the political character of these decisions that Bakongo entrepreneurs, perhaps the only ethno-regional group in Angola with extensive business experience, acquired mostly in the DRC, would not figure prominently in the business groups of the 1990s. Although closely connected with the business

concerns of MPLA notables, in a role akin to that of the Lebanese and other foreign managers of elite interests, Bakongo traders remain politically fragile, as shown by the 1993 pogrom unleashed against them in Luanda (Mabeko-Tali 1995).

17. Interview with Angolan businessman, Luanda, February 2012.

18. Interview, Luanda, February 2012.

19. Pitcher (2002).

20. The academic literature on economic reform in Africa tends to emphasize external determinants, and especially the role of Western donors and agencies such as the World Bank. Even in aid-dependent states, the extent to which domestic policy-makers proved to be agents in the character, timing and consequences of reform has been misunderstood. In the case of Angola, the role of external players was irrelevant. Angolans made the key decisions about reform and reconfigured the political economy without external input.

21. Vallée (2008: 22).

22. Aguilar (2003: 8–9).

23. Soares de Oliveira (2007a).

24. Interview with José Pedro de Morais, Luanda, November 2013.

25. Conversation with former Finance Ministry high official, Luanda, September 2012.

26. Skype interview with former IFI official with experience in Angola, August 2013.

27. Vallée (2008: 30).

28. Interview with SIC Notícias, 6 June 2013.

29. This has been underlined by the nomination to key positions in "reformist" institutions of those close to the president, including members of his family. Dealing with a Sovereign Wealth Fund headed by his son Zenu or with a National Agency for Private Investment (ANIP) led by one of his ex-wives, Luísa Abrantes, no one can fail to realize dos Santos' direct control over the postwar economy. The language of apolitical, technocratic competence is always undermined by a clear signal of who's in charge. Nothing and no one is aloof from the grasp of the presidency; nothing is beyond politics.

30. Lewis (2007).

31. This is an explicit legal requirement in oil, diamond, telecommunications and air transportation (Jover, Pinto and Marchand 2012: 22) but de facto applies to the Angolan economy more generally.

32. Jover, Pinto and Marchand (2012: 29).

33. Boone (2005: 408).

34. The sector concentration is considerable, with the top five banks controlling 80 percent of total bank assets (KPMG, 2011: 8).

35. This amounted to 11 percent of the population in 2010 (KPMG, 2011: 10), up from 6 percent in 2008.

36. Interview, Luanda, July 2009.

37. On the basis of a series of interviews, Rafael Marques (2009: 33) argues that this process of elite distribution (in banking as well as in every other major sector) is the product of a "highly sophisticated [...] task force, within the intelligence services, set up for privatization [of] state assets [that] also oversees the enrichment of selected families".

38. "Seguradora entra no capital do Standard Bank de Angola", *Jornal de Angola*, 26 July 2012.

39. In 2010, the OECD's Financial Action Task Force noted: "Angola's lack of a comprehensive AML/CFT [anti-money laundering and combating the financing of terrorism] regime poses a risk to the international financial system" (FATF, 2010). By 2013, Angola had an action plan to deal with these matters but the FATF still pointed out that "certain strategic AML/CFT deficiencies remain" (FATF, 2013).

40. BFA is a wonderful construct of Luso-Angolan finance: it is 50.1 percent owned by Portugal's BPI, while the rest is owned by Angola's UNITEL, whose main shareholder is Isabel dos Santos. In turn, Portugal's BPI itself is 19.5 percent owned by Isabel dos Santos' Santoro SPSG (she is BPI's second largest shareholder after Spain's La Caixa).

41. In its Article IV consultation, the IMF (2012) noted: "Angola's financial system faces vulnerabilities given the risky domestic and external environment in which it operates. This is due to capacity constraints in banking supervision, inadequate bank corporate governance, high dollarization, and liquidity shifts linked to large oil sector transactions."

42. US Senate (2010: 316–17).

43. Marques (2012).

44. Joaquim Gomes, "Álvaro Sobrinho com caução de meio milhão de euros", *Expresso*, 11 November 2011.

45. Lei do regime cambial aplicável ao sector petrolífero, Lei no. 2/12, 13 January 2012.

46. When it comes to the domestic economy, Sonangol's role is the subject of low-profile but persistent criticism, especially amongst Angolan businessmen who, as one self-described "victim of Sonangol" put it, "are big but not top 50" (interview with Angolan businessman, Luanda, June 2009). Sonangol has been accused of plunging headlong into any profitable sector and thus crowding out other investors. Carlos Severino, the head of the major business lobby in Angola, has been a vocal critic of Sonangol's role in this regard (interview, Luanda, July 2011). As to local content, several interviewees complained that Sonangol consistently implements this policy to the disproportionate benefit of regime insiders, including, during his tenure, CEO Manuel Vicente.

47. See Ovadia (2012) for a study of local content policy in the oil sector.

48. For an early contribution see Guerra (2003).

49. Interview, Luanda, July 2010.

50. This was the case of prominent generals of the 1990s like the Faceira brothers, Higino Carneiro, Kundi Paihama, Ndalu and De Matos, who are officially retired but remain as influential as ever with the armed forces.

51. Interview, Luanda, June 2012.

52. José Eduardo dos Santos, "Estado da Nação: Mensagem Integral do Presidente da Républica", Luanda, 15 October 2013.

53. Ironically, this was the implicit logic of many liberal economic reformists in post-socialist and developing countries during the heyday of the Washington consensus in the 1990s.

54. Conversation with the Angolan economist Manuel Alves da Rocha, Luanda, June 2009.

55. See the excellent discussion of "transparent looting" in Marques (2009).

56. Alves da Rocha (2011: 115).

57. To these one should add transfer pricing and fake accounting, practices fully indulged in by foreign companies operating in Angola as well.

58. During a March 2012 dinner at Pimms, a top restaurant in the Alvalade neighbourhood of Luanda, everyone turned around to greet a newly arrived patron. His moving on to a loud table presided over by a couple of Angolan politicians gave rise to exchanges regarding this individual's present status. Only three months earlier he had been (very) briefly imprisoned for bank fraud but was released through higher intervention and was now back in the circuit; the money simply disappeared.

59. Interview, Luanda, September 2012.

60. Interview, Luanda, June 2012.

61. Aguilar (2003).

62. Conversation with the author, Luanda, July 2009.

63. Interview with Angolan businessman, Luanda, July 2010. Carlos Severino, the head of the Angolan Industrial Association (the lobby group of Angolan businessmen), is a vocal advocate in this regard. Interview with Carlos Severino, Luanda, July 2011.

64. The quotes in this paragraph are from Jaime Fidalgo, "Gestão a Alta Velocidade", *Exame*, December 2010–January 2011.

65. Interview, Luanda, February 2012.

66. This point is made by Coronil (1997: 287) in regard to the Venezuelan bourgeoisie but applies broadly to the character of local business, and its not so hidden dependence on oil rents, in many petro-states.

67. Interview, Luanda, August 2012. An executive at a top foreign consultancy argued: "it will take at least a generation, if not two, for Angolan human resources to reach a critical mass". Interview, Luanda, March 2012.

68. Interview, Lisbon, August 2009.

69. World Bank (2012).

70. J. F. Palma-Ferreira and Ricardo Marques, "Insegurança ameaça empresários", *Expresso*, 15 September 2012.

71. Conversation with the author, Luanda, June 2012. These difficulties paradoxically illustrate why (in addition to the skills they bring) the Angolan elite likes doing business with foreigners: they can be ejected at will, whereas a genuine Angolan entrepreneurial class would be highly destabilizing for the status quo.

72. Interview, Luanda, October 2011.

73. This point, noted by Iliffe (1983) and much of the literature on African capitalism, is illustrated in the Angolan case by the travails of the Wapossoka Group, which collapsed with the untimely death of the founder Valentim Amões. After protracted disputes, one of his daughters has taken the helm of the Group and is seeking to revive it.

74. Note that this logic extends to well-networked foreign companies which, having entered Angola for one specific purpose (say, defence or construction) have used their long-standing relationships at the Palace to extend their interests across the Angolan economy. Teixeira Duarte, the Portuguese construction company, even owns a string of patisseries throughout Luanda.

75. Faustino Diogo, "Neste mundo globalizado os bancos estão abertos aos investidores", *Novo Jornal* 30 March 2012.

76. Hamilton Viage, "O Renascer do Império Amões", *Rumo*, September 2012.

77. Jaime Fidalgo, "Gestão a Alta Velocidade", *Exame*, December 2010–January 2011.

78. Interview, Luanda, February 2012.

79. "A vontade de sacar muito rápido". See Faustino Diogo, "Não expatriamos capitais investimos em Angola", *Novo Jornal* 8 March 2012.

80. Interview, Luanda, February 2012.

81. Interview, Luanda, June 2010.

82. Interview with Angolan banker, Luanda, June 2010.

83. Metz (2011) is an original study of the difficulties of Angolan SMEs in Luanda.

84. Interviews in Benguela and Huambo provinces, January 2010.

85. Interview with Angolan entrepreneur, Huambo, January 2010.

86. Iliffe (1983: 19).

87. Interview, Luanda, October 2011.

88. See Tomás (2012) for a study of the family as an "informal" but ubiquitous "institution of intermediation" in Angolan society, especially as a conduit for accessing state resources by the powerful.

89. Interview with senior MPLA member, Luanda, May 2012.

90. Interview, Luanda, May 2012.

91. *"Geração kudurista"*; *"não prestam para nada"*. Interview, Luanda, May 2012.

92. *"São inapresentáveis"*. Interview, Luanda, October 2011.

93. Interview, Luanda, October 2011.

94. Interview, Luanda, October 2011.

95. The novel by Pepetela (2005), aptly titled *Predators*, provides a lucid portrait of Angola's elite that is all too rare in contemporary Angolan literature.

96. This billboard was to be found at the top of Rua da Missão in July 2009.

97. Carla Jesus, "Casamento de amor e fortunas", *Focus*, 3 June 2009.

98. Isabel Lacerda, "Como vivem os ricos na cidade mais cara do mundo", *Sábado*, 18 August 2011.

99. Conversations with Pinóquio staff, Lisbon, August and October 2012.

100. "Angola lá fora deve bancar, para mostrar". Conversation with former high official of Sonangol, Luanda, January 2012. My interlocutor was explaining the logic behind elite beahviour, not agreeing with it.

101. Conversation with Angolan businessman, Luanda, January 2012.

102. Off Mutamba Square in central Luanda, a popular street vendor does a brisk business in old copies of *Caras*; there is a constant crowd flipping through these issues.

103. Interview, Luanda, November 2011.

104. Agualusa (2006).

105. Gustavo Costa, "Castelos de areia...", *Novo Jornal*, 1 April 2011.

106. Interview with oil services executive, Luanda, November 2011.

107. Mfonobong Nsehe, "Africa's Richest Women", *Forbes*, 5 February 2011.

108. There are few dissonant voices in this regard amongst the many interviewees with whom I have discussed Isabel dos Santos' rise.

109. See Luís Villalobos, "O rosto de Angola", *Público*, 20 July 2007; Luís Villalobos, "Isabel dos Santos: a face invisível dos negócios angolanos em Portugal", *Público*, 30 November 2009; Celso Filipe, "Isabel dos Santos: tem cara de menina mas faz negócios crescidos", *Jornal de Negócios*, 19 December 2008; "Isabel a Poderosa", *Focus* 480, 2008; and other similar articles.

110. Kerry A. Nolan, "Daddy's Girl: How An African 'Princess' Banked $3 Billion In A Country Living On $2 A Day", *Forbes*, 2 September 2013.

111. In a Wiki-leaked report on her visit to the US Embassy in Luanda for a cocktail party in December 2009, US Ambassador Dan Mozena noted that Isabel "speaks impeccable colloquial English" (he forgot to mention her posh, British-inflected accent), and "comes across as sophisticated, polished, and extremely articulate" (US State Department 2009).

112. Conversations, Luanda, August 2012 and November 2013.

113. Tom Burgis, "Lunch with the FT: Isabel dos Santos", *Financial Times*, 29 March 2013.

114. Burgis, "Lunch with the FT".

115. Great credit is due to Rafael Marques, the Angolan civil society campaigner whose website www.makaangola.org is deservedly famous for a series of author-

itative investigations of the business interests of the Angolan elite. This has earned Marques a number of lawsuits in Angola and Portugal.

116. On BAI see US Senate (2010). On CIF see Mailey (2014), Levkowitz, Ross and Warner (2009) and the relevant section in Chapter 5. On Portugal see OECD (2013) and Chapter 5. On Cobalt see, e.g., Tom Burgis, "US to probe Cobalt link in Angola", *Financial Times*, 21 February 2012; Tom Burgis, "Rival to Nigeria as prodigious source of crude", *Financial Times*, 18 July 2012; and Tom Burgis, "Cobalt's returns from Angola venture raise wider concerns", *Financial Times*, 20 November 2013.

117. "Porque se alguém alguma vez for denunciado e for levado a julgamento, por não conseguir justificar como adquiriu a fortuna, esse indivíduo, se quiser falar, levará toda a gente a julgamento e à prisão. Porque o MPLA criou uma teia, laços entre os dirigentes em que ninguém fala do outro. Porque se alguém um dia falar, vão-se todos. Porque as relações são umbilicais". Aguinaldo Brito, "Reconstrução de Angola precisa alcançar o Estado", *Folha de São Paulo*, 25 May 2010.

118. Messiant (2006: 19). In the Nigerian case, Apter refers to the same dynamics as "webs of mutual implication" (2005: 39).

119. www.club-k.net

120. Conversation with the author, Luanda, January 2010.

121. Ibid.

122. Schubert (2013).

123. Quoted in Yergin (2011: 110).

124. Ministério do Planeamento (2007b).

125. António Tomás, "A doutrina da educação", *Novo Jornal*, 27 July 2012.

126. Interview, Luanda, May 2012. He went on to say, "Angolans are as capable as everyone else if they are given the opportunity to have the same education as the foreigners, but with these universities they are bound to be unemployable".

127. "Alembamento: Um símbolo de respeito para com a mulher", *Jornal de Angola*, 10 February 2008.

128. "Bento Kangamba e Avelina dos Santos prometem casar em 2011", *Bessangana*, August 2010.

129. Comaroff and Comaroff (2000: 298).

130. Interview, Luanda, July 2011.

131. Ferguson (2006).

132. See Malaquais (2001: 112) for a fascinating study of Cameroon's picaresque *feymen* and their complex rapport with the Cameroonian elite.

133. Ferguson (2006).

134. These lines are from rapper MC K's song, "*Eu queria morar em Talatona*".

135. It is noteworthy that, while individual believers frequently attribute their disapproval of the status quo to its violation of their religious precepts, all major

Christian denominations in Angola (the Catholic Church as well as the mainline Protestant, Evangelical and African churches) have come to terms with the party-state and are deeply enmeshed in it.

136. At worst, they also exemplify the casual racism and xenophobia of the Luanda masses, an aspect less frequently underlined.

137. This includes the very frequent resort to lynching as the extra-judicial penalty for anything from petty thieving to drivers running over pedestrians, as well as other extremely brutal forms of popular justice.

138. As a blogger on Club K breathlessly claimed: "70 percent of Angolans want TO BE Bento Kangamba!"; accessed 8 August 2012.

139. This has little to do with Angolan culture, and everything to do with a historical legacy of state brutality and lack of a civic project, including in the postcolonial era. It is entirely understandable that Angolans would define their relevant moral communities in very restricted terms as those based on shared lived experiences, friendship and family, instead of abstractions with no meaning in everyday life.

140. The writer Pepetela discussed the impact of Luanda's "money culture" and the "pressures of women and family" on guerrilla commanders as they settled in Luanda in 1975. Interview, Luanda, September 2012. Most Angolan observers emphatically refer not to a generic Angolan "hedonistic culture", but to a specifically "Caluanda" one, and go on to contrast it with the "hardworking tradition" of the Highlands and Lubango.

141. Iliffe (1983: 19).

142. Interview with opposition politician, Luanda, July 2011.

143. The Angolan academic Assis Malaquias (2007: 15) ruefully noted: "Alarmingly, though expectedly, the habit of corruption that was first embraced by the elites now dominates all levels of society".

144. Literally a "fizzy drink", the Angolan euphemism for bribe money. Since the advent of the mobile phone, and equally popular euphemism is "*saldo*", i.e., phone credit.

145. Conversation with off-duty Luanda traffic policeman, Luanda, June 2012.

146. Wiig and Kolstad (2013).

147. Rich Angolans have at their disposal two state-of-the-art private clinics, Sonangol's Clínica Girassol and Clínica Sagrada Esperança, and use foreign hospitals (mostly in Portugal and South Africa) for serious medical procedures.

148. Alves da Rocha (2011: 254).

149. Interview with medical doctor, Luanda, July 2009.

150. See Paulo de Carvalho, "Universidades angolanas entre as piores da SADC", *Semanário Angolense*, 2 February 2013 and Fernando Guelengue, "Monografias à venda", *Novo Jornal*, 6 December 2013.

151. An interesting aspect of Angolan perceptions of university attendance as pri-

marily a rite of passage into a higher social echelon is what an Angolan journalist termed "the obsession with [mimicking US-style] commencement ceremonies, and the expensive partying associated with starting a degree, finishing an academic year, or graduating". Interview, Luanda, May 2012.

152. Interview with academic at a major university, Luanda, January 2012.
153. Meagher (2010: 9).
154. See quote at the start of this chapter.
155. Callaghy (1984).
156. Ricardo Soares de Oliveira, "Transparency reforms yield little change", *Financial Times*, 18 July 2012.
157. Lei da Probidade Pública, Lei no. 3/10, 29 March 2010.
158. "Agências de 'rating' atribuem notação a Angola", *Jornal de Negócios*, 19 May 2010.
159. Lewis (2007).
160. Admittedly, today's institutions of advanced capitalism proved unable and unwilling to properly regulate the banking sector in the West itself.
161. Acemoglu and Robinson (2012: 84).
162. At any rate, Angola's foreign partners are broadly content with the post-2002 management style, as explained in the next chapter.
163. Celia W. Dugger, "Battle to Halt Graft Scourge in Africa Ebbs", *New York Times*, 9 June 2009.

5. ANGOLA RISING: INTERNATIONAL STRATEGIES IN THE PEACE ERA

1. Bayart (1989: 45).
2. Arrighi (2002).
3. Clapham (1996: 3). See Walle (2001) for a landmark study on structural adjustment.
4. Castells (1996).
5. Renaissance Capital (2012) and McKinsey (2010).
6. Soares de Oliveira (2007a).
7. Trade with China went from US$11 billion to US$166 billion between 2002 and 2012 ("A hopeful continent", *Economist*, 2 March 2013).
8. Alden, Morphet and Vieira (2010).
9. Palan (2005: xii).
10. Levi and Middleton (2004).
11. Gideon Rachman, "Britain should rise above Russian money and power", *Financial Times*, 16 July 2013.
12. Bremmer (2010) is a study of contemporary state capitalism.
13. Daron Acemoglu and James Robinson, "Is State Capitalism Winning?", *Project Syndicate*, 31 December 2012.

14. Clapham (1996: 251).
15. Angola's regional relations were at their most problematic in the last years of the war, when the FAA got involved in the DRC conflict and in the process secured Kabila's hold over Kinshasa, invaded Congo Brazzaville to support their ally Denis Sassou-Nguesso, and raided the border regions of Zambia in retaliation for perceived support for UNITA.
16. An example is the 2003 nomination by JES of Pierre Falcone as Angola's ambassador to UNESCO.
17. Bayart (2004).
18. Soares de Oliveira (2007a: 253–61).
19. Interview with Angolan diplomat, Washington, DC, June 2010.
20. Conversation with foreign diplomat, Luanda, September 2012.
21. See footnote 25 in Chapter 2 for the most important contributions.
22. This was at least the case in the first decade of the new relationship. Angola's growing dependence on China as a market for its oil is likely to shift the dynamics of the relationship in China's favour. From this perspective 2004 may have constituted a tactical victory for Angola but the structural imbalances in China-Angola relations will favour China in the long run.
23. Taylor (2006: 75–92).
24. Alden, Large and Soares de Oliveira (2008).
25. Interview, Luanda, June 2009.
26. Vickers (2013: 673).
27. GAO (2013: 16).
28. http://en.expo2010.cn/c/en_gj_tpl_62.htm, accessed on 23 June 2012.
29. The Portuguese word used by JES, "*razoáveis*", conveys something closer to "acceptable" or "middling"; interview, SIC Notícias, 6 June 2013.
30. Alves and Power (2012).
31. Interview with Angolan diplomat, Washington, DC, June 2010.
32. José Eduardo dos Santos, "Estado da Nação: Mensagem Integral do Presidente da República", Luanda, 15 October 2013.
33. Conversation with the author, Brussels, February 2009.
34. Soares de Oliveira (2007a).
35. This did not prevent implicit threats (which never materialized) that the French private sector would indeed suffer consequences for Angolagate. See, e.g., "La 'mission impossible' du Medef—Angola", *La Lettre du Continent*, 10 June 2007.
36. Interview with European diplomat, Luanda, June 2009.
37. "UK/Africa High Level Prosperity Partnership: HMG promotes Angola, Cote d'Ivoire, Ghana, Mozambique and Tanzania to UK business in mutual prosperity drive", Foreign and Commonwealth Office, Press Release, 19 November 2013.
38. Interview, Luanda, November 2013.
39. "The IMF makes up with Luanda", *Africa Confidential*, 14 May 2010.

40. IMF (2011: 10).

41. In a truly embarrassing display of innuendo, Angola's inchoate accounting for this is phrased by the Fund in un-IMF language such as "it appears", "another explanation being explored by the authorities", "this may have resulted", etc. (IMF 2011).

42. IMF (2011: 10). According to the IMF, the Angolan government later accounted for US$27 billion of these US$32 billion as off-budget operations conducted by Sonangol; International Monetary Fund, Letter to Mr Arvind Ganesan and Ms Karin Lissakers, 9 April 2012 (www.imf.org, accessed 3 May 2012).

43. Interview, Luanda, September 2012.

44. Alex Vines, "Angola matters to US so what's the problem?", CNN *Global Public 4quare*, 17 May 2003.

45. US Senate (2010).

46. "Treasury targets Hizballah financial network", Press Release, Department of the Treasury, Washington, DC, 12 September 2010.

47. Josh Rogin, "37 embassies in Washington face banking crisis", *Washington Post*, 25 November 2010.

48. According to the *Washington Post*, during her visit to Angola Secretary of State Hillary Clinton "sought to emphasize the positive [...] Clinton was notably less critical of Angola's democratic failings—corruption and a lack of press freedom—than she was of Kenya's performance during her stop there last week"; Mary Beth Sheridan, "Clinton Building Ties with Angola", *Washington Post*, 10 August 2009.

49. For a broader analysis of Brazilian-African relations see Stolte (2012).

50. Interview with Brazilian expatriate, Luanda, October 2012. On Minoru's interests in Angola, see Chico Otavia and Aloy Jupiara, "Negócios de Valdomiro Minoru misturam o público e o privado", *O Globo*, 18 December 2011, and Chico Otavia and Aloy Jupiara, "Valdomiro Minoru, o brasileiro sinônimo do poder em Angola", *O Globo*, 19 December 2011. Urban legends about Minoru are legion, including that he owns Angola's ID card system and holds the rights to printing Angola's currency, the Kwanza.

51. Interview with Angolan NGO official, Luanda, July 2010.

52. David Stephen, "Guinea Bissau Coup: military play politics to defend own power", *African Arguments*, 23 April 2012.

53. Louise Redvers, "Integrating SADC: Why Angola is the odd man out", *South African Institute of International Affairs*, 21 August 2013.

54. Interview with former Angolan senior diplomat, Lisbon, December 2011.

55. Peter Fabricius, "Zuma feted on visit to Angola", *IOL News*, 21 August, 2009.

56. Conversation with the author, Paris, April 2012.

57. David Rodrigues, "Angolanos investem mais lá fora que os estrangeiros cá dentro", *Expansão*, 14 August 2013.

58. Heller (2012).

59. M.E. Ferreira, conversation, July 2013, underlined this continuity.
60. "Stash the cash", *Africa Confidential*, 14 March 2008.
61. Luís Villalobos, "Sonangol, o braço empresarial do governo angolano", *Público*, 5 September 2008.
62. Interview, Lisbon, August 2009.
63. See Soares de Oliveira (2007b) and Mateus Cavumbo, "Sonangol continuará a expandir negócios", *Jornal de Angola*, 29 February 2008.
64. Hansen-Shino and Soares de Oliveira (2010).
65. Vines, Shaxson and Rimli (2005: 15).
66. Interview with Sonangol official, Luanda, July 2009.
67. Interview with Sonangol official, Luanda, June 2009.
68. Interview with Sonangol official, Luanda, September 2012.
69. Interview with former Sonangol official, Luanda, June 2012.
70. "Lemos' landmark makeover for Sonangol", *Africa Energy Intelligence*, 4 December 2012.
71. Interview with two former senior officials of the Finance Ministry, Luanda, September 2012 and November 2013. In fact, both officials claimed not to have known about this commission until it was up and running.
72. Interview with Ricardo Viegas de Abreu, Luanda, June 2009.
73. Hansen-Shino and Soares de Oliveira (2010).
74. Fundo Soberano de Angola, "The Republic of Angola Launches US$5 Billon Sovereign Wealth Fund", Press Release, Luanda, 17 October 2012.
75. Louise Redvers, "Angolan wealth fund gets president's son on board", *Mail and Guardian*, 19 October 2012.
76. http://www.fundosoberano.ao/faqs/ (accessed 3 February 2014).
77. This scepticism was compounded by initial (unfounded) reports that Eduardo Santos, the President's nephew, was another member of the management team.
78. "Wealthy Sovereigns", *Africa Confidential*, 1 February 2013.
79. Practically the only other deal by the FSDEA was the reported acquisition of 90 percent of Escom, an all-purposes business group with close connections to the presidency and formerly owned by Portugal's Espírito Santo Group and the businessman Helder Bataglia (the Espírito Santo Group divested entirely while Battaglia kept the remaining 10 percent). It is unclear how this acquisition if it took place fits in with the official investment strategy of the FSDEA; Gustavo Costa, "Fundo Soberano compra Escom", *Expresso*, 29 June 2013.
80. Luís Villalobos, "Filho do presidente de Angola preside a fundo soberano", *Público*, 21 June 2013.
81. Interview, Luanda, July 2009.
82. In a manner reminiscent of the cooptation strategies of FESA, Sonangol and other bodies controlled by JES, the FSDEA will also include "funds for Angolan civil society" to create support and distribute patronage throughout the

MPLA-linked civil society organizations (conversation with Angolan civil society activist, Bergen, December 2012).

83. Mailey (2014: 26).
84. See especially Levkowitz, Ross and Warner (2009) and the more recent Mailey (2014).
85. In this regard, Tom Burgis' upcoming book is likely to produce an authoritative account of CIF.
86. Interview, Luanda, June 2012. This is supported by Mailey (2014: 38).
87. See among others, Levkowitz, Ross and Warner (2009) and Vines, Wong, Weimer and Campos (2009: 51).
88. While early discussions of CIF made the assumption that much of this money would come from Chinese state banks, the first major oil-backed loan involving CIF was in fact the 2005 US$3 billion Calyon syndicated loan, which has normally not been mentioned in connection with CIF; the exception is Mailey (2014). Other than this loan, there is speculation about other loans or the extent of Chinese financing in particular being funnelled into CIF, though the World Bank (2007: 50) and many other sources routinely mention a US$10 billion estimate for the total amount of the loan(s). This led an Angolan official to argue: "all along CIF brought in no money. This was all Angolan money whether money they had or money they borrowed". Interview, Luanda, June 2012.
89. Murray et al. (2011).
90. See Mailey (2014: 55) for a detailed list of known China Sonangol assets outside Africa.
91. Beth Morrissey et al, "China-based Corporate web behind troubled African resource deals", Center for Public Integrity, 9 November 2011.
92. Mailey (2014); Levkowitz, Ross and Warner (2009); "The Queensway Syndicate and the Africa trade", Economist, 13 August 2011.
93. The relationship with Sinopec was particularly close, through a joint venture with China Sonangol (Sonangol Sinopec International Ltd) as well as extensive informal links.
94. Interview, Luanda, May 2012. According to this interviewee, the Chinese officials added: "the Angola-Eximbank relationship is a privileged one. We should be your first stop for financing. Each time you go to other places you jeopardize this relationship."
95. "Outra vigarice do Palácio". Interview with Angolan academic, Luanda, January 2010.
96. Levkowitz, Ross and Warner (2009).
97. Yu Ning, Gu Yongqiang and Wang Duan, "A Legacy of Dirty Deals", Caixin, 17 October 2011.
98. Interview, Luanda, July 2010 and interview, Lisbon, March 2011.
99. Mailey (2014: 29).

100. "The Queensway Syndicate and the Africa trade", *Economist*, 13 August 2011. By this stage, the CIF network amounted to more than 60 companies, according to Laura Murray *et al*, "Africa's Safari: CIF's Grab for Oil and Minerals", *Caixin*, 17 October 2011.

101. Phone conversation, July 2013.

102. Cardenal and Araújo (2013).

103. Adding to the generally negative coverage of the Queensway Group, *The Economist* suggested that the 2005 oil-backed loans were indexed not to spot market prices, but to the (in retrospect very low) price of the oil barrel at that stage. According to the same source, the resulting profits "could amount to tens of billions of dollars". See "The Queensway Syndicate and the Africa trade", *Economist*, 13 August 2011.

104. See Costa, Lopes and Louçã (2013) and Filipe (2012) for two surveys of Angolan interests in Portugal.

105. The Angolan business group Newshold is based in Panama and the identity of its owners is unknown but assumed to be close to the MPLA. See Anabela Campos and Adriano Nobre, "Vêm do Panamá, são angolanos e querem a Cofina", *Expresso*, 23 December 2011, and Adriano Nobre, "A atração angolana pelo 4° poder", *Expresso*, 17 March 2012.

106. "Angola passa a maior investidor na bolsa portuguesa", *Expansão*, 23 August 2013.

107. Alexandra Correia *et al*, "A vida dos angolanos ricos em Portugal", *Visão*, 10 December 2009.

108. Isabel Faria and Marta Martins Silva, "Novos Colonos: Angolanos conquistam Portugal em busca de negócios e de luxo", *Correio da Manhã*, 18 September 2011.

109. Ana Taborda, "Os angolanos que mandam nas maiores empresas portuguesas", *Sábado*, 2 September 2010.

110. The references to the Freemasonry and Opus Dei are ubiquitous in my interviews and occasionally surface in the Portuguese and Angolan press. See, for instance, Celso Filipe, "Mbanga, Mboti, Sakidila, Oxoto", *Jornal de Negócios*, 11 October 2013.

111. In São Tomé and Príncipe, perhaps the closest to an actual Angolan colony, Angolan sources have been known to finance the two main political parties. See Thalia Griffiths, "Governance under scrutiny as São Tomé's EEZ licensing round closes", *African Energy* 193, 10 September 2010.

112. Jaime continued: "The Portuguese companies [present here] can testify that they are in Angola thanks to their competence, thanks to their organization, thanks to their professional commitment and not for [other reasons]." *Prós e Contras*, RTP1, 16 March 2009.

113. Lurdes Ferreira, "Sonangol diz que posição de 'patrão' na Galp ditou fim da guerra pelo controlo da Enacol", *Público*, 26 February 2008.

114. OECD (2013: 36).
115. OECD (2013: 36).
116. Joaquim Gomes, "Álvaro Sobrinho com caução de meio milhão de euros", *Expresso*, 16 November 2011.
117. Conversation, Lisbon, June 2013.
118. For an intemperate sample see "Jogos perigosos", *Jornal de Angola*, 12 November 2012.
119. Interview, SIC Notícias, 6 June 2013.
120. "Estado da Nação: Discurso Integral do Presidente da República", Luanda, 15 October 2013, http://www.mpla.ao/mpla.6/discursos.15.html accessed 2 January 2014.
121. Diogo Cavaleiro, "Machete pede desculpas a Angola por investigações judiciais, MP garante autonomia", *Jornal de Negócios*, 4 October 2013.
122. Le Billon, Malaquias and Vines (2008) correctly identified Angola's petro-economy as a more important source of international clout than its military forces.
123. This was uncharacteristically recognized by Manuel Vicente, one of the exponents of such behaviour, in a revealing TV interview for Portugal's SIC Notícias, 6 June 2013.
124. Interview with foreign diplomat, Luanda, June 2009.
125. Conversation with the author, Luanda, September 2012.
126. Interview, Luanda, July 2010.
127. Soares de Oliveira (2007a: 326–27).

6. CONCLUSION: POST-POSTWAR ANGOLA

1. Interview with MPLA official, Luanda, August 2012.
2. Interview with MPLA official, Viana, August 2012.
3. Note that this apparent tolerance applies only to the electoral game, which the ruling party masters without problem. It happens simultaneously with the MPLA's ferocious repression of street demonstrations since 2011, a much more serious threat from the viewpoint of the party-state.
4. These quotes are from Admiral Miau's press conference held at Epic Sana hotel in Luanda, 28 June 2012.
5. "UNITA critica falta de observadores da União Europeia nas eleições angolanas", *Público*, 25 August 2012. The AU and SADC missions vouched for the fairness of Angola's 2012 elections.
6. See João Fellet, "Em Angola, marqueteiro do PT busca reeleição de líder há 33 anos no poder", *BBC Brasil*, 30 August 2012, and "Marqueteiro de Dilma e Lula faz propaganda do governo angolano", *O Globo*, 1 September 2012.
7. "Verdades muito duras e campanha contra o aborto", *Jornal de Angola*, 16 August 2012.

8. "Conselho de Ministros aprova aumento de 10% salário da função pública", *ANGOP*, 30 May 2012.

9. Fernando Pacheco noted in this regard: "Either the MPLA is disorganized, or it lies, and doesn't know how many members it has, or the accusation that it is compulsory [to be in the party in order to] get a job and other perks [is true]". Fernando Pacheco, "Cartão amarelo, por enquanto", *Novo Jornal*, 7 September 2012.

10. Interview, Luanda, September 2012.

11. Interview, Luanda, September 2012.

12. Fernando Pacheco, "Cartão amarelo, por enquanto", *Novo Jornal*, 7 September 2012.

13. Soares de Oliveira (2011).

14. Jones, Soares de Oliveira and Verhoeven (2013).

15. The poor and often perverse outcomes of so many foreign-supported reconstruction processes in the post-Cold War era should give pause to anyone arguing that an international effort would have fared better than what the Angolan elite came up with. This is obviously not a statement in favour of Angola-style reconstruction but simply an acknowledgement of the disappointing character of liberal peacebuilding (see Mayall and Soares de Oliveira, 2011).

16. Interview, Lisbon, December 2013.

17. I thank Tom Burgis for this apt phrase, which is the title of his forthcoming book.

18. This mirrors a point made about early post-colonial Indonesia in Anderson (1991: 132). That said, in addition to the Cabinda issue, a federal-style relationship with the centre remains a popular aspiration in the Lunda provinces.

19. Ferreira (2005b).

20. Ricardo Soares de Oliveira, "Avoiding Africa's Oil Curse", *Foreignaffairs.com*, 16 April 2014.

21. "José Eduardo dos Santos admite que está há 'demasiado' tempo no poder", *Público*, 12 November 2013.

22. Interview with Angolan journalist, Luanda, October 2011.

23. This may be a major reason for Angola not having yet ratified the Rome Statute of the International Criminal Court.

24. JES's other children are conspicuous presences in Angolan public life but hardly presidential material. Another son, the *kuduro* manager "Coreon Du", is an amiable member of the jury of Angola's most prominent talent show. The idea that he might be the next president hasn't crossed anyone's mind, and he for one seems happy in his TV producer and singer roles. Other members of the family have dabbled in politics without much success (JES's daughter Tchizé is a member of parliament but is better known as a socialite and editor of *Caras Angola*, the jet set's glitzy magazine). Isabel, of course, has until recently preferred to stay in the shadows.

25. Conversation with senior MPLA official, Luanda, September 2012.

26. The elite never loved dos Santos but criticism used to be kept to a minimum. From 2012, however, impatience towards JES became the rule in my elite interviews. Some bluntly stated that they feared being dragged down by his unpopularity. But the elite are afraid of the transition even as they are tired of JES. In the words of a former minister, "you have to understand: this is Africa, [there will be no] orderly transition, there will be chaos". Interview, Luanda, August 2012.

27. Miguel Gomes, "Entrevista: Carlos Rosado de Cravalho e o OGE 2012", *Novo Jornal*, 16 December 2011 and OPSA (2013: 14).

28. Skype interview with security and defense expert with extensive knowledge of the FAA, July 2012.

29. CEIC (2013: 99).

30. Ernst & Young (2013).

31. Manuel Alves da Rocha, "Os grandes desafios de Angola até 2017", *Expansão*, 31 August 2012 and CEIC (2013: 54–55).

32. Much of the literature on postcolonial Africa portrays African states as inimical to this role. For different views see e.g., Mkandawire (2001) and the more recent Kelsall (2013) and Booth and Golooba (2012). The insightful paper by Sogge (2009: 24) shares this conclusion's scepticism about the likelihood of the Angolan state performing a developmental role, at least in the near future.

33. Kyle (2010).

34. Kohli (2004: 418).

35. A foreign financial consultant active in Angola since the mid-1990s noted that "there are no angels in this elite" before outlining his belief that there are nonetheless people who know that the economy can be run on different grounds without detriment to their own interests. Skype interview, August 2013.

36. Ministério do Planeamento e do Desenvolvimento Territorial (2012).

37. See the June 2013 quote at the start of the Conclusion.

38. The data and analysis are from the Observatório Politico-Social de Angola, which is now publishing an annual review of the Angolan General State Budget; see OPSA (2013).

39. Pearce (2014).

40. Karl (1997).

41. Interview, Luanda, August 2012.

42. Conversation, Lisbon, April 2012.

43. Rodrigues (2013).

44. The estimates are from UNICEF and the CIA World Factbook.

45. Fukuyama (2011).

46. The Angolan academic Assis Malaquias (2007: 21) rightly emphasizes the role of ethnicity as a "perennial backburner with tremendous explosive potential".

47. See Kennedy (1988) and Berman and Leys (1994) among others.

48. The 1977 Nito Alves coup is briefly discussed in Chapter 3.

SELECT BIBLIOGRAPHY

This bibliography lists works and sources quoted in the text and is not an exhaustive compilation of consulted materials.

Abrantes, José Mena, *José Eduardo Dos Santos e os Desafios do Seu Tempo: Palavras de Um Estadista, 1979–2004*, two vols (Luanda: Edições Maianga, 2004).

———, *José Eduardo Dos Santos e os Desafios do Seu Tempo: Palavras de Um Estadista, 1979–2009* (Luanda: Edições Maianga, 2009).

Acemoglu, Daron, and James Robinson, *Why Nations Fail* (Princeton: Princeton University Press, 2012).

Africa Economic Outlook, *Angola Country Note* (African Development Bank, OECD, UNDP and UNECA, 2012).

Agualusa, José Eduardo, *Estação das Chuvas* (Lisbon: Dom Quixote, 1997).

———, "Os pretos não sabem comer lagosta", in *Fronteiras Perdidas* (Lisbon: Dom Quixote, 1999).

———, *O Vendedor de Passados* (Lisbon: Dom Quixote, 2006).

Aguilar, Renato, "Angola's Private Sector: Rents Distribution and Oligarchy", paper presented at the Lusophone Africa Conference: Intersections between the Social Sciences, Cornell University, Ithaca, 2–3 May, 2003.

Alden, Chris, *China in Africa* (London: Zed Books, 2007).

Alden, Chris, Daniel Large and Ricardo Soares de Oliveira (eds), *China Returns to Africa* (London: Hurst, 2008).

Alden, Chris, Sally Morphet and Marco António Vieira, *The South in World Politics* (London: Palgrave Macmillan, 2010).

Alexander, Jocelyn, "The Local State in Post-war Mozambique: Political Practice and Ideas About Authority", *Africa* 67, 1 (1997), pp. 1–26.

Alves, Ana Cristina, and Marcus Power (eds) *China and Angola: A Marriage of Convenience?* (London: Pambazuka Press, 2012).

Alvesson, M., S. Bhattarai and G. Pastor, "Sources and uses of state oil revenue", in *Angola: Selected Issues and Statistical Appendix* (Washington, DC: IMF, 2003).

SELECT BIBLIOGRAPHY

Amaral, Ilídio do, *Luanda: Estudo de geografia urbana* (Lisbon: Junta de Investigações do Ultramar, 1968).

Ammann, Daniel, *The King of Oil: The Secret Lives of Marc Rich* (New York: St Martin's Griffin, 2009).

Amnesty International, *Angola—Lives in Ruin: Forced Evictions Continue*, AFR/12/001, 2007.

Amsden, Alice H., Alisa DiCaprio and James Robinson (eds), *The Role of Elites in Economic Development* (Oxford: Oxford University Press, 2012).

Amundsen, Inge, "Drowing in Oil: Angola's Institutions and the 'Resource Curse'", *Comparative Politics*, 46, 2 (2014), pp. 169–189.

Anderson, Benedict, *Imagined Communities* (London: Verso, 1991).

Anstee, Margaret Joan, *Orphan of the Cold War: The Inside Story of the Collapse of the Angolan Peace Process, 1992–93* (London: Macmillan, 1994).

António, Mário, *Luanda, "ilha" crioula* (Lisbon: Agência-Geral do Ultramar, 1968).

Apter, Andrew, *The Pan-African Nation: Oil and the Spectacle of Culture in Nigeria* (Chicago: University of Chicago Press, 2005).

Arrighi, Giovanni, "The African Crisis: World Systemic and Regional Aspects", *New Left Review* 15 (2002), pp. 5–36.

Bayart, Jean-François, *L'Etat en Afrique. La politique du ventre* (Paris: Fayard, 1989).
———, *Le Gouvernement du monde* (Paris: Fayard, 2004).

Bender, Gerald J. *Angola Under the Portuguese: The Myth and the Reality* (Berkeley: University of California Press, 1978).

Benner, Thorsten, and Ricardo Soares de Oliveira, "The Good/Bad Nexus in Energy Governance", in Jan Martin Witte and Andreas Goldthau (eds), *Global Energy Governance: The New Rules of the Game* (Washington, DC: Brookings Institution, 2010).

Berman, Paul, and John Lonsdale, *Unhappy Valley*, vol. 1 (London: James Currey, 1992).

Berman, Paul, and Colin Leys (eds), *African Capitalists in African Development* (Boulder: Lynne Rienner, 1994).

Birmingham, David, *Trade and Conflict in Angola: The Mbundu and Their Neighbours Under the Influence of the Portuguese, 1483–1790* (Oxford: Clarendon Press, 1966).
———, "Is Nationalism a Feature of Angola's Cultural Identity?", in Eric Morier-Genoud, ed., *Sure Road? Nationalisms in Angola, Guinea Bissau and Mozambique* (Leiden: Brill, 2012), pp. 217–30.

Boone, Catherine, "State, Capital, and the Politics of Banking Reform in Sub-Saharan Africa", *Comparative Politics* 37, 4 (2005), pp. 401–420.

Booth, David, and Frederick Golooba-Mutebi, "Developmental Patrimonialism? The Case of Rwanda", *African Affairs* 111, 444 (2012), pp. 379–403.

Bowerbank, Michael, "For the English to See: Decentralization and Institutional Choice in Angola" (unpublished MSc thesis, University of Oxford, 2010).

SELECT BIBLIOGRAPHY

Brautigam, Deborah, *The Dragon's Gift* (Oxford: Oxford University Press, 2009).

Bremmer, Ian, *The End of the Free Market* (New York: Portfolio, 2010).

Bridgland, Fred, *Jonas Savimbi: A Key to Africa* (London: Coronet, 1988).

Brinkman, Inge, "War, Witches and Traitors: Cases from the MPLA's Eastern Front in Angola (1966–1975)", *Journal of African History* 44, 2 (2003), pp. 303–25.

Brownlee, Jason, *Authoritarianism in an Age of Democratization* (Cambridge, Cambridge University Press, 2007).

Cahen, Michel, ed., *Bourgs et Villes en Afrique Lusophone* (Paris: L' Harmattan, 1989).

———, "The Enemy as Model: Patronage as a Crisis Factor in Constructing Opposition in Mozambique", OXPO Working Papers, 2011.

———, "Anti-Colonialism and Nationalism: Deconstructing Synonymy, Investigating Historical Processes", in Eric Morier-Genoud (ed.), *Sure Road? Nationalisms in Angola, Guinea Bissau and Mozambique* (Leiden: Brill, 2012), pp. 1–28.

Callaghy, Thomas, *The State-Society Struggle: Zaire in Comparative Perspective* (New York: Columbia University Press, 1984).

Campos, Indira, and Alex Vines, *Angola and China: a Pragmatic Relationship* (London: Chatham House, 2008).

Cann, John, *Counter-Insurgency in Africa: The Portuguese Way of War, 1961–1974* (Westport: Praeger, 1997).

Cardenal, Juan Pablo, and Heriberto Araújo, *China's Silent Army: The Pioneers, Fixers, Traders and Workers who are Remaking the World in Beijing's Image* (London: Penguin, 2013).

Carvalho, Ruy Duarte de, *Actas da Maianga* (Lisbon: Cotovia, 2003).

Castells, Manuel, *The Information Age, Economy, Society and Culture: The Rise of the Network Society* (Oxford: Blackwell Wiley, 1996).

Castelo, Cláudia, *Passagens para África: O povoamento de Angola e Moçambique com naturais da metrópole* (Oporto: Afrontamento, 2007).

Chiwale, Samuel, *Cruzei-me com a História* (Oporto: Sextante Editora, 2008).

Cilliers, J. and Chris Dietrich (eds), *Angola's War Economy: The Role of Oil and Diamonds* (Pretoria: ISS, 2000).

Clapham, Christopher, *Africa and the International System* (Cambridge: Cambridge University Press, 1996).

———, "Controlling Space in Ethiopia", in W. James *et al* (eds), *Remapping Ethiopia* (Oxford: James Currey, 2002), pp. 9–30.

Clarence-Smith, William G., *Slaves, Peasants and Capitalists in Southern Angola, 1840–1926* (Cambridge: Cambridge University Press, 1979).

———, "Capital Accumulation and Class Formation in Angola", in D. Birmingham and P. Martin (eds), *History of Central Africa*, vol. 2 (Harlow: Longman, 1983).

———, *The Third Portuguese Empire* (Manchester: Manchester University Press, 1985).

SELECT BIBLIOGRAPHY

CMI and CEIC, *Public Construction Projects: Angola* (Christian Michelsen Institute and Centro de Estudos e Investigação Científica, May 2011).

Comaroff, Jean, and John L. Comaroff, "Millennial Capitalism: First Thoughts on a Second Coming", *Public Culture* 12, 2 (2000), pp. 291–343.

Cooper, Fred, *Africa Since 1940* (Cambridge: Cambridge University Press, 2002).

Corkin, Lucy, *Uncovering African Agency: Angola's Management of China's Credit Lines* (London: Ashgate, 2013).

Coronil, Fernando, *The Magical State: Nature, Money and Modernity in Venezuela* (Chicago: University of Chicago Press, 1997).

Corruption Watch, *Deception in High Places: The Corrupt Angola-Russia Debt Deal* (Corruption Watch and Associação Mãos Livres, 2013).

Costa, Jorge, João Teixeira Lopes, and Francisco Louçã, *Os Donos Angolanos de Portugal* (Lisbon: Bertrand, 2014).

Cramer, Christopher, *Civil War is not a Stupid Thing: Accounting for Violence in Developing Countries* (London: Hurst, 2006).

Crocker, Chester, *High Noon in Southern Africa: Making Peace in a Rough Neighborhood* (New York: W.W. Norton, 1993).

Croese, Sylvia, "One Million Houses? Chinese Engagement in Angola's national Reconstruction", in Ana Cristina Alves and Marcus Power (eds), *China and Angola: A Marriage of Convenience* (Oxford: Pambazuka Press, 2012), pp. 124–144.

Crystal, Jill, *Oil and Politics in the Gulf* (Cambridge: Cambridge University Press, 1995).

Dias, Jill R., "Uma Questão de Identidade: Respostas Intelectuais às Transformações Económicas no Seio da Elite Criola de Angola Portuguesa entre 1870 e 1930", *Revista Internacional de Estudos Africanos* I (1984), pp. 61–94.

———, "Angola", in Joel Serrão and A. H. de Oliveira Marques (eds), *O Império Africano 1825–1890, Nova História da Expansão Portuguesa*, vol. VIII (Lisbon: Editorial Estampa, 2001), pp. 319–556.

Downs, Erica, 'The fact and fiction of Sino-African energy relations', *China Security*, 3, 3 (2007), pp. 42–68.

Duarte, Ana, "The Ambivalent Character of Reconstruction: Winners and Losers of the Lobito Transport Development Corridor", *Journal of US-China Public Administration*, 10, 3 (2013), pp. 1–13.

Ernst & Young, *Angola: More than an Oil and Gas Story* (Ernst & Young, 2013).

European Union, *Angola Final Report: Parliamentary Elections 5 September 2008* (Luanda: EU Election Observation Mission, 2008).

Feijó, Carlos, *A Coexistência Normativa entre o Estado e as Autoridades Tradicionais na Ordem Jurídica Plural Angolana* (Coimbra: Almedina, 2012).

Ferguson, James, *Global Shadows: Africa in the Neoliberal World Order* (Durham: Duke University Press, 2006).

SELECT BIBLIOGRAPHY

Ferreira, Manuel Ennes, "O processo de privatização em Angola", *Política Internacional*, I, 10 (1994/1995), pp. 177–196.

———, "La reconversion économique de la nomenklatura pétrolière", *Politique Africaine* 57 (1995), pp. 11–26.

———, *A Indústria em Tempo de Guerra* (Lisbon: Cosmos, 1999).

———, "Realeconomik e realpolitik nos recursos naturais em Angola", *Relações Internacionais* 6 (2005a), pp. 3–31.

———, "Development and the Peace Dividend Insecurity Paradox in Angola", *The European Journal of Development Research* 17, 3 (2005b), pp. 509–524.

———, "China in Angola: just a passion for oil?", in C. Alden, D. Large and R. Soares de Oliveira (eds), *China Returns to Africa* (London: Hurst, 2008), pp. 275–94.

Filipe, Celso, *O Poder Angolano em Portugal* (Lisbon: Editorial Planeta, 2013).

Financial Action Task Force, *FAFT Public Statement* (Paris, February 2010).

Financial Action Task Force, *Improving Global AML/CFT Compliance: On-going Process* 18 October 2013 (Paris, 18 October 2013).

Freeland, Chrystia, *Sale of the Century: The Inside Story of the Second Russian Revolution* (London: Abacus, 2005).

Fukuyama, Francis, *The Origins of Political Order* (New York: Farrar, Straus and Giroux, 2011).

GAO, *Sub-Saharan Africa: Case-Studies of US and Chinese Economic Engagement in Angola, Ghana and Kenya; A Supplement to GAO-13–199* (Washington, DC: United States Government Accountability Office, 2013).

George, Edward, *The Cuban Intervention in Angola, 1965–1991: From Che Guevara to Cuito Cuanavale* (London: Frank Cass, 2005).

Global Witness, *All the President's Men: The Devastating Story of Oil and Banking* in *Angola's Privatised War* (London: Global Witness, 2002).

Global Witness, *Time for Transparency* (London: Global Witness, 2004).

Guerra, Henrique, *Angola: Estrutura Económica e Classes Sociais* (Lisbon: Edições 70, 1979).

Guerra, A. Morais, "Para uma política de fomento empresarial petrolífero privado angolano", Comunicação ao Primeiro Forum Nacional dos Quadros Angolanos do Petróleo, Soyo, July 2003 (unpublished paper).

Hansen-Shino, Kjetil and Ricardo Soares de Oliveira, "Political Economy of the Petroleum Sector in Angola", in Tuan Le Minh (ed.), *The Political Economy of the Natural Resource Paradox in Africa: Governing Extractive Industries for Sustainable Development* (Washington, DC: World Bank Publications, forthcoming).

Heimer, Franz Wilhelm (ed.), *Social Change in Angola* (Munich: Weltforum Verlag, 1973).

Heimer, Franz Wilhelm, *The Decolonization Conflict in Angola 1974–76: an essay in political sociology* (Geneva: Institut Universitaire de Hautes Etudes Internationales, 1979).

SELECT BIBLIOGRAPHY

Heller, Patrick, "Angola's Sonangol: Dexterous Right Hand of the State", in David G. Victor, David R. Hults, and Mark C. Thurber (eds), in *Oil and Governance: State-Owned Enterprises and the World Energy Supply* (Cambridge: Cambridge University Press, 2012).

Herbst, Jeffrey, *States and Power in Africa: Comparative Lessons in Authority and Control* (Princeton: Princeton University Press, 2000).

Heydemann, Steven, *Upgrading Authoritarianism in the Arab World* (Washington, DC: Brookings Institution, 2007).

Heywood, Linda, *Contested Power in Angola, 1840s to the Present* (Rochester: University of Rochester Press, 2000).

Hibou, Béatrice (ed.), *Privatising the State* (London: Hurst, 2004).

———, *La force de l' obéissance: Economie politique de la répression en Tunisie* (Paris: Editions La Découverte, 2006).

Hobsbawm, Eric, *The Age of Capital, 1848–1875* (London: Weidenfeld and Nicholson, 1995).

Hodges, Tony, *Angola: Anatomy of an Oil State* (Oxford: James Currey, 2004).

Human Rights Watch, *Angola Unravels* (London: Human Rights Watch, 1999).

———, *Angola: Between War and Peace in Cabinda* (London: HRW, 2004).

———, *"They Pushed Down the Houses": Forced Evictions and Insecure Land Tenure for Luanda's Urban Poor* (London: HRW, 2007).

———, *"They Put Me in a Hole": Military Detention, Torture and Lack of Due Process in Cabinda* (London: HRW, 2009).

———, *Transparency and Accountability in Angola: An Update* (London: HRW, 2010).

Iliffe, John, *The Emergence of African Capitalism* (Minneapolis: University of Minnesota Press, 1983).

International Crisis Group, *Dealing with Savimbi's Ghost: The Security and Humanitarian Challenges in Angola* (Brussels: ICG, 2003a)

———, *Angola's Choice: Reform or Regress* (Brussels: ICG, 2003b).

International Monetary Fund, *Angola: Staff Report (Confidential) for the 2002 Article IV Consultation* (Washington, DC: IMF, 2002).

———, *Angola: Fifth Review Under the Stand-By Agreement* (Washington, DC: IMF, 2011).

Jamba, Sousa, *Patriots* (London: Penguin, 1992).

JMJ Angola, *Análise do Sector de Agricultura* (Luanda: Banco Mundial, 2011).

Jover, E., A. Lopes Pintos and Alexandra Marchand, *Angola: Perfil do Sector Privado do País* (Tunis: African Development Bank, 2012).

Kang, David C., *Crony Capitalism: Corruption and Development in South Korea and the Philippines* (Cambridge: Cambridge University Press, 2002).

Karl, Terry Lynn, *The Paradox of Plenty* (Berkeley: University of California Press, 1997).

Keese, Alexander, "Dos abusos às revoltas? Trabalho forçado, reformas portuguesas, política 'tradicional' e religião na Baixa de Cassange e distrito do Congo (Angola), 1957–1961", *Revista Africana Studia* 7 (2004), pp. 247–76.

Kelsall, Tim, *Business, Politics and the State in Africa* (London: Zed Books, 2013).

Kennedy, Paul, *African Capitalism: The Struggle for Ascendancy* (Cambridge: Cambridge University Press, 1988).

Kohli, Atul, *State-Directed Development: Political Power and Industrialization in the Global Periphery* (Cambridge: Cambridge University Press, 2004).

Kolstad, Ivar, and Arne Wiig, "Is it both what you know and who you know? Human capital, social capital, and entrepreneurial success", *Journal of International Development* (2013).

Kyle, Steven, *Angola's Macro-economy and Agricultural Growth* (Working Paper, Department of Applied Economics and Management, Cornel University, January 2010).

Laban, Michel, *Mário Pinto de Andrade: Uma Entrevista* (Lisbon: Edições João Sá da Costa, 1997).

Le Billon, Philippe, "Angola's political economy of war: the role of oil and diamonds, 1975–2000", *African Affairs* 100, 398 (2001), pp. 55–80.

Le Billon, Philippe, Assis Malaquias and Alex Vines, "Au delà du petro-militarisme: la stratégie extérieure angolaise d'après-guerre", *Politique Africaine* 110 (2008), pp. 102–21.

Levi, Michael, and David J. Middleton, "The Role of Solicitors in Facilitating 'Organized Crime': Situational Crime Opportunities and Their Regulation", *Crime, Law and Social Change* 42 (2004), pp. 123–61.

Levkowitz, Lee, Martha McLellan Ross and J.R. Warner, *The 88 Queensway Group: A Case Study in Chinese Investors' Operations in Angola and Beyond* (Washington, DC: US-China Economic and Security Review Commission, 2009).

Lewis, Peter M., *Growing Apart: Oil, Politics and Economic Change in Indonesia and Nigeria* (Ann Arbor: University of Michigan Press, 2007).

Linz, Juan J., *Totalitarian and Authoritarian Regimes* (Boulder: Lynne Rienner, 2000).

Lonsdale, John, "States and Social Processes in Africa", *African Studies Review*, 24, 2–3 (1981), pp. 139–225.

Mabeko Tali, Jean-Michel, "La 'chasse aux Zaïrois' à Luanda", *Politique Africaine* 57 (1995), pp. 71–84.

———, *O MPLA Perante Si Próprio*, two vols. (Luanda: Nzila, 2001a).

———, "La question de Cabinda: Séparatismes éclatés, habiletés luandaises et conflits en Afrique central", *Lusotopie* (2001b), pp. 49–62.

McGregor, Richard, *The Party: The Secret World of China's Communist Rulers* (London: Penguin, 2010).

MacQueen, Norrie, *The Decolonization of Portuguese Africa: Metropolitan Revolution and the Dissolution of Empire* (London: Longman, 1997).

Maier, Karl, *Angola: Promises and Lies* (London: Serif, 1996).

SELECT BIBLIOGRAPHY

Mailey, J. R., *Corporate Vultures and Fragile States: The Queensway Syndicate and the Anatomy of the Resource Curse* (Washington, DC: National Defense University, forthcoming 2014).

Malaquais, Dominique, "Arts de feyre au Cameroun", *Politique Africaine* 82 (2001), pp. 101–18.

Malaquias, Assis, *Rebels and Robbers: Violence in Postcolonial Angola* (Uppsala: Nordiska Afrikainstitutet, 2007).

Mann, Michael, "The Autonomous Power of the State", *Archives Européennes de Sociologie*, 25, 2 (1984), pp. 185–213.

Marcum, John P., *The Angolan Revolution*, two vols. (Cambridge: MIT Press, 1969 and 1978).

Marques, Rafael, *MPLA Sociedade Anónima* (MAKA Angola, 2010).

———, *The Transparency of Looting in Angola* (Unpublished MSc thesis, University of Oxford, 2009).

——— BAI: *The Regime's Banking Laundromat* (MAKA Angola, 2012).

———, *Diamantes de Sangue* (Lisbon: Tinta da China, 2011).

Marques Guedes, Armando, *et al.*, *Pluralismo e Legitimação* (Coimbra: Almedina, 2003).

Ministério da Administração do Território, *Encontro Nacional Sobre a Administração Local em Angola, 30 de Agosto—02 de Setembro 2004* (Luanda: MAT, 2004).

MAT and PNUD, *Desconcentração e Descentralização em Angola* (Luanda: Ministério da Administração do Território and Programa das Nações Unidas para o Desenvolvimento, 2007).

Matloff, Judith, *Fragments of a Forgotten War* (London: Penguin, 1997).

Matos, João de, "Retratos de Angola", *Política Internacional* 25 (2002), pp. 81–92.

Mayall, James, and Ricardo Soares de Oliveira (eds), *The New Protectorates: International Tutelage and the Making of Liberal States* (London: Hurst, 2011).

McKinsey and Company, *Lions on the Move: The Progress and Potential of African Economies* (McKinsey Global Institute, 2010).

Meagher, Kate, *Identity Economics: Social Networks and the Informal Economy in Nigeria* (Oxford: James Currey, 2010).

Melman, Yossi, and Julio Godoy, *Making a Killing: The Influence Peddlers* (Washington, DC: International Consortium of Investigative Journalists, 2002).

Messiant, Christine, "Angola, les voies de l'ethnisation et de la décomposition. I. De la guerre à la paix (1975–1991): le conflit armé, les interventions internationales et le peuple angolais", *Lusotopie* 1994, pp. 155–210.

———, "Angola, les voies de l'ethnisation et de la décomposition. II. Transition à la démocratie ou marche à la guerre? L'épanouissement des deux 'partis armés' (mai 1991-septembre 1992)", *Lusotopie*, 1995, pp. 181–212.

———, "La Fondation Eduardo dos Santos: à propos de l'investissement de la société civile par le pouvoir politique", *Politique Africaine* 73 (1999), pp. 82–101.

SELECT BIBLIOGRAPHY

————, 1961. *L'Angola Colonial, histoire et société. Les prémisses du mouvement nationaliste* (Basel: P. Schlettwein Publishing, 2006).

————, *L'Angola postcolonial 1: Guerre et paix sans démocratisation* (Paris: Karthala, 2008a).

————, *L'Angola postcolonial 2: Sociologie politique d'une oléocratie* (Paris: Karthala, 2008b).

Metz, Forrest, "The Challenging Business Environment: Experiences of Angolan Small and Medium Sized Enterprises", paper presented at "The Study of Angola" conference, University of Oxford, 1–2 July 2011.

Miller, Joseph, "The paradoxes of impoverishment in the Atlantic zone", in D. Birmingham and P. M. Martin (eds), *History of Central Africa*, vol. 1 (Harlow: Longman, 1983), pp. 118–59.

————, *Way of Death: Merchant Capitalism and the Angolan Slave Trade, 1730–1830* (Madison: University of Wisconsin Press, 1988).

Ministério do Planeamento, *Angola 2025. Angola um país com futuro: Estratégia de Desenvolvimento a Longo Prazo*, volume 1 (Luanda: Ministério do Planeamento, 2007a).

Ministério do Planeamento, *Angola 2025. Angola um país com futuro: Estratégia de Desenvolvimento a Longo Prazo*, volume 2 (Luanda: Ministério do Planeamento, 2007b).

Ministério do Planeamento e do Desenvolvimento Territorial, *Plano Nacional de Desenvolvimento, 2013–2017* (Luanda: República de Angola, 2012).

Mkandawire, Thandika, "Thinking about developmental states in Africa," *Cambridge Journal of Economics* 25, 3 (2001), pp. 289–314.

Morice, Alain, "Commerce parallèle et troc à Luanda", *Politique Africaine* 17 (1985), pp. 105–20.

MPLA, *Manifesto Eleitoral* (Luanda: MPLA, 2008).

MPLA, *Angola a Crescer Mais e a Distribuir Melhor: Manifesto Eleitoral* (Luanda: MPLA, 2012).

Muekalia, Jardo, *Angola, A Segunda Revolução. Memórias da luta pela Democracia* (Oporto: Sextante, 2010).

Nascimento, Lopo do, "O país começa agora?", *Política internacional* 25, 2002.

Newitt, Malyn, *Portugal in Africa: The Last Hundred Years* (London: Hurst, 1981).

————, "Angola in Historical Context", in P. Chabal and N. Vidal (eds), *Angola: The Weight of History* (London: Hurst, 2007), pp. 19–92.

Palan, Ronen, *The Offshore World: Sovereign Markets Virtual Places, and Nomad Millionaires* (Ithaca: Cornell University Press, 2005).

OECD, *Portugal: Phase 3—Final Report. Final Report on the Implementation and Application of the Convention on Combatting Bribery of Foreign Public Officials in International Business Transactions and the 2009 Recommendations for Further Combatting Bribery* (Paris: Directorate for Financial and Enterprise Affairs, Organizations for Economic Co-operation and Development, 2013).

SELECT BIBLIOGRAPHY

Oliveira, J. E. da Costa, *Memórias de África 1961–2004* (Lisbon: IPAD, 2005).

OPSA, *Posição do OPSA e da ADRA sobre o OGE 2014* (Luanda: Observatório Politico-Social de Angola, 2013).

Orre, Aslak, "Fantoches e Cavalos de Tróia: Instrumentalização das Autoridades Tradicionais em Angola e Moçambique", *Cadernos de Estudos Africanos* 16/17, 2008, pp. 141–78.

———, *Entrenching the Party-State in the Multiparty Era: Opposition parties, traditional authorities and new councils of local representatives in Angola and Mozambique* (PhD thesis, University of Bergen, 2010).

Otayek, R. "Décentralisation et résilience des autoritarismes en Afrique: une relation de cause à effet?", in M. Camau et G. Massardier (eds), Démocraties et autoritarismes (Paris: Karthala, 2009),pp. 121–140.

Ovadia, Jesse, "The dual nature of local content in Angola's oil and gas industry: development vs. elite accumulation", *Journal of Contemporary African Studies* 30, 3 (2012), pp. 395–417.

Pacheco, Fernando, "Autoridades Tradicionais e Estruturas Locais de Poder em Angola", paper presented at Friedrich Ebert Stiftung workshop, (2002a).

———, "Caminhos para a cidadania: poder e desenvolvimento a nível local na perspectiva de uma Angola nova", *Política internacional* 25 (2002b), pp. 43–50.

Pawson, Lara, *In the Name of the People: Angola's Forgotten Massacre* (London: I. B. Tauris, 2014)

Pearce, Justin, *An Outbreak of Peace: Angola's Situation of Confusion* (Claremont: New Africa Books, 2005).

Pearce, Justin, "L'Unita à la recherche de "son people": Carnets d'une non campagne sur le planalto", *Politique africaine* 110 (2008), pp. 47–64.

———, "Rebel Movements, Identity and Peace Building in Angola" (unpublished DPhil thesis, University of Oxford, 2011).

———, "UNITA after the first decade of peace", paper presented at the "New Directions in Angolan Research" conference, St Peter's College, Oxford, 17–18 March 2014.

Péclard, Didier, "L'Angola dans la paix: autoritarisme et reconversions", *Politique Africaine* 110 (2008), pp. 5–20.

———, "Culture, Modernity and Nationalism: The Politics of Social Imaginaries in 20th Century Angola", paper presented at the African History and Politics Seminar, University of Oxford, 10 March (2014a).

———, *Les incertitudes de la nation en Angola: Aux racines sociales de l'Unita* (Paris: Karthala, forthcoming 2014b).

Pélissier, René, *La colonie du Minotaure: Nationalismes et révoltes en Angola, 1926–1961* (Orgeval: Editions Pélissier, 1978).

———, *História das Campanhas de Angola* (Lisboa: Editorial Estampa, 1986).

Pepetela, *Predadores* (Lisbon: Dom Quixote, 2005).

SELECT BIBLIOGRAPHY

Pimenta, Fernando Tavares, *Angola no Percurso de um Nacionalista: Conversas com Adolfo María* (Porto: Afrontamento, 2006).

Pitcher, M. Anne, *Transforming Mozambique: The Politics of Privatization, 1975–2000* (Cambridge: Cambridge University Press, 2002).

Pomeranz, Kenneth, "Imperialism, Development, and 'Civilizing' Missions, Past and Present," *Daedalus*, 134 (2), (2005), pp. 34–45.

Porto, Nuno Gomes, Imogen Parsons and Chris Alden, *From Soldiers to Citizens: The Social, Economic and Political Integration of UNITA ex-Combatants* (Pretoria: Institute for Strategic Studies, 2007).

Power, Marcus, "Angola 2025: the future of the 'world's richest poor country' as seen through a Chinese rear-view mirror", *Antipode: a radical journal of geography* 44, 3 (2011), pp. 993–1014.

Pushal, N. and V. Foster, *Angola's Infrastructure: A Continental Perspective* (Washington, DC: World Bank, 2011).

Rela, José Manuel Zenha, *Angola entre o Presente e o Futuro* (Lisbon: Escher, 1992).

Reno, William, *Corruption and Politics in Sierra Leone* (Cambridge: Cambridge University Press, 1995).

Reno, William, *Warlord Politics and African States* (Boulder: Lynne Rienner, 2000a).

———, "The real (war) economy of Angola", in J. Cilliers and Chris Dietrich (eds), *Angola's War Economy: The Role of Oil and Diamonds* (Pretoria: ISS, 2000b), pp. 219–35.

Robertson, Charles, *et al*, *The Fastest Billion: The Story Behind Africa's Economic Revolution* (London: Renaissance Capital, 2012).

Rocha, Manuel Alves da, *Alguns Temas Estruturantes da Economia Angolana* (Luanda, Editorial Kilombelombe, 2011a).

———, *Desigualdades e Assimetrias Regionais em Angola- os Factores de Competitividade Regional* (Luanda: UCAN/CEIC, 2011b).

Rodrigues, Cristina Udelsmann, "Youth in Angola: Keeping the Pace Towards Modernity", *Cadernos de Estudos Africanos*, 18, 19 (2013), pp. 165–79.

Roque, Fátima, *et al.*, *Economia de Angola* (Lisbon: Bertrand, 1991).

Roque, Paula Cristina, "Angola's Façade Democracy", *Journal of Democracy* 20, 4 (2009), pp. 137–150.

Sakala, Alcides, *Memórias de um Guerrilheiro* (Lisboa: Dom Quixote, 2006).

Scott, James, *Seeing Like a State* (New Haven: Yale University Press, 1998).

Shaxson, Nicholas, *Poisoned Wells: the Dirty Politics of African Oil* (New York: Palgrave McMillan, 2007).

———, "Angola's Homegrown Answers to the Resource Curse", in Jacques Lesourne and William C. Ramsay (eds), *Governance of Oil in Africa: Unfinished Business* (Paris: IFRI, 2008).

Schubert, Jon, "A Culture of immediatism" (unpublished paper, 2013).

Sciascia, Leonardo, *The Moro Affair* (London: Granta, 2002).

SELECT BIBLIOGRAPHY

Slater, Dan, *Ordering Power: Contentious Politics and Authoritarian Leviathans in Southeast Asia* (Cambridge: Cambridge University Press, 2010).

Smith, Benjamin, "Life of the Party: The Origins of Regime Breakdown and Persistence Under Single-Party Rule", *World Politics* 57 (2005), pp. 421–51.

Soares de Oliveira, Ricardo, *Oil and Politics in the Gulf of Guinea* (London: Hurst, 2007a).

———, "Business Success, Angola-Style: Postcolonial Politics and the Rise and Rise of Sonangol", *Journal of Modern African Studies* 45 (4), 2007b, pp. 595–619.

———, "Illiberal Peacebuilding in Angola", *Journal of Modern African Studies* 49 (2), 2011, pp. 287–314.

———, "'O Governo está aqui': Post-war statemaking in the Angolan Periphery", *Politique Africaine* 130 (2013a), pp. 165–87.

———, "Grand Colonic Tour: Theroux Does Angola", *openDemocracy.net* (2013b).

Sogge, David, *Angola: "Failed" yet "Successful"* (Madrid: FRIDE Working Paper 81, 2009).

Soromenho, Castro, *Viragem* (Lisbon: Cotovia, 2010).

Stolte, Christina, *Brazil in Africa: Just another BRICS country seeking resources?* (London: Chatham House, 2012).

Taylor, Ian, *China in Africa: Engagement and Compromise* (London: Routledge, 2006).

———, *China's New Role in Africa* (Boulder: Lynne Rienner, 2009).

Theroux, Paul, *Last Train to Zona Verde* (London: Hamish Hamilton, 2013).

Tilly, Charles (ed.), *The Formation of National States in Western Europe* (Princeton: Princeton University Press, 1975).

———, "War Making and State Making as Organized Crime", in P. Evans *et al.* (eds), *Bringing the State Back In* (Cambridge: Cambridge University Press, 1985), pp. 169–91.

Tomás, António Andrade, *Refracted Governmentality: Space, Politics and Social Structure in Contemporary Luanda* (unpublished PhD thesis, Columbia University, 2012).

UCAN, *Relatório Económico de Angola 2008* (Luanda: Centro de Estudos e Investigação Científica da Universidade Católica de Angola, 2009).

———, *Relatório Económico de Angola 2009* (Luanda: Centro de Estudos e Investigação Científica da Universidade Católica de Angola, 2010).

———, *Relatório Económico de Angola 2010* (Luanda: Centro de Estudos e Investigação Científica da Universidade Católica de Angola, 2011a).

———, *Relatório Energia em Angola* (Luanda: Centro de Estudos e Investigação Científica da Universidade Católica de Angola, 2011b).

UCAN, *Relatório Económico de Angola 2012* (Luanda: Centro de Estudos e Investigação Científica da Universidade Católica de Angola, 2013).

UNSA, *Angola: the post-war challenges: common country assessment 2002* (Luanda: United Nations System in Angola, 2002).

US Senate, *Keeping Foreign Corruption out of the United States: Four Case Histories*

(Washington, DC: Permanent Sub-Committee on Investigations, United States Senate, 2010).

US State Department, "Isabel dos Santos: Bio Note" (Luanda: US Embassy, December 2009).

Vallée, Olivier, "Du palais au banques: La reproduction élargie du capital indigene en Angola", *Politique Africaine* 110, 2008, pp. 21–46.

Vandewalle, Dirk, *Libya Since Independence: Oil and State-building* (Ithaca: Cornell University Press, 1998).

Vickers, Brendan, "Africa and the Rising Powers: Bargaining for the 'Marginalized Many'", *International Affairs* 89, 3 (2013), pp. 673–93.

Vidal, Nuno, "The Angolan regime and the move to multiparty politics", in Patrick Chabal and Nuno Vidal (eds), *Angola: The Weight of History* (London: Hurst, 2007), pp. 124–74.

———, and Justino Pinto de Andrade (eds), *Sociedade Civil e Política em Angola: enquadramento regional e internacional* (Luanda and Lisbon: Firmamento and Universidade Católica de Angola, 2008).

———, and Justino Pinto de Andrade (eds), *Economia Política e Desenvolvimento em Angola* (Luanda: Chá de Caxinde, 2011).

Vines, Alex, "The siege of Cuito: a visit", in Joanna Lewis and Keith Hart (eds), *Why Angola Matters* (London: James Currey, 1995), pp. 156–159.

———, N. Shaxson and L. Rimli, *Angola: drivers of change, an overview* (London: Chatham House, 2005).

———, and Bereni Oruitemeka, "Bullets to ballots: The reintegration of UNITA in Angola", *Conflict, Security and Development* 8, 2 (2008), pp. 241–63.

———, Lilian Wong, Markus Weimer and Indira Campos, *Thirst for African Oil: Asian National Oil Companies in Nigeria and Angola* (London: Chatham House, 2009).

Vu, Tuong, "Studying the State Through State Formation", *World Politics* 62, 1 (2010), pp. 148–75.

Walle, Nicolas van de, *African Economies and the Politics of Permanent Crisis, 1979–1999* (Cambridge: Cambridge University Press, 2001).

Weber, Eugen, *Peasants Into Frenchmen* (Stanford: Stanford University Press, 1976).

Wells, Jill, *Political Economy and the Construction Sector in Angola* (draft, 6 December 2011).

Wheeler, Douglas, and René Pélissier, *História de Angola* (Lisbon: Tinta da China, 2009).

World Bank, *Angola: issues and options in the energy sector* (Washington, DC: Report No. 7408–ANG, Report of the Joint UNDP/World Bank Energy Sector Assessment Program, 1989).

———, Private *Solutions for Infrastructure in Angola: a country framework report* (Washington, DC: World Bank, 2005).

————, *Angola: Country Economic Memorandum. Oil, Broad-Based Growth and Equity* (Washington, DC: World Bank, 2006).

————, *International Development Association Interim Strategy Note for the Republic of Angola* (Washington, DC: Report No. 39394–AO, World Bank, 2007).

Yergin, Daniel, *The Quest: Energy, Security, and the Remaking of the Modern World* (London: Penguin Books, 2011).

INDEX

INDEX

INDEX

INDEX

BAE Systems 193
BAI (Banco Angolano de
  Investimentos) 138, 139, 153, 185
bailundos 217
bairros 114
Bakongo 9–10, 103, 110
Baku, Azerbaijan 41
Bank of America 179
banking 36–40, 54–5, 67, 105, 134,
  137–40, 146, 147, 151, 153, 162, 168,
  171, 179, 185, 186–93, 196
Barcelona, Spain 207
Battaglia, Helder 190
Battle of Cuito Cuanavale 11, 103
Beijing, China 143, 190
Belgian Congo 10
Bembe, António Bento 125
Ben Ali, Zine El Abidine 81
Bengo, Angola 117
Benguela, Angola 6, 59, 60, 61, 109,
  148, 158, 203
Benin 7
Bento, Bento 109
Bermuda 168
'Bermuda Triangle' 39, 189
BESA (Banco Espírito Santo Angola)
  139, 196
Bessangana 157
betrothal ceremonies 150, 157
BFA (Banco de Fomento Angola) 138
BIC Bank 193
Bicesse Accords (1991) 14
Black Power, General 111
Bloco Democrático 110, 113–14
BNA (Banco Nacional de Angola) 37,
  138, 139, 162, 187, 188
Boone, Catherine 137
Botswana 187
bourgeoisie 4, 13, 80, 82–3, 88, 93,
  116, 132–5, 140, 155, 161, 184, 206,
  213, 214
Bowerbank, Michael 120
BP 78
BPI (Banco Português de
  Investimento) 193

BPN (Banco Português de Negócios)
  193
Brautigam, Deborah 56
Brazil 61, 63, 64, 70, 75, 78, 84, 85, 86,
  98, 114, 123, 149, 155, 174, 175, 180,
  181, 182, 183, 184, 187, 196, 202
Brazzaville, Republic of Congo 40, 181
Bretton Woods 54
bribery 160, 196
bricolage 86
BRINDE (Brigada de Informação e
  Defesa do Estado) 12
Brownlee, Jason 99
Bulgaria 68–9, 74
Bush, George Walker 55, 180

CABGOC (Cabinda Gulf Oil
  Company) 30, 33
Cabinda, Angola 9, 10, 14, 18, 29, 34,
  36, 98, 103, 109, 110–11, 117, 124–5,
  128, 205
  Cabinda City 125
  FLEC (Frente para a Libertação do
    Enclave de Cabinda) 9, 18, 124–5
  Treaty of Simulambuco (1885) 124
Cacanda, Lunda Norte 73
  Cacanda project 69–70
CACS (Conselhos de Auscultação e
  Concertação Social) 120
Cacuaco, Luanda 203
Café, Maria Mambo 44
Calulo, Kwanza Sul 123
Cameroon 98
Campus Universitário 62
Canada 177
Capapinha, Job 109
Cape Verde 42
capital accumulation 131–64
capital flight 168, 176
capitalism 2, 14, 23, 30, 35, 38, 88, 98,
  131–64, 165, 169, 177, 197, 205, 212
Caracas, Venezuela 155
Caras Angola 150, 151
Carnation Revolution (1974) 11, 26–7

INDEX

INDEX

education 12, 62, 152, 153, 156, 160–1,
214
Egypt 113
elections
1992 14, 93, 97, 98, 110, 128
2008 18, 67, 93, 98, 110, 118, 119–20,
128, 201
2012 18, 59, 93, 98, 110, 111, 112, 113,
118, 120, 159, 201–3
electricity sector 4, 58, 60, 62, 63, 73,
80, 85, 87, 212
Elf Aquitaine 15, 33, 39, 124
elite 2, 3, 5–7, 9, 13, 19, 20, 22–4, 26,
35, 38–9, 42, 46, 49, 54, 56, 65–6,
71, 73–4, 76, 80, 82–6, 88–9, 92–3,
97–9, 101, 104, 111, 118, 122, 126–7,
130, 131–64, 177, 179, 203, 208, 215,
216
embezzlement 120
empresários de confiança (trustworthy
businessmen) 134–5, 137, 144
energy sector 32, 64, 69, 193, 195
ENI 31
ENSA (Empresa Nacional de Seguros
de Angola) 105
enticement tactics 111, 112
entrepreneurs 82, 132, 140, 141, 144,
145, 148, 151, 154, 156, 160, 206
Equatorial Guinea 98, 208
Ernst & Young 76, 210
Escola Francesa, Luanda 153
Escola Internacional, Luanda 153
Escola Portuguesa, Luanda 153
Escom group 190
Espírito Santo Bank 139
Ethiopia 126, 204
European Union (EU) 78, 195
Exame 143–4
exchange rate manipulation 133–4
Executive Outcomes 15
Exim Bank 56, 57, 171, 191
Expansão 106
expatriates 2, 23, 73–9, 89, 145, 217
export licenses 144

Expresso 194
Exxon 35, 179

FAA (Forças Armadas Angolanas)
15–16, 45–6, 52, 53, 68, 108, 124,
125, 126, 133, 149, 158, 170, 181, 182,
198, 203, 209
FAC (Forças Armadas de Cabinda)
125
Facebook 113, 153
Faceira, Antonio and Luis 46
FALA (Forças Armadas de Libertação
de Angola) 12
Falcone, Pierre 38, 190
FAPLA (Forças Armadas Populares
de Libertação de Angola) 45
fashion shows 75, 150
Fastest Billion, The 167
Feijó, Carlos 43, 120, 122
Ferguson, James 83, 158
Ferreira Ramos, José 143–4
Ferreira, Manuel Ennes 29, 148, 216
FESA (Fundación Eduardo dos
Santos) 107
de Figueiredo, Elísio 170
filhos da terra 7
Finance Ministry 33, 37, 38, 44, 187,
191
financial crisis (2008–10) 59, 60, 65,
66, 162, 167, 186, 194, 195, 216
Financial Times 75, 152
Flash 157
FLEC (Frente para a Libertação do
Enclave de Cabinda) 9, 18, 124–5
FAC (Forças Armadas de Cabinda)
125
FLEC-Renovada 125
FNLA (Frente Nacional de
Libertação de Angola) 10, 11, 12, 18,
95, 102, 110
FOCAC (Forum on China–Africa
Cooperation) 174
football 61, 72, 108, 114, 125
Forbes 152

INDEX

INDEX

INDEX

INDEX

INDEX

INDEX

Nunda, Geraldo Sachipengo 46
Nunes Júnior, Manuel 213

OAA (Ordem dos Advogados) 106,
 142–3
Obiang (Teodoro Obiang Nguema
 Mbasogo) 208
Odebrecht 70, 123, 180
OECD (Organisation for Economic
 Co-operation and Development)
 172, 195, 196
Office for National Reconstruction
 (GRN) 45, 57, 61, 63, 64, 65, 66, 67
oil 3, 5, 11–12, 15, 18, 24–5, 28–40,
 51, 54–7, 78, 80, 81–3, 87–9, 104,
 124, 129–31, 137, 146–8, 153–5, 161,
 163, 165, 167, 169, 170, 173–7, 179,
 180, 184–6, 189–90, 199, 205–7,
 209–11, 216
 Elf Aquitaine 15, 33, 39, 124
 Exxon 35, 179
 Gulf Oil 30, 33
 National Commission for the
  Restructuring of the Petroleum
  Sector 30
 OPEC (Organization of the
  Petroleum Exporting Countries)
  154, 182
 Petrochina 186
 Petrofina 30
 Petroleum Ministry 31, 33
 Sinopec 191
 Sonangol 17, 22, 29–40, 43, 46,
  47, 49, 63, 66–7, 105, 108, 138,
  139–40, 166, 169, 174, 184–93,
  205, 207, 208
 Texaco 30
 Thales 177
 Total 177
oligarchs 132, 138, 146, 149, 150–51,
 152–64, 165, 169, 195, 216
Oliveira, Eduardo Costa 84
OM (Ordem dos Médicos) 106
OMA (Organizacao da Mulher de
 Angola) 97, 114

OPEC (Organization of the
 Petroleum Exporting Countries)
 154, 182
Open Society Institute 54, 55
opposition 109–114, 201–3, 212, 214,
 215
optic fibre 64
Opus Dei 194
Organization of African Unity 94
Ovimbundu 9, 13, 101, 111, 112, 217

Pacavira, Rosa 126
Pacheco, Fernando 122, 203
PAIGC (Partido Africano da
 Independência da Guiné e Cabo
 Verde) 27
Palanca, Luanda 108, 109
parallel system 22, 23, 26, 36, 37, 39,
 48, 49, 55, 56, 57, 89, 165, 171, 187,
 189, 209
Paraná, Brazil 63
parastatal organizations 105, 151
Paris Club 56
peace dividend 92, 207
Pearce, Justin 129
PEP (Politically Exposed Person) 196
Pepetela (Artur Carlos Maurício
 Pestana dos Santos) 47, 113, 149
Petrochina 186
Petrofina 30
Petroleum Ministry 31, 33
philanthropy 151
Pinóquio, Lisbon 150
Pinto, Inglês 142
PIR (Policia de Intervenção Rápida)
 15, 46
Pitcher, Anne 97, 134
Pitra, António 213
poder popular militias 15
police 15, 118, 126, 133, 160
Politburo 29, 41, 100, 101, 106, 120
Ponto de Reencontro 103
Portugal 1, 3, 6–12, 14, 18, 24, 61, 64,
 74, 75, 76, 77, 78, 84, 93, 138, 144,

INDEX

INDEX

INDEX

INDEX